SHAMBHALA DRAGON EDITIONS

The dragon is an age-old symbol of the highest spiritual
essence, embodying wisdom, strength, and the divine power
of transformation. In this spirit, Shambhala Dragon Editions
offers a treasury of readings in the sacred knowledge of Asia.
In presenting the works of authors both ancient and modern,
we seek to make these teachings accessible to lovers of
wisdom everywhere.

THE
LOTUS-BORN
The Life Story of Padmasambhava

Composed by Yeshe Tsogyal
Revealed by Nyang Ral Nyima Öser

Foreword by His Holiness Dilgo Khyentse Rinpoche
Clarification of the Life of Padmasambhava
by Tsele Natsok Rangdröl

Translated from the Tibetan by Erik Pema Kunsang
Edited by Marcia Binder Schmidt

SHAMBHALA
Boston & London
1993

Shambhala Publications, Inc.
Horticultural Hall
300 Massachusetts Avenue
Boston, Massachusetts 02115

9 8 7 6 5 4 3 2

Printed in the United States of America

⊗ This edition is printed on acid-free paper that meets the American National
Standards Institute Z39.48 Standard.

Distributed in the United States by Random House, Inc. and in Canada by
Random House of Canada Ltd.

Library of Congress Cataloging-in-Publication Data
Ye-śes-mtsho-rgyal, 8th cent.
[Padma bka' than. English]
The lotus-born: life story of Padmasambhava / composed by Yeshe Tsogyal;
revealed by Nyang Ral Nyima Öser; foreword by His Holiness Dilgo Khyentse
Rinpoche; clarification of the life of Padmasambhava by Tsele Natsok Rangdröl;
translated from the Tibetan by Erik Pema Kunsang; edited by Marcia Binder
Schmidt—1st ed.
p. cm.   Translation of: mam thar zangs gling ma.
Includes bibliographical references and index.
ISBN 0-87773-909-9 (alk. paper)
ISBN 0-87773-869-6 (paperback)
1. Padma Sambhava, ca. 717-ca. 762.
2. Lamas—China—Tibet—Biography—Early works to 1800.
3. Priests, Buddhist—India—Biography—Early works to 1800.
I. Ñan-ral Ñi-ma-'od-zer, 1124–1192, II. Kunsang, Erik Pema.
III. Schmidt, Marcia Binder. I V. Title.
BQ7950.P327Y4713 1992   91-52516
294-3'923'092—dc20 CIP
[B]

Eight years after I pass into nirvana, I will reappear in the country of Uddiyana bearing the name Padma-sambhava. I will become the lord of the teachings of Secret Mantra.

—BUDDHA SHAKYAMUNI, from the *Tantra of the Perfect Embodiment of the Unexcelled Nature*

Contents

CONTENTS

CONTENTS

CONTENTS

Foreword

❀

His Holiness Dilgo Khyentse

Guru Padmasambhava, the glorious Master of Uddiyana and king of the Dharma, is the single embodiment of the activity of the victorious ones throughout the three times. According to the ways in which sentient beings perceive reality, there exists an inconceivable number of life stories of the three mysteries of his body, speech, and mind. Among them, the Sanglingma Life Story entitled The Jewel Garland Dharma History and Biography, revealed from the profound terma of Ngadag Nyang, is like the king.

The *Sanglingma* places emphasis on how Padmasambhava converted disciples in the dark country of Tibet. It condenses all the biographies and histories of Guru Rinpoche and contains the profound key points of the nine vehicles of Sutra and Mantra. It is the most authoritative scripture regarding how the teachings of Sutra and Mantra spread to the Snowy Land of Tibet.

The *Sanglingma* also contains oral instructions and advice that the Great Master of Uddiyana left as his profound and detailed testament to help the Buddhadharma and people of future generations.

This biography, containing Padmasambhava's final advice concerning practice, the quintessence of the teachings of Sutra and Mantra, has been carefully translated into English by Erik Pema Kunsang of Denmark with the single, pure intention of furthering the Buddhadharma.

The gate to the benefit and good qualities of Guru Rinpoche's life

I

story having been opened to people of all times and races, may everyone who sees, hears, or thinks of him obtain insight into the sacred Dharma of scriptures and realization and be assured of becoming a child of the victorious vidyadhara on the Glorious Copper-Colored Mountain on Chamara.

> This was written at the glorious temple of Ngagyur Shechen Tennyi Dargye Ling by Dilgo Khyentse on the fifteenth day of the first month of the Year of the Iron Horse. May it be virtuous.

Translator's Preface

T HE LOTUS-BORN: THE LIFE STORY OF PADMASAM-
BHAVA, commonly called *Sanglingma*, is a translation of a
biography of the great master recorded by his foremost
Tibetan disciple, the dakini Yeshe Tsogyal. The name *Sanglingma*
means "Copper Temple." It refers to a temple built at Samye by one
of King Trisong Deutsen's queens. Yeshe Tsogyal concealed this
biography in the ninth century under the statue of the tantric deity
Hayagriva on the temple's shrine. The terma treasure was revealed
by Nyang Ral Nyima Öser (1124–1192). In later centuries it became
known after its place of discovery.

Jamgön Kongtrül the First (1813–1899) felt this life story of
Padmasambhava was important enough to be the first text in the first
volume of his famous collection of terma treasures known as *Rinchen
Terdzö*. The *Sanglingma* itself belongs to the Kathang literature, a class
of Buddhist scriptures that narrates the biography of Padmasambhava as it was written down by his close Tibetan students. Many
of these biographies were concealed as terma treasures to protect
them against the changes of time. Centuries later they would be
revealed by a *tertön*, a reincarnation of an accomplished student of
Padmasambhava who had made the aspiration to benefit people in
future generations. The *Sanglingma* is a religious scripture read by
devoted followers of Padmasambhava to keep his miraculous deeds
and great compassion in mind.

Why was Padmasambhava so important? Due to his great realization and spiritual power, he created the conditions for the propaga-
tion of the Vajrayana teachings in this world. In Tibet, he tamed

spirits hostile to the Buddhadharma and pacified negative forces, allowing for the completion and consecration of the magnificent temples of Samye. Moreover, through Master Padma's unfailing compassion and diverse skillful means, he hid numerous teachings for future generations. These terma teachings would be revealed when the conditions were auspicious and the benefit most appropriate for the people of that particular time. Even in recent times, Padmasambhava's treasure teachings continue to be revealed. Judging from the past and discerning the present, the impact of Padmasambhava is inconceivable.

To clarify doubts about Padmasambhava I would like to suggest to the reader to investigate the concise version of Padmasambhava's life by Jamgön Kongtrül the First as contained in *Dakini Teachings*.[1] Secondly, there are several English books available that are mentioned at the end of the bibliography. Finally, I will present a condensation of the writings of Tsele Natsok Rangdröl concerning the Lotus-Born Master.

During the latter part of his life, Tsele Natsok Rangdröl, who is also reputed to be one of Jamgön Kongtrül's prior incarnations, was asked eighteen questions about the life story of Padmasambhava contained in the Kathang literature. Several of his replies are directly relevant to the translation of the *Sanglingma* presented in this book. I have therefore taken the liberty to extract and summarize the most pertinent parts of his eminent advice on how to view the historical and personal background of the Lotus-Born Master. They are presented in the following essay entitled "Clarifying the True Meaning."

In the back of the book I have included a bibliography of Tibetan historical source material related to Padmasambhava, Vimalamitra, and Vairochana. Together with the oral teachings I have been fortunate enough to receive, these precious writings form the basis for the notes and the explanations in the glossary. I sincerely wish that enclosing the names of these scriptures may inspire further translations to illuminate the historical background for the precious Vajrayana teachings.

To conclude, I would like to thank His Holiness Dilgo Khyentse Rinpoche for his encouragement to undertake this translation, the most venerable Tulku Urgyen Rinpoche for clarifying many difficult points, and the current upholders of Guru Rinpoche's teachings who have given priceless inspiration, especially Tulku Pema Wangyal and Orgyen Tobgyal Rinpoche. Out of gratitude for their kindness, I engendered the wish to share this wondrous life story of the eminent master Padmasambhava. My deepest thanks go also to everyone who helped with the translation of the *Sanglingma*, especially to my wife Marcia, who checked all stages of the production; to Phinjo Sherpa, who repeatedly typed the manuscript and entered numerous corrections; to Franz-Karl Erhard for help in locating existing manuscripts; and to Carol Faust for many helpful suggestions.

Finally, I am pleased with the coincidence that this translation was completed on the auspicious day of the consecration of Samye Monastery in Tibet by His Holiness Dilgo Khyentse Rinpoche on September 29, 1990.

ERIK PEMA KUNSANG
Ka-Nying Shedrup Ling Monastery
Boudhanath, Nepal

Clarifying the True Meaning

Tsele Natsok Rangdröl

Buddhas and bodhisattvas throughout all times
    and directions,
Embodiment of all objects of refuge, Padma Thö-
    treng Tsal,
Consider all beings and myself with your loving
    kindness.
May every wish we make be effortlessly fulfilled.
Strengthen the Dharma and increase auspicious
    conditions
So that true awakening will swiftly be attained.

The Birth of Padmasambhava

THE WORD *padma* is Sanskrit. It was preserved as a Tibetan word and means lotus flower. *Sambhava* means "born from." Padmasambhava's usual name in Tibetan, is Pema Jungney, translated from the Sanskrit name Padmakara, which means "originated from a lotus."

When Padmakara was born from a lotus flower and, also, while being led back by King Indrabhuti, wherever he was set down, a lotus spontaneously sprung up. The king exclaimed, "This child is truly a lotus-born one!" Therefore he became renowned as Padmakara.[2]

His ordination name was Shakya Senge. Later, when he became learned in the fields of knowledge and presided as the head of five hundred great panditas, he was known as Padmasambhava, the

Lotus-Born. Thus he is indeed named after his manner of birth.

It is universally renowned that the Precious Master took birth from a lotus flower in a way that is called instantaneous birth. Instantaneous birth in itself is nothing to marvel about since all beings take rebirth through one of the four modes of birth: womb birth, egg birth, moisture birth, and instantaneous birth. But this master's birth was superior to ordinary instantaneous birth. The reason is that the lotus flower from which he was born, in the center of Lake Danakosha, had been fused with the combined light rays of compassion of Buddha Amitabha and all the buddhas of the ten directions.

This is not just an exaggerated praise tenaciously offered by old ignorant followers of the Nyingma School; Padmakara was foretold by Buddha Shakyamuni himself in many sutras and tantras. If it was the case that those predictions are found only in the Nyingma tantras, it would be difficult for other people to have full trust in them, so here is a quotation from the *Immaculate Goddess Sutra:*

> The activity of all the victorious ones of the ten
>   directions
> Will gather into a single form,
> A buddha son, who will attain marvelous
>   accomplishment,
> A master who will embody buddha activity,
> Will appear to the northwest of Uddiyana.

Padmasambhava is also prophesied in the *Sutra of Inconceivable Secrets:*

> A manifestation of the buddhas of the three times,
> With marvelous deeds in this Good Aeon,
> Will appear as a vidyadhara
> In the center of a wondrous lotus flower.

The *Tantra of the Ocean of Ferocious Activity* says:

A holder of the secrets of all the buddhas,
The king of the deeds of indestructible wrath,
A miraculous form without father or mother,
Will appear as a vidyadhara
In Lake Kosha of Uddiyana.

There exists a vast number of similar quotations, but since these will suffice for gaining understanding, I shall refrain from further elaborations. The heart of the matter is that these quotations establish that he was miraculously born from a lotus flower.

For people who could not be converted by someone miraculously born, Padmasambhava showed himself as taking birth through a womb. In that version he was born as the son of King Mahusita of Uddiyana and given the name Danarakshita. When reaching maturity, he wanted to leave in order to practice the Dharma, but his parents did not permit him to do so. Unable to find any other way, he saw that he could only escape through some felonious action. He killed one of the king's children and was then banished as punishment.[3] Taking ordination from the pandita Shakyabodhi, he was named Shakya Senge.

Whatever the case, Master Padma was not an ordinary, material person. We should understand that all his deeds and life examples are a magical display shown to convert people according to their individual inclinations. By regarding him as a normal human being, we will fail to perceive even a fraction of his enlightened qualities.

Padmasambhava's Stay in Tibet

Differing accounts exist regarding the length of time Master Padma remained in Tibet. One story narrates that he remained for one hundred and twenty years. Other sources state he was asked to leave due to the slander of evil-minded ministers after respectively six or three years, eighteen or three months. As I mentioned already, an ordinary person cannot measure the deeds of the victorious ones; remember that also here.

In the past, Buddha Shakyamuni taught the *Saddharma Pundarika Sutra*. The sutra describes that the Buddha performed a miracle, making the duration of teaching, which was one morning, appear as if it were fifty aeons. The Buddha could also transform one moment into an aeon and one aeon into one moment. How can our intellect grasp that?

In the general perception of people and as narrated in the shorter and longer *Bashey Annals*, Master Padma came to Tibet, performed a ritual for taming the land around Samye, and twice made a ritual fire offering to tame the gods and demons. When about to perform the ritual a third time, some manipulative ministers prevented him from doing so. Master Padma gave the king and a few worthy people advice. When Padmakara was about to turn the dunes into meadows, the desert into fields, and plant trees and so forth, the ministers misinterpreted this and prohibited it. Without having fulfilled his purpose, he was escorted to the Sky Plain Pass by two religious ministers. On the way, Master Padma overcame some murderers sent by antagonistic ministers by paralyzing them with his gaze. Leaving from the Sky Plain Pass, Master Padma flew through the air toward the southwest.

These narrations are exclusively what is described in the shorter and longer *Bashey Annals*. The *Bashey Annals* are only comprised of superficial perceptions of the ministers of that time which I do not consider fully authentic. Try to understand this comparison: the Buddha's twelve deeds and so forth differ in the traditions of Hinayana and Mahayana. We only take the Mahayana version to be truly accurate. The Hinayana version is what was perceived through the limited vision of Hinayana disciples. This is the same as the analogy of a white conch seen to be yellow by a person suffering from jaundice. The person with healthy eyesight will see it as it truly is. Here, similarly, we should not regard an impure perception as true, but place our trust in the impeccable words of the Great Master himself.

In this regard, it should be mentioned that there is no conflict in the uncorrupted terma teachings that unanimously say Master Padma remained in Tibet for one hundred and eleven years. Since Indians then counted six months as one year, these "years" should be regarded as "half-years," meaning that Guru Rinpoche stayed for fifty-six years.

Some ministers and faithless people perceived that Guru Rinpoche only spent a few months in Tibet. They only saw that Padmakara tamed the land of Samye, performed its consecration, and gave teachings to the king and some fortunate disciples. The major part of the time the Great Master stayed in Tibet he spent visiting, blessing, concealing termas, and so forth in the principal sacred places and areas. For these reasons it seems that most Tibetan commoners did not meet him.

From our point of view, when Padmasambhava was about to leave Tibet for the land of rakshasas in the southwest, he consecrated all the temples. He was escorted to the Sky Plain Pass in Mang-yul by Prince Lhasey and many other disciples, where he gave many predictions and instructions. On the tenth day of the Monkey month, he was led through the sky to the continent of Chamara by dakas and dakinis carrying offerings.

Padmasambhava Being an Enlightened Buddha

Ordinary beings to be trained perceive the buddhas of the three times as taking birth among different types of sentient beings in the different worlds. Moreover, the buddhas enact the deeds of gathering the accumulations and purifying the obscurations over incalculable aeons. We can find evidence of this in the stories of the past lives of the Buddha. If we regard the words of the Buddha as authentic, we also can trust in his statements found in many sutras and tantras concerning the Great Master Padmakara as the embodiment of the compassion of all the buddhas. There is no great need to suffer by stubbornly objecting.

Padmasambhava's Appearance into This World

According to the scriptures mentioned above and other texts, including the *Tantra of the Perfect Embodiment of the Unexcelled Nature*,[4] there are varying statements about exactly when Master Padma would appear. Most sources seem to agree on twelve years after the passing of the Buddha. The *Nirvana Sutra* says:

> Twelve years after
> I pass into nirvana,
> A person who is superior to everyone
> Will appear from the anthers of a lotus flower
> In the immaculate Lake Kosha
> On the northwestern border of the country of
> Uddiyana.

The Buddha also said in the *Sutra of Predictions in Magadha:*

> I will pass away to eradicate the view of per-
> manence.
> But twelve years from now, to clear away the view
> of nihilism,
> I shall appear from a lotus in the immaculate Lake
> Kosha
> As a noble son to delight the king
> And turn the Dharma wheel of the unexcelled
> essential meaning.

This is the version unanimously agreed upon in all the narrations found in authentic terma teachings.

It is difficult for myself to identify correctly the exact year when the Buddha was born and passed away. There are many discrepancies in the various treatises, but all the histories of the Nyingma School tell that Buddha Shakyamuni passed away in the Year of the Iron

Bird and that Padmasambhava was born in the Year of the Earth Monkey. Between these two events are twelve years so I consider that to be the correct version.

One version of the Kathang mentions that Padmasambhava took ordination from Ananda in the presence of the arhat Nyima Gungpa and Kashyapa the Elder. Other reliable and uncorrupted terma teachings do not include this story. I myself, though old and uneducated, have read quite a few of the shorter and longer versions of Guru Rinpoche's biographies. In particular, I have carefully examined the manuscript of Ngadag Nyang's terma that is renowned as the *Sanglingma Life Story*. My sources say that Padmakara stayed five years in the royal palace in Uddiyana and five years in Cool Grove. After that time he went to many different charnel grounds such as Joyful Grove and Sosaling where he received empowerment and blessings from the wisdom dakinis Vajra Varahi, Sustainer of Peace, and Subduer of Mara. Here he also bound under oath the mundane dakinis and karma dakinis and employed them as his servants.

Although the Buddhadharma and all topics of knowledge arose spontaneously within Padmasambhava's mind, he nevertheless pretended to study languages, healing, logic, craftsmanship, and so forth to instill confidence in ordinary followers. After this, he took ordination in a cave in Sahor from the preceptor Shakyabodhi, who is more known as the great master Prabhahasti, and he was given the name Shakya Senge. The reason Guru Rinpoche became a monk was to safeguard ordinary people from giving rise to wrong thoughts. Padmakara then received the empowerments, tantric explanations, and oral instructions on Yoga Tantra from Master Prabhahasti. These details are indisputable and trustworthy.

Criticism of Followers of the Nyingma School

The teachings of the Secret Mantra of the Early Translations are profound, extensive, and marvelous. Unfortunately their followers fool themselves with pursuing the upkeep of livelihood and attainment of temporary aims, instead of endeavoring through practice to gain realization. Leading the life of a householder, they neither belong to the category of sutra nor tantra. They are nothing but a dishonor to the Early Translations. This is exactly the reason why followers of the Sarma Schools, both learned and ignorant, not only expel the teachings and followers of the Nyingma School from the confines of Buddhism, but find them as loathsome as beholding a pool of vomit.[5] Due to these circumstances, the flawless words of Padmakara, the Second Buddha, have been corrupted by people's individual corrections, omissions, additions, presumptions, and guesswork. The Secret Mantra has become like precious sandalwood turned into charcoal for trade.

In this dark age it seems that no one engages in teaching, studying, or practicing the flawless older termas. The volumes of books have become worms' nests. The teachers waste their lives chasing after the novelty of so-called new termas or anything that resembles a terma, which nowadays proliferate like mushrooms on a summer meadow. On seeing this sad state of affairs, an old ignorant monk like me can do nothing but shed tears.

The Reliability of the Kathang Literature

Nowadays, there are two renowned versions of Padma Kathang. One, by Orgyen Lingpa, is in poetry, and the other by Sangye Lingpa is in prose. Their effect on the land of Tibet has been immense. Although the main part of these two texts surely is the words of the Great Master, obviously some uneducated and foolish people have interpolated them with colloquial terms and phrases of their invention. Similarly, the famous *Five Chronicles* are unmistakenly a terma by Orgyen Lingpa. However, no matter how you examine the verbiage and meaning, it is unlike authentic terma teachings. For example, the assertion that Guru Rinpoche had a son and the predictions of people who later appeared I personally find implausible. The various versions of Padma Kathang are for the most part comprised of the teachings of Master Padmasambhava. Of course they possess great blessings, but it is simply hard for me to regard them as reliable historical sources.

In general, it is impossible for ordinary people to measure buddhas and great siddhas who can transform time, show numerous manifestations of their bodily form, and display inconceivable kinds of miracles. Sometimes a single teaching or deed of the Buddha is perceived in different ways by various disciples due to their capacity and caliber. For instance, when the Buddha displayed the great miracles, Hinayana followers saw them as lasting only one day while the people of the Mahayana perceived them for half a month.

People generally accept only three turnings of the wheel of the Dharma. Yet, extraordinary people saw the Buddha give an inconceivable number of other teachings, such as the *Avatamsaka*, *Kalachakra*, and so forth. Until one attains the eye of Dharma, it is inappropriate to try to judge the Buddhadharma or other people.

Here is a story to illustrate the huge difference between the scope of perception of Hinayana and Mahayana:

Once noble Manjushri had spent the rainy season retreat in the company of King Salgyal's assemblage of queens. Later, Mahakashyapa criticized him, sounded the gong, and said, "Bodhisattva, you offender, don't stay among the sangha of monks!" The Buddha himself then exhorted Manjushri to reveal the power of his qualities. By his power, it was seen how a Manjushri was present near each buddha in each realm in the ten directions. It was also seen that a Mahakashyapa was sounding a gong in each realm as well. The Blessed One then said, "Mahakashyapa, are you going to expel all these forms of Manjushri or only this one?" Mahakashyapa felt remorse. He wanted to throw down the gong but was unable to do so. The gong itself continued to sound. Asking the Buddha for forgiveness, the Buddha told him to ask forgiveness from Manjushri.

According to this story, when even a great arhat like Mahakashyapa is unable to judge the character of another person, how can ordinary people like ourselves do so? It is really important to avoid creating more obscurations!

Padmasambhava's Level of Realization

The Great Master of Uddiyana said that he was not an explicit buddha but a buddha who had attained the four results of spiritual practice. Some people, displeased with that statement, made various objections. It does not lie within my power to present a claim about whether Padmasambhava specifically realized the fruition of an arhat. Yet, the position of the Nyingma School on this definitely is that he is an embodiment of the compassion of all the buddhas of the ten directions. Padmasambhava appeared as a nirmanakaya to tame the beings of the dark age. This is not just our personal opinion that we stubbornly uphold with deluded obsession. The Great Master was foretold by the Buddha himself. There is no need to elaborate on this or to define him as an ordinary person who had to journey the path in stages, such as achieving the result of an arhat or a pratyekabuddha.[6]

Padmasambhava's Five Superior Qualities

Buddha Shakyamuni extolled the virtues of the forthcoming incarnation Padmasambhava. He described him as possessing five qualities that made him superior to other emanations of the buddhas. The following quotation is from the *Nirvana Sutra*.

> Kyeho! Listen, whole retinue, with one-pointed
> mind.
> This emanation of myself

Will be superior to other emanations in the three
  times.
Not subject to age and decline,
His eminent form will be superior to other emanations.

From the very first vanquishing the four maras,
His wrathful power will be superior to other
  emanations.
Teaching the greater vehicle of buddhahood in
  one lifetime,
His realization will be superior to other emanations.

Converting the central and surrounding lands of
  the Jambu continent,
His benefit for beings will be superior to other
  emanations.
Beyond passing away in this Good Aeon,
His life span will be superior to other emanations.
This is because he is an emanation of Amitabha.

The line that mentions Padmasambhava "teaching the greater
vehicle of buddhahood in one lifetime" does not mean that he
attained enlightenment in one life. It means that Padmasambhava is
superior by being someone who teaches the profound instructions
of Secret Mantra through which buddhahood can be attained in this
very body and lifetime.

Primordial Buddhahood According
to Vajrayana

According to the Nyingma School, the ultimate source of all buddhas is called Buddha Unchanging Light. This buddha is all-encompassing wakefulness, the realization of all the victorious ones
throughout the three times without a single exception. This wakeful-

ness is primordially beyond delusion, the original state of supreme and changeless great bliss that transcends the confines of mental constructs. It is also known as the dharmakaya Samantabhadra, the great forefather of all the buddhas.

The unceasing, natural expression of this wakefulness manifests as wisdom forms, free from obscuration. These wisdom forms are Buddha Vajradhara, the victorious ones of the five families of sambhogakaya, and so forth who are endowed with the seven aspects of union. They can only be perceived by the great bodhisattvas on the ten levels.

The compassionate energy of the sambhogakaya buddhas appears as a magical display. This display is inexhaustible and unending, the incarnate emanations and the nirmanakayas of supreme enlightenment, such as Buddha Shakyamuni. This display of emanations appears unceasingly for as long as there are sentient beings to be benefited.

In this way all the infinite mandalas of the victorious ones in the ten directions and in particular in this Saha world-system, as exemplified by the thousand buddhas who successively appear during the Good Aeon, are of one identity in being the vast dharmadhatu of innate wakefulness. The magical display of emanations simply appears according to those who have the fortune to be influenced. Such buddhas are not ordinary people, who necessarily must attain enlightenment through traversing the path gradually.

If this is truly so, one might question the Mahayana sutras that say the Buddha first aroused the intent to attain supreme enlightenment, next he gathered the accumulations of merit and wisdom during three incalculable aeons, and finally he attained buddhahood while enacting the twelve deeds. The answer is that those Mahayana teachings were an exercise in expedient meaning for the benefit of ordinary disciples to communicate that each action yields a particular result.

Just like Buddha Shakyamuni, Padmasambhava was an emanation of all the buddhas. Padmasambhava appeared to convert the beings of the dark age, like the moonlight of compassion on the lake of the disciple's faith.[7] From this angle, the debates about whether he was born from a womb or appeared miraculously, whether he attained the level of an arhat, and whether he became enlightened within one lifetime or the like—all such refutations and affirmations are like a child trying to fathom the sky.

Most important and trustworthy are the words of the Buddha: "Rely not on the expedient but on the definitive meaning. Rely not on the conditioned but on the unconditioned. Rely not on the words but on the meaning."

How Padmasambhava Received Empowerment

As mentioned earlier, we should keep in mind that Guru Rinpoche was not an ordinary person. To begin with, when he was born from a lotus flower in Danakosha, all the eight classes of gods and demons of this world-system paid homage to him and presented offerings. The victorious ones of the ten directions appeared, like cloud banks assembling, and conferred empowerments and blessings upon him.

Not only did he receive empowerment for Yoga Tantra from the master Prabhahasti, but later while residing in the eight great charnel grounds he had the complete teachings of the Three Inner Tantras of Secret Mantra clarified by Garab Dorje, Manjushrimitra, Shri Singha, the dakini Leykyi Wangmo, and many other great masters. In addition, he journeyed to the dharmadhatu palace of Akanishtha where he received the Three Inner Tantras in the presence of the teachers of the three kayas, Samantabhadra, Vajradhara, and Vajrasattva.

When Padmasambhava went to Maratika and engaged in the sadhana of longevity, his aim was not to attain immortality out of fear of birth and death, but to bring benefit to future generations of followers. Acting as if practicing the sadhana of longevity, he then received the tantras, sadhanas, and oral instructions from Buddha Amitayus and accomplished an immortal body. Not only Padmasambhava himself, but also Princess Mandarava reached this attainment. She became renowned as the single mother and queen of siddhas and had numerous followers. The practices she taught are still applied by the New Schools.

This was just one example of how Padmasambhava manifested the attainment of the vidyadhara level of longevity. The three other vidyadhara levels to be accomplished according to the Nyingma School are the vidyadhara level of maturation, the vidyadhara level of mahamudra, and the vidyadhara level of spontaneous perfection.

Historical Details

Much detailed analysis can be made about the exact time King Trisong Deutsen invited the Great Master and when Samye was built. Other issues to be raised are whether Padmakara remained secretly ruling the country for some years after the king passed away at the age of fifty-six, how long Master Padma stayed during the reign of Prince Lhasey, whether Guru Rinpoche consecrated the Vajradhatu Temple at Karchung after its completion, and what he was doing while the dispute broke out between the systems of Indian and Chinese Buddhism.

The truth is that the numerous well-known historical writings all differ on many points, and it is hard to decide on which to rely. It is also difficult to discern whether the statements made in the Kathang are corrupt or authentic, so we are still in want of reliable sources.[8]

Nevertheless, historical narrations from the uncorrupted terma teachings of the Nyingma School mention that Trisong Deutsen was born in the Year of the Horse. At the age of seventeen he gave rise to the thought of Dharma and invited the pandita Shantarakshita to lay the foundation for a temple. When hostile gods and demons interrupted the building, Shantarakshita proclaimed that Guru Rinpoche should be invited.

Padmasambhava arrived in the later part of the Year of the Tiger and tamed the building site. The foundation was established in the Year of the Rabbit, and the construction then went on for five years. The consecration was celebrated for a whole twelve-year cycle.

While the Buddhadharma was being translated, the Great Master spent approximately ten years at Samye and Chimphu. He brought worthy disciples to ripening and liberation. Moreover, there are convincing descriptions that he stayed in all the sadhana places of the country of Tibet.

Padmasambhava was not present during the dispute between the Indian and Chinese systems. Shantarakshita predicted a certain master by the name of Kamalashila was predestined to solve that conflict and should therefore be invited to Tibet. After Kamalashila defeated the Chinese teacher Hashang, he reestablished the earlier system of the Buddhadharma.

To ensure that Trisong Deutsen's life span would last for as long as the sun and moon would shine, Padmakara prepared the empowerment and elixir of longevity. But when he was about to present it to the king, some evil ministers protested and the auspicious coincidence was undone. Later, the king regretted this and made another request. By receiving the empowerment of longevity, his life was extended for thirteen years. Although he was not meant to live for more than fifty-six years, he remained till the age of sixty-nine.

Prince Muney Tsenpo, the oldest of the king's three sons, was then placed on the throne. He established four major places to worship the Tripitaka and the abhisambodhi. He attempted the remarkable feat of equalizing rich and poor. Later, he was poisoned by his own mother.

The middle son was known under the names of Mutig Tseypo, Muri Tsenpo, Hutse Tsenpo, or as Lekpey Lodrö, the name he was given by Padmasambhava. He was young but dignified. He was enthroned at the age of thirteen. He became known as Seyna-lek Jing-yön, and he built the nine-storied Vajradhatu Temple at Karchung. His queen, Ngangchungma, had the Tsenthang Temple in Yarlung constructed. Padmakara consecrated both temples.[9]

The youngest son was Murub Tseypo or Prince Virtuous Protector. Padmasambhava gave him the name Prince Damdzin. He was strong-headed and wrathful. He became a general and was appointed to the task of guarding the borders in the four directions. After he had brought all enemies under his command, on his return, he had a fight with a minister's son. The son died and Prince Damdzin was sentenced to exile in the district of Kongrong for nine years.

Mutig Tseypo was young and had great faith in Padmasambhava. He asked for advice in all matters. That is the reason Master Padma is said to have ruled the kingdom. Padmasambhava stayed for three years during the reign of Mutig Tseypo.

Prince Lhajey was the oldest of Mutig Tseypo's five sons and received many oral instructions and predictions from Padmakara. Both he and his brother Lhundrub died at an early age. The third son, Tsangma, took ordination as a monk. Since Langdarma was unsuitable to rule, Tri Ralpachen was later appointed king. Most of the historical sources agree on this. Anyhow, Padmasambhava left Tibet while Prince Mutig was still young.

The Dependency of Perception

Of course it is impossible for any ordinary person to measure fully the virtuous qualities of even a single pore of the Buddha's body, since it defies the reach of ordinary thought. The inconsistencies and dissimilarities in the life stories of enlightened beings come about because those beings are perceived differently by the different levels of people who are to be influenced. It is therefore totally inappropriate to make fixed generalizations.

In the past, the buddha by the name Indomitable appeared with a body the size of eighty cubits, while the tathagata King of Stars was the size of one inch. The sugata Boundless Life lived for one hundred billion years while the sugata Lord of Assemblies appeared as living for just one day. These buddhas were definitely unlike ordinary people who have different life spans and degrees of merit. The buddhas appeared in those ways because of the different karmic perceptions of the different followers.

The superior qualities of our teacher, Buddha Shakyamuni, were perceived in varying ways, respectively, by common people, the shravaka followers of Hinayana, and the bodhisattva followers of Mahayana. Devadatta and the heretics perceived the Buddha only with their impure thoughts. This does not mean that the Buddha himself had different degrees of qualities, but only proves the individual perceptions of different people.

Master Padma was a supreme nirmanakaya. He appeared free from faults and fully endowed with all eminent qualities. He surely does not remain within the reach of people's solid fixation on a permanent reality, but appeared according to those to be tamed. Consequently, the clinging to absolutes concerning whether he took birth from a womb or was born miraculously, whether his different names and deeds in the Indian countries agree with one another, whether there are inconsistencies in the duration he remained in Tibet and so forth are nothing but causes to exhaust oneself and prove one's ignorance while attempting to conform the inconceivable to fit within the confines of conceptual thinking.

The Great Master expressed the real essence of this in his advice named the *Precious Garland of Gold*:

> I, Padmakara, came to benefit Tibet.
> By miraculous displays, I have tamed the vicious
>   spirits
> And established many destined people on the path
>   of ripening and liberation.
> The profound terma teachings shall fill Tibet and
>   Kham with siddhas.
>
> Pass and valley, mountain and cave, everywhere
>   down to the size of a hoof,
> I have consecrated to be a place of sadhana.

Creating the auspicious coincidence for lasting
    peace in Tibet and Kham,
I shall nurture beings with an unceasing stream of
    emanations.
My kindness to Tibet is great but it will not be
    appreciated.

Padmakara also said:

In the future, some incorrigible people with wrong
    views,
Foolish and corrupt, with the pretense of learning,
Babbling self-praise and disdain for others,
Will claim that I, Padma, did not stay long in
    Tibet.
Some will say that I stayed one month, some will
    say two weeks,
Some will claim that the Master of Uddiyana
    returned
With a load of gold after ten days.
That is not true; I stayed for one hundred and
    eleven years.

In all of Tibet, center and border land, the three
    valleys, down to the size of one arm span,
There is not any place I didn't visit.
Intelligent people, have trust when you discern
Whether I protect Tibet with kindness!

He also said:

Once in the future, some haughty and ignorant
    people
Will claim that Padmakara the Younger came to
    Tibet
While Padmakara the Elder never arrived in Tibet.

There is not a Younger and an Elder; in essence
they are the same.

Just let people with wrong views say what they
want.

If you have faith and devotion, supplicate me
constantly.

You will then receive the blessings, people of future
generations.

This is how Padmasambhava spoke, and in that I have full trust.

The Lotus-Born

Prologue

Homage to the divinities of the three kayas:
To dharmakaya Amitabha,
To sambhogakaya Great Compassion,
   noble Avalokiteshvara,
And to nirmanakaya Padmasambhava.

T HE NIRMANAKAYA PADMASAMBHAVA was emanated
by Buddha Amitabha for the benefit of beings from Sukhavati in the western direction, a realm superior to all pure
realms. He was emanated to the southern Jambu continent in this
Saha world-system, the domain of the nirmanakaya Shakyamuni,
into the countries of Uddiyana and India, and especially to Tibet,
so that noble Avalokiteshvara could tame the entire Land of Snow.

If you ask with which supreme qualities this Lotus-Born nirmanakaya was endowed and what were the details of his life, then
I shall describe them as follows.

I

IN THE WESTERN DIRECTION OF INDIA, in the country of glorious Uddiyana, in the city called Glowing Jewels, there was a palace of lapis lazuli decorated with many kinds of precious substances. Within this palace lived the Dharma king Indrabodhi, who ruled his kingdom from a great throne of shining gems, surrounded by his hundred and eight queens, his inner, outer, and intermediate ministers, as well as innumerable servants.

As the king was without a son, he bade all the court chaplains to assemble and perform an extensive offering ceremony before the three jewels on the fifteenth day of the first month of summer. Having recited once the *Cloud of Dharma Sutra*, the king promised to perform a great act of generosity to benefit all.

Many years passed during which he gave out the wealth of his treasury as alms, and the treasury drew close to empty. The flow of giving ceased, but the flow of beggars did not cease.

The ministers said, "The treasury is completely emptied and there is nothing left."

But the beggars retorted, "If that is so and you do not give us anything, all the alms previously given to others will have been in vain."

The king then reflected, "On an island in the great ocean lives the naga king's daughter known as Lovely Maiden, in whose possession there is a precious jewel that knows no limits for granting all needs and wants. She will give it if asked by a bodhisattva practicing generosity for the sake of Dharma. I must therefore request it and continue to give alms to the people." Thinking this, he had a sea-going vessel prepared, commanded by a captain who had fetched precious stones from the great ocean often in the past. As the king was about to depart with his retinue, all his ministers and subjects tried to dissuade him from leaving, but he would not listen. The king entered the ship, and four sails were raised in the four directions.

When a favorable wind blew the vessel would sail. When an unwanted wind blew it would not, and four great anchors of lead hanging from ropes made of camel hair were lowered in the four directions. By thus directing the ship, the king and his retinue found their way to the great ocean. The big sail was then hoisted and a favorable wind sent them on their way. They continued their journey with the speed of a strongly loosened arrow.

When they reached an island of precious gems, the retinue was left behind while the king and the captain continued the journey in a smaller boat. A white mountain came into sight and the king asked, "What kind of mountain is that?"

"That mountain is made of silver," was the answer.

They proceeded further and a blue mountain appeared so he asked, "What kind of mountain is that?"

"It is a mountain of lapis lazuli," was the answer.

After that, they saw a yellow mountain and the king asked about it.

"That is a mountain of gold; we are going to that place," the captain said.

They went there and saw that the earth was made of golden sand and that in front of the mountain there was a castle made of various kinds of precious substances.

The captain then told the king, "You should proceed while I stay here. The castle is surrounded by seven rings of lakes. When crossing them, you will meet many vicious animals, such as poisonous snakes, so contemplate bodhichitta while walking. In the center of the lakes is a wall made of iron and many different precious substances, which has four gates. A naga girl is the gatekeeper. Beseech her and she will open the gate. On the door of the palace inside, there is a vajra knocker. Use it to knock. One hundred deva maidens will then appear and present you with precious stones. Do not converse with them; knock again on the door. Finally the naga girl, a beautiful bluish girl, decorated with gem-studded ornaments and called Lovely Maiden, will arrive. Ask her to lend her ears to your story, and then request the jewel from her. She will present you with the precious jewel that is blue and shines with five-colored rays of light. Accept it immediately and, without letting it slip away, wrap it respectfully in your sleeve and return here. That is the precious gem that will fulfill all your wishes." Thus the captain instructed the king and sent him on his way.

The king then went on as prescribed, and, crossing first the seven rings of lakes, he reached the place of the poisonous snakes. Here the king meditated on bodhichitta and was therefore unharmed by the peril of the venomous breath of the serpents. At the wall he made a supplication to the naga girl guarding the gate, and it opened. Using the vajra knocker he knocked on the door of the palace. After a short while the naga girl Lovely Maiden appeared.

"Few people have ever reached my palace. You must be a man of great merit. What do you want?" she said.

After the king had told his whole story in detail, he said, "I have come to get the precious jewel."

The girl rejoiced and, pulling out the precious gem from the crown on her head, she gave it to the king who took it and departed. By the power of the jewel he did not need to walk back. Instantly reaching where the captain was, he said, "You have been most kind, captain!" Then the king and the captain arrived in a moment to where the retinue was waiting.

Afterward, the captain, who was skilled in examining gems, separated the precious stones from the semiprecious and gave them to the retinue, saying, "If we have too many, the boat will sink and it will cost us our lives. Please be content." With the captain steering the vessel, the king and his retinue set out in the direction of land.

On an island in the ocean grew a multicolored lotus flower upon which sat a little boy child, only eight years of age, beautiful to behold, ornamented with the major and minor marks and holding a vajra and a lotus in his hands. Seeing him they were struck with wonder and the king asked the little boy:

> Little boy child, who is your father and who is
>   your mother?
> What is your caste and what is your country?
> What food do you live on and what is your
>   purpose here?

In reply to these questions the boy said:

> My father is the wisdom of spontaneous awareness.
> My mother is the Ever-Excellent Lady, the space
>   of all things.
> I belong to the caste of indivisible space and
>   awareness.
> I have taken the unborn dharmadhatu as my
>   homeland.
> I sustain myself by consuming the concepts of
>   duality.
> My purpose is the act of killing disturbing
>   emotions.

Thus he spoke, and the king, filled with wonder, thought, "This must be a miraculous emanation!" He said, "I will make you my son and object of veneration." He then put the boy on a silken cloth and cut off the lotus. With both, the king returned to his country.

His servants and subjects were overjoyed and gave an enormous welcoming party. The king then took the precious jewel in his hand and made a wish with these words, "If this precious gem that I have found is an unmistaken wish-fulfilling jewel, may my little boy child

34

be seated upon a huge throne made of the seven precious substances and decorated with a parasol of costly gems." As soon as these words were uttered, the throne and parasol appeared. The boy was seated upon the throne, empowered as prince and given the name King Padma Vajra.

Again the king said, "If this precious gem is the unmistaken and priceless wish-fulfilling jewel, may all the empty treasuries from where I formerly distributed alms become as full as they once were!" Instantaneously his treasure houses were again filled, just as before. Then the king let the great drum resound and the good news be announced in all directions: "I, King Indrabodhi, proclaim that the fulfillment of all needs and wants will rain down by the grace of my precious wish-fulfilling jewel. Come and receive whatever you wish for and whatever you may need!"

The king washed the jewel in cleansing water, attached it at the top of a victory banner, enveloped it in fragrant fumes of camphor and sandalwood, and put out a vast display of offerings before it. He then bathed, donned clean clothing, and, having paid homage to the divinities of the four directions, made the following prayer. "If this priceless gem that I have found is truly the unmistaken and precious wish-fulfilling jewel, may whatever humans and all other beings desire shower down like falling rain!" Immediately upon exclaiming these words, winds rose from the four directions and swept away all dirt. A gently falling rain ensured that no dust would rise, and thus all was perfectly cleansed.

Foods endowed with one hundred flavors fell from the jewel, satisfying all who were starving. A cascade of clothing fell, satisfying all who were cold, and after that a shower of gems rained down, satisfying all wishes.

The king then gave this command to everyone under his power: "Everyone must now embrace the teachings of the Mahayana." Thus, everyone developed bodhichitta and achieved the fruition of nonreturn.

This was the first chapter in the immaculate life story of the Lotus-Born Master, telling how he became the son of King Indrabodhi and ascended the royal throne.

2

❁

THE PRINCE NIRMANAKAYA considered that by ruling the kingdom, he would not benefit beings. Consequently, he performed some actions of yogic discipline to avert the attachment of the king and ministers. He adorned his naked body with bone ornaments, in his hands he thrust up the damaru drum of united bliss and emptiness and a three-pronged khatvanga, the annihilator of the three poisons, and began to dance on the palace roof.

Many spectators gathered. One day he let the khatvanga slip from his hand. It hit the head of the son of Kamalatey, the most influential among the ministers, and killed him.[10]

Whoever broke the law of the kingdom had to be punished. All the ministers assembled and said to the king, "Although this boy was crowned as monarch he has conducted himself in an improper fashion. He has killed a minister's son. Now the prince himself must be punished by impalement."

The king replied, "I do not know whether the prince is a child of a nonhuman or whether he is a miraculous emanation. It would be improper to kill him; let him be banished."

The ministers sentenced the prince to exile. Due to this, the king grew very sad and full of sorrow. But, as the law of the kingdom was strongly enforced, he was powerless not to banish the prince. He summoned the prince and treated him with all kinds of food and drink. Afterward, the king spoke in these poetic words:

> From a lotus flower amidst the precious waters
> You appeared, without father or mother, emanation
> boy child.

Lacking the fortune of a son, I crowned you in the
    royal palace,
But your action, prince, caused a minister's son to
    expire.
The ministers have sentenced you by the royal law.
As you are to be expelled, go now to wherever you
    please.

Saying these words, tears streamed forth from the king's eyes. The prince gave the best pieces of food to his father the king and said:

In this world, a father and mother are precious.
You have been my parents and given me the
    throne.
As a karmic debt the minister's son was killed,
And it is correct to be exiled under my father's
    strict law.
Yet, I have no fear, as mind knows neither birth
    nor death.
Not having attachment to a homeland, to be exiled
    does not intimidate me.
Remain always in happiness, my father and mother.
By our karmic connection we will meet again in the
    future.

The prince paid homage to his father and mother and then also shed tears. The parents thought, "He is really a nirmanakaya!" Feeling extremely unhappy, they veiled their heads and lay down to sleep.

The ministers led away the prince and escorted him to the great charnel ground known as Cool Grove, in the eastern direction of the country of Uddiyana. It was a most frightening and terrifying place, filled with spirits, corpses, carrion-eating birds, and ferocious predators.

Following the local religious customs, when dead people were brought to that charnel ground and left there, each corpse was wrapped in a sheet of cotton cloth as clothing and accompanied by a bushel of rice-pap as food. The prince now acted as a yogi of Secret Mantra. He wore the clothing of the corpses as his dress and ate the food given to the dead. He remained in the samadhi called Unshakable and thus stayed in great happiness.

After some time, a widespread famine broke out in that area. Most of the people died. The numerous corpses were carried in without the sheet of cloth and without the provision of rice-pap. Therefore the prince flayed human skin for clothes and ate the corpses for food. Through this he brought all the mamo dakinis dwelling in the charnel ground under his command and remained practicing the actions of yogic discipline.

During this time, in the district of Uddiyana known as Gaushö, there was an evil king named Shakraraja. He was forcing the people under his domain onto an errant path from which later they would go to the lower realms. The prince considered that there was no other way to convert them than through subjugating and wrathful activity. He tied up the hair on his head with a snake, donned a human skin as his shirt, and made a tiger skin his skirt. Holding in his hands five iron arrows and a bow, he went to that country of evil deeds. The prince killed all the males he came across, ate their flesh, drank their blood, and united with all the females. He brought everyone under his power and performed the tanagana ritual of union and liberation. Therefore he was named Rakshasa Demon.[11]

The evil king gathered the local people and conspired to go hunting in the cemetery to kill the Rakshasa Demon. The king himself took his sword Taramashi. A skilled archer from the area was placed on guard at the lower end of the charnel ground while all the others, carrying their armor and weapons, started to hunt from its upper end. Rakshasa Demon shot the guardsman with an arrow and fled. He was then given the name Youthful Escapee.

Padmasambhava now went to the country of Sahor where he practiced in the great charnel ground Joyful Grove while living off the corpses. Here he was empowered and blessed by the dakini Subduer of Mara.

Following that, he went to the charnel ground Sosaling, situated to the south of Uddiyana. There he practiced yogic discipline and was empowered and blessed by the dakini Sustainer of Peace. Later, he went back to the island in the ocean where previously he had been born from a lotus flower. By practicing the dakini sign language of Secret Mantra, he magnetized the four classes of dakinis dwelling on the island. All the ocean nagas and the planetary spirits in the heavens promised to be his servants and were bound under oath.

After this, he practiced at the charnel ground Rugged Grove in Uddiyana and had a vision of Vajra Varahi who empowered him. The four classes of dakinis and the dakas and dakinis of the three levels bestowed attainments and transmission upon him. All the dakinis blessed him and taught him the Dharma. Thus he became a powerful yogi. The dakinis gave him the secret name Dorje Drakpo Tsal, Powerful Vajra Wrath.

This was the second chapter in the immaculate life story of the Lotus-Born Master, telling how he practiced in the charnel grounds and was blessed by the dakinis.

3

PADMASAMBHAVA then went to the Vajra Seat in India.
Sometimes he transformed himself into many hundreds of
monks making offerings to the shrine, sometimes into many
hundreds of yogis performing various practices. The people, therefore, asked him who his master was, whereto he replied:

> I have no father and I have no mother.
> I have no teacher nor do I have a master.
> I have no caste and I have no name.
> I am a self-appeared buddha.

Everyone became doubtful and said, "Someone who displays
miracles without having a teacher must be a demon."

Master Padma reflected, "Although I am a self-appeared nirmanakaya, to show future generations the necessity of a master, I
must act as if seeking all the outer and inner teachings of Secret
Mantra from the learned and accomplished masters of India."

Thinking this, he went toward the dwelling of Master Prabhahasti. On the road, he met the two monks Shakyamaitri and
Shakyamitra, who were on their way to receive teachings from
Master Prabhahasti. After paying homage, he requested teachings
from them.

The two monks thought, "The rakshasa demon has come back!",
and they became frightened.

Padmasambhava said, "I am not doing any more evil actions;
please accept me."

They answered, "If that is so, first give us your weapons." Then he handed over the bow and iron arrows. The monks said, "The time has not come for us to teach you. Go to Red Rock Garuda where our master Prabhahasti lives."

He arrived before Prabhahasti, from whom he received ordination and was named Shakya Senge. The master taught him the three great sections of Yoga Tantra: *Sundha Jnanaya, Yogacharyava,* and *Tattvasamgraha.*[12] Although he understood these scriptures the moment they were taught, he studied them eighteen times in the pretense of purifying obscurations. At the same time, even without having practiced, he had visions of the thirty-seven divinities of Yoga Tantra.

Shakya Senge reflected, "I will practice the teaching of Mahayoga and accomplish both the vidyadhara level of longevity and the supreme vidyadhara level of mahamudra." Thinking thus, he went to the great master Manjushrimitra who was living at Mount Malaya.

He requested the teaching, but the master said, "The time is not yet right for me to teach you. You must go to the charnel ground named Sandal Grove where the nun Kungamo lives. She is a wisdom dakini endowed with great blessings and skilled in conferring the outer, inner, and secret empowerments. Go there and request the empowerments." Thus he was instructed.

Shakya Senge then went to charnel ground Sandal Grove where he met the maid Young Damsel, who was fetching water. He presented the letter requesting the bestowal of the outer, inner, and secret empowerments. Having gotten no response, he asked, "Have you forgotten my message?" Still, she did not utter a word, so Master Padma applied his power of concentration, nailing down her buckets and crossbar.

Being unable to lift the buckets, she drew a white crystal knife from her waist and said, "You have quite some power, but I can do something more amazing!" Exclaiming these words, she cut open her chest revealing the forty-two peaceful deities in her upper part and the fifty-eight herukas of wrathful deities in her lower torso, thus vividly displaying the hundred peaceful and wrathful divinities.

"She must be the nun," he thought and began to pay her homage and to circumambulate her.

Yet, she said, "I am just a maid-servant. Go inside."

He went inside and met the nun Kungamo, who was seated on a throne. Flanked by dakas she wore bone ornaments and held a skull cup and a wooden drum in her hands. Surrounded by thirty-three maidens, she was performing a feast offering. After having offered a mandala, prostrating, and circumambulating Kungamo, he requested the outer, inner, and secret empowerments. She then turned Shakya Senge into the syllable HUNG and, swallowing him, she conferred the empowerments within the mandala of her body. Emitting the HUNG through the secret lotus, she purified the obscurations of his body, speech, and mind.

Empowering him externally as Buddha Amitabha, Kungamo gave the blessing to attain the vidyadhara level of longevity. Empowering him internally as the noble Avalokiteshvara, she gave the blessing to attain the vidyadhara level of mahamudra. Empowering him secretly as glorious Hayagriva, she blessed him to magnetize all the mamo dakinis, worldly devas, and haughty demon spirits. Finally, she also gave him the secret name of Loden Chogsey.

Loden Chogsey went back before Manjushrimitra, with whom he studied all the inner and outer teachings of Manjushri. Following this, he had a vision of Manjushri. Then, he journeyed to the master Humkara and studied all the teachings of Vishuddha. From the great master Prabhahasti, Loden Chogsey received all the teachings of Vajra Kilaya and had a vision of the Kilaya deities. Afterward, he proceeded to the great master Nagarjuna, where he learned all the causal philosophical teachings and the teachings on Lotus Speech. Having gone before the great master Buddhaguhya, he studied all the teachings on the magical display of the peaceful and wrathful ones. Later, he traveled to the great master Mahavajra and received all the teachings on Nectar Quality. Having gone before the great master

Dhana Sanskrita, he learned all the teachings on the universal Mother Deities. Next, he went before the great master Rombuguhya Devachandra, with whom he studied all the teachings on Mundane Worship. Having gone before the great master Shantigarbha, he received all the teachings on the Maledictory Fierce Mantra and the fierce and subjugating mantras of the guardians of the Dharma. Later, he journeyed to the great master Shri Singha, with whom he studied all the teachings on the sacred Great Perfection.[13] He gained immediate comprehension of these teachings and, without having to practice, he had visions of all the deities. He was now famed under the name Loden Chogsey.

This was the third chapter in the immaculate life story of the Lotus-Born Master, on how he followed his gurus, received teachings, and showed the manner of mind-training.

Thank You for Visiting KPC's Stupa Peace Park

Some of the things you will come across on the land include:

✦ **Stupas** (sacred Buddhist monuments) considered to be the Mind of the Buddha in physical form. Walk around them in a clockwise direction (keep the Stupa on your right). Make prayers and wishes for the benefit of beings. It is good to make offerings—fruit, candles, incense, etc.,—at the stupas. Please feel welcome to do so, but do not disturb the offerings that are present.

✦ **Walking trails** on 65 acres of woodlands.

✦ **Color Gardens** corresponding to the five directions and purifications of the five poisons.

West	Red	Desire	Discriminating wisdom
North	Green	Jealousy	All-accomplishing wisdom
East	Blue	Anger	Mirror-mind wisdom
South	Yellow	Pride	All-equalizing wisdom
Central	White	Ignorance	Dharmadhatu wisdom

✦ **Prayer Wheels** filled with thousands of mantras (prayers). Give them a spin in a clockwise direction.

✦ **Prayer Flags** whose thousands of prayers are carried by the wind to bring benefit everywhere.

✦ **Wildlife** that is protected from hunting.

Some facts about the land:

✦ The land is naturally recovering from past over-farming; fast-growing cedar trees are in abundance; the next phase will be the growth of more deciduous (leafy) trees.

✦ It was part of a parcel of land once owned by George Washington's brother.

✦ The walking trails, roads, gardens, bridges, prayer wheels and stupas require ongoing maintenance. In addition, the land was severely damaged by last winter's storms, and much effort is being focused on reclaiming trails and clearing the dead wood. Sponsorships or donations toward these projects are gratefully appreciated.

KPC is a 501(c)(3) tax exempt organization, supported by the generosity of its friends, members and visitors. Your financial contributions are always welcome, much appreciated, and tax-deductible to the full extent allowed by law.

TO HELP PROTECT THIS SACRED LAND, PLEASE CONSIDER MAKING A TAX-DEDUCTIBLE DONATION

Make checks payable to KPC Stupa Peace Park or complete the credit card information below. Drop in the offering box inside KPC's front door, on the right, or mail to the address at the bottom of this form.

Name on credit card: _____ Amount of Gift $_____

E-mail: _____ Today's date: _____

Type of card: ❑ Visa ❑ MasterCard ❑ American Express + 4 digit # on front _____

Credit Card Number_____

Expiration Date _____ Signature _____

KUNZANG PALYUL CHÖLING ✦ 18400 RIVER RD., P.O. BOX 88 ✦ POOLESVILLE, MD 20837
(301) 710-6259 ✦ WWW.TARA.ORG

Guide to KPC's Stupa & Peace Park

Welcome to the Stupa Peace Park. This sacred land is dedicated to the benefit of all beings. Please invite your family and friends to come and enjoy the Park. Times indicate a leisurely pace between gardens.

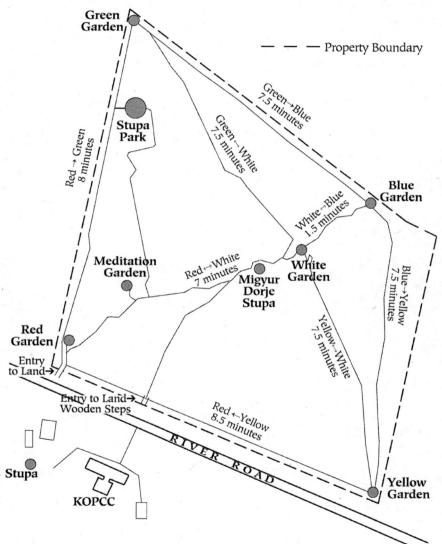

KPC's Stupa Park

The park is open to all during daylight hours,
seven days a week.

(Please see reverse for additional information.)

4

L ODEN CHOGSEY then contemplated, "By Secret Mantra, I will now accomplish the vidyadhara level of longevity beyond birth and death. I must cause all the people of Uddiyana and India to enter the Buddhadharma."

In order to practice the Secret Mantra, one must have a genuine spiritual consort, so he went to the country of Sahor. Here Arshadhara, the king of Sahor, had a daughter called Mandarava Flower, a sixteen-year-old maiden endowed with the qualifying marks. Master Padma magnetized her and took her along as his *mudra*, a spiritual consort and support in practice.

South of Mount Potala, the palace of noble Avalokiteshvara, lies the cave known as Maratika. It faces south, and a rain of flowers constantly falls. Enveloped in a dome of rainbows, the scent of incense permeates the air. It has a grove of sandalwood trees and is blessed by the Lords of the Three Families. The master and his consort went to this place and, disclosing the mandalas of Buddha Amitayus, they performed the practice of vidyadhara longevity.

After three months, they had the vision of Amitayus. He placed the nectar-filled vase of immortal life upon the heads of Master Padma and his consort and, by pouring the nectar into their mouths, their bodies became vajra bodies beyond birth and death. He blessed Master Padma to be the daka Hayagriva and the consort to be Vajra Varahi. Thus they reached the attainment of vidyadhara life.

In order to cause the people of Sahor to enter the Buddhadharma, Master Padma and his consort then went to the city to beg for alms. While doing that the people became envious and said, "This is the stray foreign mendicant, who in the past killed the males and coupled with the females. He has carried off the king's daughter and adulterated the royal caste. Again, he will create havoc; he must be corrected!"

Saying this, the people gathered sandalwood with a drey of oil for each load of wood. After that, they burned Master Padma and his consort in the center of a village.[14]

Normally, when people were burned, the smoke would cease after three days, but now even after nine days the smoke did not stop. As people came for a closer look, the fire blazed up, burning the entire royal palace. The oil had turned into a lake, with the inner part covered by lotus flowers. Upon an open lotus, in the middle of the lake, Master Padma and his consort sat fresh and cool. Here, the king and his ministers, struck with wonder offered the following praise:

> HUNG
> Your body is the changeless vajralike body.
> Your speech is the changeless Brahma-like voice.
> Your mind is the changeless skylike mind.
> Your body, speech, and mind are the immortal
>   vajrakaya.
> We praise and prostrate to you, Padma Vajra.
> Out of ignorance, we have wronged you; please
>   forgive us.
> Be kind to establish our country in peace.

By praying in that way, the flames in the town calmed down and everything became even more beautiful and pleasant than before. The master was then given the names Padmakara and Padmasambhava, the Lotus-Born.

He caused the whole country of Sahor to embrace the Buddhadharma and established everyone on the level of nonreturn.

Master Padma then thought, "Now, I must make everyone in the land of Uddiyana enter the Buddhadharma." The master and his consort went to the kingdom of Uddiyana in order to beg for alms.

The local people recognized him and said, "In the past, this man broke the royal law and killed the son of our minister. He will again bring harm; he must be punished!"

The minister whose son had been killed, along with many towns-people, tied up Master Padma and his consort. They gathered sandalwood with a drey of oil for each load of firewood and burned the master and his consort. In the past, the smoke had ceased after seven days of burning, but now even after twenty-one days, the smoke did not stop. The king told his ministers to go and investi-gate. No one had the courage to go and look. The king, formerly Master Padma's father, became doubtful and thought, "If the master really is a miraculous emanation, then he should not burn."

With his retinue the king went to look for himself. There, in the center of the lake, which was created from the oil, amidst a huge dome of embers, sat Master Padma and his consort upon a lotus flower, fresh, cool, and shining with dew drops. In order to liberate the beings through compassion, they were adorned with garlands of skulls. The king and the others were filled with wonder and, after prostrating and circumambulating the master, they offered this praise:

> Having achieved the supreme accomplishment, your
>   body is a great marvel.
> Transcending birth and death, you took birth from
>   a lotus bud.
> You wear a garland of skulls to free samsara
>   through compassion.
> We praise your bodily form, Padma Vajra.

The king placed the foot of Master Padma above his head and requested him to become the supreme object of veneration at the court, but the master replied:

To take birth in the three realms of samsara is a
    dungeon of misery.
Even to be born as a dharma king is mere bustle
    and distraction.
If you do not know that your mind is the unborn
    dharmakaya,
Samsaric rebirth does not end, and you circle un-
    ceasingly.
Great king, look into your empty and cognizant
    nature!
Then you shall soon attain the perfect enlight-
    enment.

In the same moment as Master Padma spoke, the king realized
his mind to be dharmakaya. Realization and liberation occurred
simultaneously, and the father-king, with his retinue, achieved the
"acceptance of the nature of nonarising." The king then offered this
praise:

HUNG
Great wondrous one, who has attained the supreme
    accomplishment,
Through your eminent and unsurpassable reali-
    zation,
You have unfolded the great mystery of all the
    instructions of the tathagatas.
I offer you my prostrations and praises!

After this praise, as he was wearing a garland of skulls, the master
was named Padma Thötreng Tsal, the Powerful Lotus of the Garland of Skulls. Since he had previously been the son of the king, he
was named Lotus King. After this, he remained for thirteen years as
the supreme object of veneration at the court of his father the king,
and he established the whole kingdom of Uddiyana in the Buddhadharma. King Indrabodhi, his queens and ministers, as well as five

hundred merchants achieved the supreme vidyadhara level of mahamudra.

Master Padma then went to practice in the charnel ground of Jalandhara. At this time, there were some heretical teachers called the four great sorcerers, each surrounded by five hundred followers, who approached the four sides of the Vajra Seat to debate.

They said, "If we, the non-Buddhists, win, then you shall embrace our doctrine. If you, the Buddhists, win, then we shall become Buddhists."

The four gate-keeping panditas at Vajra Seat and all the other panditas thought, "Although we can win in debate, we cannot win in the contest of magical powers." Thinking thus, no one dared to speak.

While the panditas at Vajra Seat held a conference in the king's palace, a blue-tinged woman appeared holding a broken stick in her hand. "You can only win the contest with these heretics if my brother comes here," she said.

They asked her, "Who is your brother and where does he stay?"

"My brother is called Padma Vajra and he is practicing in the charnel ground of Jalandhara."

Then they asked, "If that is so, then how can we invite him?"

She replied, "You cannot bring him here by sending a messenger. Instead assemble in the Mahabodhi Temple, arrange an extensive offering ceremony, and pray. I shall go and invite him."[15]

Having said these words, the woman disappeared. All the panditas then gathered in the temple and, just as she had prescribed, they arranged for an offering ceremony and made supplications in the following words:

> In front of Vajra Seat, the site where the buddhas
>   of the three times appear,
> A dispute has broken out with the demonic legions
>   of heretics.
> We lack a savior who can send the enemy aflight.
> Please protect us, noble being, lion of men!

Thus they prayed. At the first break of dawn, Master Padma arrived at the palace of Vajra Seat, alighting like a bird upon a branch. The master remained in the samadhi of complete victory over demonic forces and beat a wooden drum with his hand.

In the four directions, four heretics with knowledge of sound said, "This morning an unpleasant sound is heard, unlike anything in the past."

Asked what the sound meant, the one with knowledge of sound in the eastern direction said, "Sounding the great drum of the bodhichitta of love overthrows the foxlike heretics."

The one with knowledge of sound in the southern direction said, "Sounding the great drum of the bodhichitta of compassion overpowers the demonic legions of false guides."

The one with knowledge of sound in the western direction said, "Sounding the great drum of the bodhichitta of joy annihilates the disputing hordes of savages."

The one with knowledge of sound in the northern direction said, "Sounding the great drum of the bodhichitta of impartiality reduces all dark forces to dust."

As the sun rose, the non-Buddhists and the Buddhists began the debate. Master Padma himself remained in the palace of Vajra Seat, absorbed in the concentration of complete victory over demonic forces, while displaying four different manifestations in the four directions. Thus he entered the debate, surrounded by five hundred panditas. After the Buddhists had won, the four heretical teachers, along with a few of their attendants who possessed miraculous powers, flew up in the air. Master Padma directed the menacing scorpion gesture at them and, spinning a wheel of fire in the sky, he made the four heretical teachers flee, each into his own castle. All their followers embraced the Buddhist teachings.

The four heretical teachers then said, "You might be greater in logic and miracles, but we will make sure you die seven days from now!" Having said this, they began to utter evil mantras.

Master Padma performed a feast offering for the dakinis and

prayed. At dawn, the dakini Subduer of Mara placed an iron-nailed casket of rhino hide in the master's hand. She instructed him in the method to tame all demons and heretics. Within the rhino casket, he found the subjugating mantras of the dakinis including the instructions on magical wheels, hail storms, and lightning. Master Padma then brought down a flash of meteors on the dwelling places of the heretical teachers. They were completely burnt down and reduced to dust. Thus he bestowed a great favor upon the Buddhist teachings. All the panditas at Vajra Seat regarded him as their crown jewel and named him Roaring Lion.

This was the fourth chapter in the immaculate life story of the Lotus-Born Master, on how he converted people by means of miracles, tamed the heretics, and vastly benefited the Buddhist teachings.

5

❀

ASTER PADMA then reflected, "I have attained the yoga
vidyadhara level of longevity; now I must accomplish the
supreme vidyadhara level of mahamudra."

Master Padma then went to the Cave of Yangleshö, situated half
way between India and Nepal. It is a very auspicious and blessed
place, where flowers do not wither, even in the winter time. Here,
he took along Shakyadevi, daughter of the Nepalese King Virtuous,
as his mudra and spiritual support in practice.

First, he disclosed the mandala of nine-faced glorious Vishuddha
Heruka, but three kinds of obstacles arose. The naga Gyongpo, the
yaksha Gomakha, and Logmadrin of the ethereal realms began to
make obstacles. For three years, not one drop of rain fell from the
skies. Because of that, the earth yielded neither vegetables nor crops.
Throughout the lands of India, Nepal, and Tibet famine, diseases,
and plagues gathered like dark clouds, killing both men and cattle.
Master Padma pondered, "These conditions cannot have a natural
cause. The local deities must be trying to hinder my achieving the
accomplishment of mahamudra."

Padmakara furnished his two Nepalese disciples Jilajisa and Kun-
lakunsa with a drey of gold dust as a gift and dispatched them to
his former masters in India. The disciples were instructed to convey
this message, "Three spirits have risen to obstruct my attainment of
the accomplishment of mahamudra. I request you to send a teaching
to clear away these hindrances."

The Indian panditas answered, "The master Prabhahasti has the
teaching of Vajra Kilaya as a remedy against obstacles. Go and
request it."

They went to Master Prabhahasti and asked for the teaching. Master Prabhahasti selected, from amongst the hundred thousand sections of Kilaya teachings, two loads of sadhanas that subdue enmity and obstructing forces. The disciples returned with these scriptures.

The moment the disciples arrived at the Cave of Yanglesho, the three obstructing spirits were pacified. Vapors arose from the ocean, the soil grew warm, clouds mounted in the skies, and rain started to fall. Grass, trees, crops, and fruit all ripened simultaneously and, by merely eating the fruit, diseases of both men and animals were eliminated. The famine dissipated and everyone in the land was joyful.

Then Master Padma had a vision of the glorious Vishuddha and the Kilaya deities. Vishuddha is like a merchant engaging in trade; the achievement can be great, but so can the obstacles. Kilaya is like an armed escort; he is needed to overcome the obstacles. Considering this, Master Padma composed a combined sadhana of Vishuddha and Kilaya based on the *Heruka Galpo Tantra* and the hundred thousand sections of Kilaya teachings known as *Unexcelled Knowledge*. Then he performed the sadhana and attained the accomplishment of mahamudra.

At the time of dusk, the four shvana sisters offered the core of their lives to Master Padma and were bound under oath. At midnight, the four remati sisters offered the core of their lives and were bound under oath. At dawn, the four semo sisters offered the core of their lives and were bound under oath. Moreover, the male and female powerful sey, chak, and dung spirits all offered the core of their lives, were bound under oath, and appointed as guardians of the Vajra Kilaya teachings.

Master Padma, with his body as the mandala of deities, overpowered all the haughty spirits. With his speech as the mandala of mantras, he magnetized all the haughty spirits. With his mind as the mandala of dharmata, he naturally pacified and spontaneously cleared away all the discursive thoughts of the five poisons. Thus, he remained unmoved from the realization of mahamudra.

This was the fifth chapter in the immaculate life story of the Lotus-Born Master, on how he accomplished the vidyadhara level of mahamudra by means of Vishuddha and Kilaya.

6

❀

NOW FOLLOWS the story of how Master Padma was invited to Tibet.

King Trisong Deutsen of Tibet, an emanation of noble Manjushri, invited Master Padma to his country to tame the land for the construction of the glorious temple of Samye.

Prior to this, the lord of knowledge, noble Manjushri, while dwelling at the Five-Peaked Mountain in China, turned his face toward Tibet and thought, "I must convert the people of the snowy land of Tibet. In the past, the Great Compassionate One incarnated as King Songtsen Gampo, who built one hundred and eight temples, such as Lhasa Trülnang and Ramochey, as well as many other major and minor temples, thus instigating the tradition of the sacred Dharma. Now, I must cause the Dharma to spread and flourish in the snowy land of Tibet by an incarnation of noble Manjushri. He shall incarnate as a strong king and gather everyone under his power."

Contemplating in this way, he gazed with his wisdom eyes from the Five-Peaked Mountain in China and perceived that Tridey Tsugten was the present ruler of the country of Tibet. While King Tridey Tsugten and his consort, Lady Angchung of Mashang, were lying asleep on their throne made of costly materials, in the palace at Red Rock, noble Manjushri emanated from his heart center a five-colored ray of light, upon whose tip was a golden boy-child, the size of a finger. The child entered the womb of Lady Angchung of Mashang and was conceived. Simultaneously, she dreamed that rays of light, resembling a rising sun, appeared with a baby boy at the tip of the rays and entered her belly. After recounting the dream to her husband the king, he said, "A divine being from the skies has come to be our son. It is an extremely excellent dream." The king was overjoyed.

Without any sense of discomfort, Lady Angchung then began to feel movements and throbbing. Her body became blissful and light and her mind clear, without disturbing emotions. After nine months, the incarnation was born in the palace at Red Rock, causing no pain at all to the mother.

The infant prince had many teeth and, at the top of his head, in his shiny black hair, there was a right-turning curl. The infant prince was beautiful, like a child of the gods. He was born just as the sun arose in the sky, on the day of the Victorious constellation, in the first month of spring, in the Year of the Horse. The name of Trisong Deutsen was bestowed upon him.

When the prince was thirteen years old, his father, King Tridey Tsugten, passed away, and the prince ascended to the throne. He was given three brides to marry, Lady Margyen of Tsepang, Lady Jangchub Men of Tro, and Lady Gyalmo Tsün of Pho-gyong. For seven years, he ruled the kingdom by guarding the borders outwardly and maintaining the law inwardly.

This was the sixth chapter of the immaculate life story of the Lotus-Born Master, on how the king of Tibet took hold of his kingdom.

7

❀

I<small>T WAS IN THE</small> Y<small>EAR OF THE</small> O<small>X</small> when King Trisong
Deutsen, who had reached the age of twenty, gave rise to the
thought of practicing the holy Dharma, and this deep aspiration
took root in him: "The former king, Songtsen Gampo, constructed
many temples in this pitch-black darkness of Tibet. He had many
texts of the holy Dharma translated, and he was extremely kind to
Tibet. Now, I shall cause the holy Dharma to spread and flourish!
I will construct a temple that will be a palace for the three jewels,
a site of devotion and respect for all the people. I shall build a temple
to fulfill my sacred aspiration. What kind of temple should I
construct?" He then decided, "I shall build a temple that resembles
the four continents and Mount Sumeru, surrounded by the ring of
iron mountains!"

King Trisong Deutsen laid the foundation stone in the Year of
the Tiger, after having turned twenty-one. He then heard that in
India, there lived a famous bodhisattva known as Master Bodhisattva, endowed with extremely great wisdom. The king furnished
Jnana Kumara, a translator who knew both Tibetan and Sanskrit,
with a drey of gold dust as a gift and dispatched him with two
servants to invite this master to Tibet.

Jnana Kumara met Master Bodhisattva in the temple of glorious
Nalanda, offered him the gold dust, and made this supplication,
"The king of Tibet wishes to build a temple and has sent me to
invite you to tame the construction site. Master, please come!"

Master Bodhisattva replied, "I have a karmic connection with the
Tibetan king from former lives, so I must go." Having said this, he
left for Tibet.

Master Bodhisattva was escorted to the palace at Red Rock and offered a welcome by King Trisong Deutsen, who said, "Great Master, I wish to construct a castle that will be a shrine for the Three Jewels, the fulfillment of my vow, and an object of respect and veneration for all people. Please bestow your blessings on the construction site."

Master Bodhisattva replied, "The Tibetan devas, spirits, and local deities are savage. I shall try to convert them with bodhichitta, but whether I will succeed or not, I do not know. Your Majesty, lay down the foundation stones."

Master Bodhisattva then disclosed the Vajradhatu Mandala of Peaceful Deities and consecrated the site. King Trisong Deutsen put on a gown of white silk and started to dig with a golden hoe. About one cubit under the ground, he discovered a bushel of white rice and some nectarlike paste with different kinds of sweet tastes. The king himself ate some and smeared some on his head. "My aspiration will surely be fulfilled. The teachings of the Dharma will flourish in Tibet," he said.

The foundation was laid and they began to build, but powerful male and female yaksha spirits of Tibet, such as the twenty-one genyen and others, began to create obstacles. What the king's men built by daylight, the spirits destroyed and leveled each night. Thus, the construction could not progress.

Master Bodhisattva then said, "It seems to me that the construction cannot be completed." King Trisong Deutsen asked, "Isn't there something that can be done?"

Master Bodhisattva replied, "Great king, I know all the teachings of the causal philosophical vehicles without exception, and I have mastered bodhichitta; but it looks as though I have not yet tamed the savage and malicious gods and spirits. Still, there is something to do."

> This was the seventh chapter in the immaculate life story of the Lotus-Born Master, on how the king awakened faith in the Dharma, invited Master Bodhi-sattva to Tibet to fulfill his aspiration, and laid the foundation for the temple.

8

❀

MASTER BODHISATTVA SAID, "These malicious gods and demons of Tibet must be tamed by wrathful means. In the Cave of Yangleshö in Nepal stays a siddha, who became the son of the king of Uddiyana. He is the incarnated Padmasambhava, who possesses great spiritual strength and overwhelming power. He lives by practicing the disciplines of Secret Mantra. If you can invite him, he will fulfill your aspiration and subjugate the local spirits. Your Majesty, pretend that these directions were revealed to you in a dream."

Later, King Trisong Deutsen proclaimed to his subjects, inner and outer attendants, "Last night, I had a dream about a master from Uddiyana by the name of Padmasambhava, who lives in the Cave of Yangleshö on the border of India and Nepal. My aspiration will be fulfilled if he is invited to Tibet. You must send someone to invite him. Call a council to discuss the dispatching of three emissaries."

The subjects pondered and discussed, but could not agree to send emissaries. King Trisong Deutsen himself gave directions to Mangjey Selnang of Bey and Lhalung of Sengey Go. He furnished them with three servants and a drey of gold dust and sent the five of them on their way.

At the same time, all the guardians of the Buddhadharma made a personal request to Master Padma, "The Tibetan king will beseech you to build a temple at the base of Mount Hepori in the land of Tibet. He is sending five emissaries to meet you, but they are tired and weary. Master, please prepare to go and meet them at the border of Sky Plain."

With his miraculous powers, Master Padma journeyed through the sky and remained for three months on the plateau of Sky Plain in Mang-yul. When the master met with the emissaries, although he knew who they were and where they were going, he still questioned them.

Mangjey Selnang of Bey replied, "We have been sent by the king of Tibet to invite Master Padmasambhava. Is that you?"

Master Padma said, "Well, well! Three months ago, I received a request from the guardians of the Buddhadharma. They were afraid that you emissaries were tired out, so I waited for you here. You really have taken a long time! Now, give me whatever you have to offer!"

They all did prostrations and offered one drey of gold dust. Master Padma said, "Give me some more!" The emissaries stripped off their clothes and offered them, but the master again said, "Still give me whatever you have!"

The emissaries replied, "The king did not supply us with more than this. Also we do not have any more ourselves, so now we offer you our body, speech, and mind in your service." They then made prostrations and circumambulated Master Padma and placed his foot at the crown of their heads.

The master was pleased by this and said, "I was checking whether or not the faith of Tibetans is fickle. For me all appearances are gold." While saying this he stretched out his right arm in the direction of Sky Plain in Mang-yul, and the mountains on the left side shifted to the right. When he stretched his left arm to the west, the earth and rocks all turned into zi stones, agate, coral, gold, and turquoise, some of which he gave to the emissaries. Assuming a gaze, he made the sun and moon sink to the ground and, with a threatening gesture, he made the river reverse its flow. "This is the type of miraculous power and ability I possess! You should have trust in this. I have no need for your gold, but in order to fulfill the king's aspiration and to allow him to gain merit, I should keep some." Saying that, Master Padma flung some gold toward Mang-yul and

Nepal. "Later, Tibetan gold will be plentiful in the areas of Mang-yul and the direction of Nepal."

At first, the emissaries mistrusted the gold and turquoise given by Master Padma, believing it to be fake. Later, as they walked along and examined it privately, they found it was genuine and gained faith in Padmasambhava.

This was the eighth chapter in the immaculate life story of the Lotus-Born Master, on how Padmasambhava went to Tibet out of compassion and met with the emissaries.

9

❀

PROCEEDING, MASTER PADMA and his attendants arrived at the pass at the upper end of Mang-yul. Here the war goddess of Shangshung called Mutsamey tried to create obstacles. She disguised herself as two mountains and proceeded to squeeze Master Padma and attendants. But the master made way by striking his walking stick on the rock. When the war goddess came out downward, head first, she became perplexed and frightened. Then she offered the core of her life and pledged to be a guardian. Padmakara then gave her the secret name Great Glacier Lady of Invincible Turquoise Mist.

When they were traveling down to Heavenly Plain at the north, Nammen Karmo brought down lightning on Master Padma. But the master placed a mirror in the palm of his hand and raised it. When it struck, the lightning was rendered powerless and became as small as seven peas. Stunned, Nammen Karmo became bewildered and fled down into the Lake of Splendor. Master Padma directed the scorpion gesture at the lake and visualized it to be a mass of fire. With this the lake began to boil wildly, separating the flesh from her bones. Again she tried to escape, but Master Padma flung a vajra from his hand and hit her in the right eye. She then exclaimed, "Successor of the Buddha, Vajra Thötreng Tsal, I shall not create obstacles; please accept me!" Thus she offered the core of her life, was bound under the oath, and named Fleshless One-Eyed Vajra Lady of the White Glacier.

Following that, as Padmasambhava and entourage came down from O-yuk, the tenma goddesses tried to press the group between the mountains. Master Padma directed his threatening gesture at the mountains and proceeded. The tenma goddesses were unable to move the mountains and fled. At the lower end of O-yuk, they broke down the rocks of the mountain tops and sent them rolling down, but the master pointed his threatening gesture and continued. All the rocks and stones went back, destroying the dwelling places of the tenma goddesses, such as the slate mountains, rocky mountains, and snow mountains. The twelve tenma goddesses, the twelve kyongma goddesses, and the twelve yama goddesses, with their respective retinues, offered the core of their lives and were bound under oath. Giving each a secret name, Padmasambhava empowered them to be guardians of the Buddhadharma.

Afterward, when going on to the valley of Chephu Shampo, Yarlha Shampo manifested himself as a white yak the size of a mountainside. With his nose steaming like assembling clouds, his roar like thunder, and his breath storming like a blizzard, he brought down lightning and hail. He then assumed a formidable stance. Master Padma caught the yak by the nose with the hook gesture, bound his middle with the lasso gesture, laid his legs in shackles with the chain gesture, and beat and hacked him with the bell gesture. By that, Yarlha Shampo turned into a young boy with white silken braids. He offered the core of his life and was bound under oath.

Next Master Padma proceeded to Sky Plain of Lhaitsa where Tanglha imposed his presence upon the master. Manifesting himself as an enormous yaksha, he approached, attempting to swallow up the master. When Master Padma made a threatening gesture, Tanglha turned into a child with turquoise locks and was bound under oath. Master Padma said, "Listen! Here is the one called White Skull Naga Forefather or Five-Braided Gandharva King. Sometimes he is also known as Nyenchen Tanglha. I must fetch him a meal." Saying this, he left. Around the evening meal time, he returned carrying some tasteless flat cookies and various other foods in the fold of his sleeve. Thus he brought Tanglha under his command.

They continued on toward the valley of Phen in the north. The male and female yakshas headed by Tingting Tinglomen, Takmen Sordongma, and Changphukma gathered all the icy winds of the three northern plains into one and blew them on Master Padma and his retinue. The retinue was almost paralyzed, and even the master felt a slight chill. Master Padma spun a wheel of fire on the fingertip of his threatening gesture. All the snow mountains where these yakshas lived melted like butter touched with a red-hot iron. By that, all the male and female yakshas of Tibet offered the core of their lives and were bound under oath.

Later, they went to the Trambu Forest in the Tölung Valley. At that place, Master Padma was met by a welcome escort of twenty-one subjects. Proceeding to the lower end of the Tölung Valley, the master and the subjects intended to take lunch, but found no water. Master Padma struck his staff into the rocky ground and water burst forth. It was named Divine Valley Water.

Remaining one night at Khala Cliff, Padmakara bound all the *tsen* spirits under oath. The following day, the master and entourage stayed at Sulphuk, where all the demon spirits were bound under oath. At Slate Mountain Ridge they remained one day, and Padmakara bound all the *gyalpo* and *gongpo* spirits under oath.

This was the ninth chapter in the immaculate life story
of the Lotus-Born Master, telling how Master Padma
bound all the gods and demons of Tibet under oath.

10

❀

MASTER PADMA proceeded to Hepori, where the
Tibetan king and his subjects had formed a welcome
reception. King Trisong Deutsen weighed this thought
in his mind, "I am the ruler of the black-headed Tibetans. I am the
lord of the beasts with a mane. As I am also a king who upholds the
Dharma, the master will pay homage to me!"

Master Padma thought, "I am a yogin who has reached attainment and, since I am invited to be the king's master, he will pay
homage to me!" Their greeting was not in harmony, so Master
Padma then sang the song "I Am the Great and Powerful":

NAMO RATNA-GURU
Listen here, ruler of Tibet!
I see the deaths of the six classes of sentient beings
And have accomplished the splendorous yoga, the
      vidyadhara level of longevity.
I am the immortal Padmakara,
Possessing the instruction on accomplishing in-
      destructible longevity.

In the mandala of mind manifest as appearance,
I employ the eight classes of gods and demons as
      my servants.
I am the king Padmakara,
Possessing the instruction on controlling the three
      realms.

From appearances, the book of samsara and
      nirvana,

I conduct lectures on the expedient and the
    definitive meaning.
I am the scholar Padmakara,
Possessing the instruction on separating samsara
    and nirvana.

On the natural parchment of mind essence,
I inscribe the letters beyond words.
I am the writer Padmakara,
Possessing the instruction on the teaching beyond
    words.

On the wall surface of whatever appears,
I sketch the drawing of nonduality.
I am the artist Padmakara,
Possessing the instruction on undivided appearance
    and emptiness.

The people seized by the sickness of the five
    poisons
I cure with the medicine of the unconditioned.
I am the physician Padmakara,
Possessing the instruction of the elixir that revives
    the dead.

Embodying the aims of those who have great faith,
I accomplish their welfare for both present and
    future lives.
I am the chief Padmakara,
Possessing the instruction on cutting the root of
    samsara.

Carrying the weapon of the essence of knowledge,
I subdue the enemy of perverted thought.
I am the heroic warrior Padmakara,
Possessing the instruction on victory in the battle
    with samsara.

The hostile five poisons, materializing as opponents,
I imprison in the magic pit of the five wisdoms.
I am the sorcerer Padmakara,

Possessing the instruction on annihilating the five
    poisons.

King of Tibet, you red-faced savage,
Your mind is bloated with worldly conceit.
Pride is the cause of taking birth in samsara.
Isn't that you, the ruler of Tibet,
Who is bedecked with the ornaments of the five
    poisonous kleshas?

Your lungs are inflated with your great dominion.
I will not prostrate to the king of Tibet,
But I pay homage to the clothing you wear.

Having sung this, Padmakara raised one hand in the gesture of
homage, and light rays from his hand scorched the king's dress. The
king's ministers all became terrified, and King Trisong Deutsen
himself bowed down.

Master Padma was then escorted to the palace, where he sat upon
a golden throne. He was served a variety of drinks, food, and cakes
and was offered a maroon cape of brocade to wear. As a present,
King Trisong Deutsen offered a mandala of gold and turquoise and
said:

EMAHO, NAMO lord guru.
I am the king of the red-faced rakshasas.
Since the people of Tibet are hard to tame,
I am building a shrine for the sacred Dharma.
You, nirmanakaya, please preside as the vajra master
And consecrate the foundation ground.

Thus he requested, and Master Padma replied, "Great sovereign
king, this country Tibet is a demon-land of male and female yakshas.
On the way, I bound under oath the male and female gods and
demons of Tibet. But, on that mountain over there lives a naga king
who controls the whole of Tibet and Kham. So I must establish a
naga treasure there."

Saying that, he went to the lower end of Maldro Valley and performed the ritual of Shaking Samsara from Its Depths. Having manifested the glorious mandala of Purifying the Lower Realms, he performed the ritual of clearing away the obscurations of the king and his subjects. Going to the upper end of Maldro Valley, he performed the ritual of establishing a treasure for the majestic naga of Maldro. Then, having gone to Hepori, Master Padma magnified through meditative concentration a water torma in a bowl of onyx. Bringing all the gods and demons of Tibet under his command, he sang this song of subjugating all the haughty spirits:

HUNG
Listen, I am the Lotus-Born One,
Untainted by a womb, I am Padma Vajra.
My body, invulnerable to the sickness of the four
    elements,
Has attained the longevity of an immortal vidya-
    dhara.

Manifesting my body, speech, and mind as a deity,
I possess the power of outshining haughty spirits.
By realizing all discursive thoughts to be mind,
The threat of horrifying gods and demons does not
    intimidate me.

Within the vast mandala of space,
The four elements are easily accommodated.
They are accommodated, yet still there is vastness.
Within the empty mandala of mind essence,
Appearance and existence, gods and demons, are
    easily accommodated.
They are accommodated, yet still there is vastness.

Within the empty mind essence, beyond concepts,
Neither gods nor demons exist.
Whichever magical trickery you display before me,
I am not moved even the slightest.

68

There is no way you can destroy the nature of
    mind.

To prevent you from transgressing my command,
I entitle each of you with my mantra to receive
This great offering torma
That has been multiplied through my samadhi.
Through the gesture, you will transcend loss and
    gain, strife and quarrel.[16]
Receive it through the truth of my words.
Accept the torma and give your consent to use this
    site.

Gods and demons, help building the temple!
Fulfill the aspiration of Trisong Deutsen.
Do not break the command of this mantradhara.
Respectfully and humbly, go assemble for work!

Singing that, he brought all the gods and demons under his command. When binding them under oath, Machen Pomra did not obey the order to come, so Master Padma summoned him by catching him in the heart with the hook gesture. Having done this, Machen Pomra, also known as the Monkey-Faced Chieftain of Shang suddenly descended in front of the master, dressed in a coat of wolf skin. He placed one leg on Yarmo Plain in Kham and one leg on Mount Hepori and said, "Young monk, I also have a great oath, but since you have made such an insistent order, I could not disobey. Here I am. Now, give me the command for what I should do."

Master Padma replied, "Accept this offering and fulfill the wishes of the king."

Machen Pomra said, "I will do as you command. But, I am very greedy and quite fond of valuables. This torma made of water poured around the bottom of rotten dough does not satisfy me. Give me some valuables!"

Master Padma then made filings of five precious substances on a silver plate, blessed it, and bound him under command and oath.

This was the tenth chapter in the immaculate life story of the Lotus-Born Master, telling how Padmasambhava was invited to the palace of Red Rock and tamed the building site.

II

MASTER PADMA then bound under oath all the powerful spirits, such as the twenty-one genyen of Tibet, the twenty-one mother deities dwelling in the slate mountains, snow mountains, and rock mountains, and the twenty-one male and female rakshasas of Tibet. He brought under his command all the divinities of the planets and stars. The spirits gathered earth and rocks from the mountains and valleys.[17]

When laying the foundation stones for the temple, King Trisong Deutsen had the Triple-Storied Central Temple laid in the style of Mount Sumeru. The encircling structure was laid in the style of the seven golden mountains. The two Yaksha Temples were laid in the style of the sun and the moon. The four major and eight minor temples were laid in the style of the continents and subcontinents.

As to the three special temples, Lady Gyalmo Tsün of Pho-gyong built the Golden Orphan Temple, Lady Margyen of Tsepang built the Khamsum Copper Temple, and Lady Jangchub Men of Tro built the Gegye Jema Temple.

The four major and eight minor temples to be erected were: Manjushri Temple, Exalted Palo Temple, Maitreya Temple, Vajrapani Temple, Amitabha Temple, the Temple of Purification, Meditation Temple, Translation Temple, Pekar Temple, Mara-Taming Mantra Temple, Vishva Temple, and Bodhi Temple.

In the four corners, the foundations for four stupas were laid. In the four directions, four protector shrine rooms were established. At the four gates, four great pillars were raised, and upon them were placed four big hounds made of copper. Lastly, the foundation for the outer surrounding wall was built.

71

Master Padmasambhava remained in meditation, commanding the eight classes of gods and demons to assist in the construction. They rolled down rocks from the mountain side into the valley. What the gods and demons built during the night exceeded what the humans built during the day.

Master Padma pondered, "Have I now bound under oath the body, speech, and mind of the eight classes of gods and demons?" Resting in meditation he saw that the body, speech, and mind of the eight classes of gods and demons were bound under oath and carrying out his orders. He also perceived that the nagas, with their bodies bound under oath, were building Samye, and with their speech bound under oath, they were claiming to obey Padmasambhava's command. But since their minds were not bound under oath, they were creating all kinds of havoc. So the master entered the samadhi of subjugating all nagas.

At this time, the building masters Hashang Mahayana, Yag Krakama from Mongolia, and others had completed the construction of the walls. The master carpenters, headed by Langtsang from China and Vasu from Nepal, swung their axes over their heads and said, "King, where is the wood? The wood is used up."

King Trisong Deutsen, wrought with anxiety, thought, "Where can we find that much wood?" He became quite disheartened.

The naga at the Gyachang Forest of Surphuk came to create obstacles for King Trisong Deutsen. He transformed himself into a white man on a white horse. As such, the naga met the king and said, "King, I will offer you all the wood you need for Samye. Please ask Master Padmasambhava for his approval."

The king, thinking, "This is a divine gift," granted his promise, took an oath of acceptance, and proclaimed, "Master Padma will definitely give his consent."

King Trisong Deutsen went before Master Padma in Tregu Cave of Chimphu. He asked, "Master, please give permission," but Padmakara did not assent. "By all means, please give your consent. What I have achieved is a marvelous divine gift." Master Padma permitted

King Trisong Deutsen to speak and he narrated the above story.

The master responded, "The wood for the temple would have come automatically. I have bound under oath the body, speech, and mind of the eight classes of gods and demons. But, since the nagas' minds were not bound under oath, I intended to bind them. When the time of the last five-hundred-year period comes, all the land will be controlled by nagas. Internally, eighteen kinds of leprosy will run rampant. All the border temples and human dwellings will be governed by nagas and destroyed. Everywhere, on and below the earth, will be controlled by nagas."

When King Trisong Deutsen arrived down at Samye, all the wood given by the naga had been carried by the Tsangpo river and landed on the banks near the Samye Temple. In this way, the king founded the temple. The building was begun in the Year of the Tiger, when he was twenty-one. It was completed in the Year of the Horse.[18]

The top floor of the Triple-Storied Central Temple was built in the Indian style, as India was the source of the tradition of Dharma. The middle story was built in the Chinese style, as China was the matriarch. The lower story was built in the Tibetan style, as Tibet was the patriarch.

The surrounding structure was fashioned after the seven golden mountains. The two Yaksha Temples were made to be like the sun and moon. The four major and eight minor temples were arranged to be like the continents and subcontinents. With three special temples and the outer wall, this entire temple complex was completed exactly according to the aspiration of King Trisong Deutsen and, therefore, named the Glorious and Spontaneous Fulfillment of Boundless Aspiration.

Padmasambhava performed the consecration in the Year of the Sheep, and five special blessings occurred: The Vairochana image in the Bodhi Temple rose up in the sky, and all the divinities of the central temple spontaneously came outside. The king became afraid and thought, "Now they cannot get back in," but Master Padma snapped his fingers and all the divinities went back in directly. The four huge hounds of copper on the stone pillars at the four gates leaped once into the four directions and barked three times. The bamboo at the surrounding structure did not grow up gradually, but appeared all at once. The sky was filled with vividly present sugatas, who sent out beams of light, which dissolved into the deities. The divine servants of the celestial regions showered down a rain of flowers.

This was the eleventh chapter in the immaculate life story of the Lotus-Born Master, on how His Majesty the King and Master Padma erected glorious Samye and performed its consecration.

12

When Padmasambhava and Khenpo Bodhisattva then intended to return to the land of India, Master Padma spoke to King Trisong Deutsen in this way:

You, King Trisong Deutsen, were born in the
    center of Tibet,
The learned Bodhisattva arrived from the region
    of Sahor,
And I, Padmakara, came from the land of
    Uddiyana.
In our past lives, we three were born
As three misbegotten brothers in Magadha.
We built a stupa and made aspirations.

Due to the karmic ripening of our respective
    rebirths,
Khenpo Bodhisattva was born as a brahman,
The king was born in the family line of rishis,
And I was born as a *tramen* savage.

When the three of us gathered
At that stupa in the past,
We arrayed a vast amount of offerings
And made these aspirations.

The rishi son made this aspiration:
"May I, in my next life,
Be born as a Dharma king in the icy country
    of Tibet

And establish the teachings of the Enlightened
    One."
Because of uttering this aspiration,
You are now born as a king who upholds the
    Dharma.

The brahman son made this aspiration:
"I wish to be a learned pandita,
A master skilled in the five sciences,
Who can establish the Buddhadharma of the
    Victorious One."
Therefore, you are now a bodhisattva.

The tramen son made this aspiration:
"May I be a powerful mantradhara
And protect the Buddhadharma of the monarch."
In those words, I formed that aspiration,
And have now accomplished your wish.

Through the power of the aspirations we made,
Although born in the different countries
Of Uddiyana, Tibet, and Sahor,
We became master, disciple, and court priest.

This temple of Samye, your sacred aspiration,
Was founded in the Year of the Tiger and
    completed in the Horse Year,
In five years, it was established and the hindrances
    removed.

Samye, the Boundless Aspiration, has now been
    spontaneously accomplished,
And your wish has been fulfilled.
Khenpo Bodhisattva and I, Padmakara of Uddiyana,
Now ask your permission to leave for India.

After Padmakara had spoken, King Trisong Deutsen filled two
silver vessels each with a drey of gold dust and presented them to
the two masters along with many other worldly gifts. He bowed
down, circumambulated them, shed tears, and offered this request:

THE LOTUS-BORN

EMAHO!
Please listen to me, both of you masters!
In past lives we made aspirations,
When we were born in the land of India.
Through our different wishes,
Both of you masters took birth in India,
The country of the sacred Dharma.

Due to my karma, I was born as king in Tibet,
The land of the red-faced ones.
Due to great merit, I became lord of the
        black-headed people,
And at Red Rock, in the Year of the Horse,
I took birth from Lady Angchung of Gya.

At the age of thirteen, I lost my father
And, reaching twenty, virtue arose in my mind.
At twenty-one, in the Tiger Year, I laid the
        foundation.
Although Master Bodhisattva
Performed the consecration of the building site,
The obstructing forces did not allow the
        completion.
I then invited Master Padma
To fulfill my royal aspiration.

According to Khenpo Bodhisattva's prediction,
You arrived through the force of former vows
And from the Tiger to the Horse Year completed
        the building.

Although your kindness has already been great,
Please, both of you, emanation body and womb-
        born body,
Do not leave me yet.
You two masters, do not depart.
Change your intentions, I beg your approval.

As King Trisong Deutsen made this request, the two masters conferred, and Master Padma said, "Your Majesty, since we, the three brothers, again have this connection as we had in past lives, I shall not turn back your request."

Khenpo Bodhisattva declared, "Very good, I will do likewise!"

Master Padma then told the king:

> The three of us, masters and disciple,
> Have come together in Tibet through the ripening
>   of karma
> From the aspirations of our three lives.
> In the past, I have pleased Your Majesty
> And in the future, I shall not turn back your
>   request.

Upon hearing this, King Trisong Deutsen became overjoyed.

The king then requested the two masters to teach the Dharma. Master Padma took seat upon a golden throne, and Khenpo Bodhisattva took a seat upon a silver throne. The king, himself, was seated in the middle row. In the left row, sat Chokro Lui Gyaltsen and Kawa Paltsek upon thrones of silken cushions.

To each of the two masters, King Trisong Deutsen made an offering of a gold mandala the size of one cubit, with heaps of turquoise for Mount Sumeru and each of the four continents. He offered to both the two translators a mandala of precious stones. Having done so, he made this request for them to teach the Dharma:

> EMAHO!
> Taking birth in the land of India,
> You became learned and accomplished panditas
> And attained mastery over the sacred Dharma.
> You, two great masters,
> Please expound in full, until we are satisfied,
> All the teachings of Mantra and Philosophy.
> You, two translators, please interpret.

Please kindle the torch of Dharma
In the dense darkness of Tibet.
Please shower down the rain of Dharma
On the scorching flames of disturbing emotions.

Thus he requested them to teach the Dharma, and the two masters replied: "EMAHO! Great King, the Tibetan people do not have great faith, the ministers are opposed to the Dharma, and the elemental forces create obstacles. We will therefore arrange the auspicious coincidence for being free from obstacles, so you, the king, should establish a Dharma law." King Trisong Deutsen then instigated religious law.

From the Year of the Sheep to the end of the Year of the Monkey,[19] Master Padma and Chokro Lui Gyaltsen translated the Eighteen Inner Tantras of Secret Mantra and other scriptures.

First, they translated the *Majestic Blazing Retreat Tantra* to prevent obstacles from arising against the practice of Secret Mantra. Next they translated the *Sacred Peace Deity Tantra* to liberate samsara into the innate nature and to accomplish the body as a divine mandala, because fixation on ego is the cause of samsara. After that they translated the *Blazing Cosmic Fire Tantra* to annihilate maras, heretics, rakshasas, and haughty spirits and to accomplish enlightened body. Following that they translated the *Embodiment of Great Power Tantra* to accomplish enlightened speech, the *Wrathful Blue Lotus Tantra* to accomplish enlightened mind, the *Nonstraying Goddess Tantra* to accomplish enlightened qualities, and the *Vidyadhara Accomplishment Tantra* to accomplish enlightened activity. They also translated the *Tantra of the General Accomplishment of Knowledge Mantras*, the *Tantra of the Glorious Assemblage of Herukas*, the tantra of Manjushri Body known as *Secret Black Moon*, the tantra of Lotus Speech known as *Supreme Steed Display*, the tantras of Vishuddha Mind known as *Heruka Galpo* and the *Supramundane Scripture*, the tantras of Nectar Quality known as the *Major and Minor Nectar Display* and the *Scripture in Eight Chapters*, the tantra of Kilaya Activity known as the *Hundred Thousand Sections of*

Unexcelled Knowledge, and the tantra of Liberating Sorcery of Mother Deities known as the *Hundred Thousand Tika Scripture.*[20]

Furthermore, they translated the tantras and transmission texts of the Six Sadhana Sections. To amend the activities and attach ornaments, they translated the *Tantra Adorned with Thousandfold Knowledge.* To demonstrate how to enact the ocean of activities, they translated the *Activity Garland Tantra.* To perfect the accumulations of merit and wisdom, they translated the *Major and Minor Gathering Tantra.* To consecrate offerings to be an inexhaustible treasure, they translated the *Sky Treasury Consecration Tantra.* To spontaneously purify the act of freeing, they translated the *Tantra of Powerful Liberation.* To spontaneously purify the act of uniting, they translated the *Essence Tantra of the Expanse of Bliss.* To make yogic discipline fierce, they translated the *Rampant Elephant Tantra.* To make fire offering for auspiciousness, they translated the *Sporting Devourer Tantra.* Since the torma is the prelude for all activities, they translated the *Major and Minor Torma Tantra.* To enjoin to action all the guardians of the mandala periphery with access to the residual offerings, they translated the *Glorious Blazing Wrathful Goddess Tantra.* To subdue and overpower enemies and obstructing forces, they translated the *Tantra of the Liberation of the Ten Objects.* These were the tantras of Mahayoga.

As to the tantras of Anu Yoga, they translated the Four Scriptures and the Summation, five in all: the *Assemblage of Knowledge Scripture,* the *Scripture of the Wisdom Wheel of Awesome Lightning,* and the *Scripture of the Play of the Cuckoo Bird of the Charnel Ground,* and the *Scripture of the Great Prophecy of Awakened Mind.* As the summation of all the teachings, they translated the *Scripture of the Embodiment of the Realization of All Buddhas.*

Additionally, they translated the Six Secret Sections known as the body tantra of *Sarvabuddha Samayoga,* the speech tantra called *Secret Moon Essence,* the mind tantra titled *Assemblage of Secrets,* the quality tantra known as *Magical Net of Vairochana,* the activity tantra called *Activity Garland* and, as the concluding tantra to summarize their meaning, the *Tantra of the Four Vajra Thrones.*[21]

Following those they translated the Eight Maya Sections: the

Essence of Secrets to teach mind and wisdom in their natural modes, the *Forty Magical Nets* to clarify the activities in their completeness, the *Unsurpassable Magical Net* to realize mastery, the *Leulag Magical Net* to demonstrate the oral instructions endowed with the sacred commitments, the *Eightfold Magical Net* to explain the abbreviated meaning, the *Magical Net of the Goddess* to accomplish the manifestation, the *Magical Net in Eighty Chapters* to fulfill incompleteness in the others, and the *Magical Net of Manjushri* to elucidate that wisdom is the ultimate.

These, the Inner Tantras of Secret Mantra, were translated by Master Padmakara and the translator Chokro Lui Gyaltsen. Through his miraculous powers, Master Padma fetched the Sanskrit manuscripts that were housed in the glorious Indian monastery of Nalanda. Not leaving them in India, they were safeguarded in the treasury of Samye.[22]

Master Bodhisattva and the translator Kawa Paltsek translated all the teachings of Outer Secret Mantra. First the six general kriya tantras: the framework of all knowledge mantras known as the *Kriya Tantra of Eminent Courage*, the empowerment of all knowledge mantras known as the *Vajrapani Command Tantra*, the elucidation of all knowledge mantras known as the *Supreme Knowledge Tantra*, the synopsis of all knowledge mantras known as *Susiddhikara: The Tantra of Excellent Accomplishment*, the activity of all knowledge mantras known as the *Tantra of Victory Over the Three Realms*, and the teaching on the intent of all knowledge mantras known as the *Later Meditation Tantra*.

Next, they translated the specific kriya tantras. Among the cycles of the Lords of the Three Families, the cycle of Avalokiteshvara was as follows: the *Lotus Crown Root Tantra*, the *Tantra of the Lotus Mound Mantra*, the *Tantra of the Profound Mantra Ritual*, the *Wish-Granting Jewel Monarch Tantra*, the *Amogha Pasha* known as the *Meaningful Lasso Tantra*, the *Tantra of the Major and Minor Casket Array*, and others.

From the cycle of Manjushri, they translated the *Manjushri Tantra of Immaculate Wisdom Being*, the *Manjushri Tantra of Sharp Intelligence*, the *Manjushri Web-Cutting Tantra*, the *Manjushri Nama Sangiti Tantra Expressed in Songs of Praise*, and others.

From the cycle of Vajrapani, they translated the *Vajrapani Empowerment Tantra*, the *Vajra Under Earth Tantra*, the *Vajra Above Earth Tantra*, the *Tantra of Taming the Elemental Forces*, the *Vajra Pestle Tantra*, the *Tantra of Indestructible Blissful Wrath*, the *Vajra Sharpness Tantra*, the *Tantra of the Indestructible Secret Teaching*, the *Tantra of the Blazing Vajra Mountain*, and others. Furthermore, the *Five Sets of Sacred Incantations*, the *Three Hundred and Sixty Sacred Incantations*, and others were translated.

They then translated the Four Ubhaya Tantras: the *Tantra of the Full Enlightenment of Vairochana*, the *Tantra of the Blazing Mass of Fire That Consumes the Kleshas*, the *Vajra Bearer Empowerment Tantra*, and the *Nonconceptual Mind Tantra*.

From Yoga Tantra, they omitted translating the three hundred sections of great root texts,[23] but instead translated the Four Major Sections of Yoga Tantra: the *Tattvasamgraha Root Tantra*, the *Vajra Pinnacle Tantra*, the *Glorious Supreme Primal Tantra*, and the *Compendium of Conception Tantra*.

Master Bodhisattva and the lotsawa Kawa Paltsek translated these Outer Tantras of Secret Mantra, and all the manuscripts of the tantras were installed in the treasury of Samye.

> This was the twelfth chapter in the immaculate life story of the Lotus-Born Master, on how the two masters, Padmasambhava and Khenpo Bodhisattva, and the two translators, Kawa Paltsek and Chokro Lui Gyaltsen, translated and established the teachings of Secret Mantra.

13

MASTER PADMA THEN REFLECTED, "In order for the Tibetan king and subjects to have trust in my teachings, they must be brought from India to Tibet." He said to King Trisong Deutsen, "Your Majesty, in order for the Tibetan king and subjects to have trust in my teachings and in order for you to cut through mental constructs, you must send someone to request the Vajrayana teachings of the Secret Mantra, the instructions for attaining the supreme accomplishment of mahamudra in a single lifetime, from the learned and accomplished Indian masters. If no siddhas appear here in Tibet, the future generations will not have faith."

King Trisong Deutsen agreed to this. Master Bodhisattva ordained five Tibetans: Namkhai Nyingpo of Nub, Epagsha of Drugu, Palgyi Yeshe of Lang, Singharaja of Ruley, and Gyalwey Lodrö of Drey. The king took pebbles from below their feet and placed them on his head. He issued the edict that these five should be venerated as supreme objects of respect. The king had them train in translation from the Indian languages into Tibetan. He entrusted each of them with a drey of gold dust and sent them to India to search for the teachings of the Secret Mantra.

On their journey to India, the lotsawas underwent hardships. In the eastern area of Kamarupa, they met an Indian woman and asked, "What are the names of the masters who have attained accomplishment in the teachings of Secret Mantra nowadays?"

The woman replied, "In the Golden Rock Garuda Forest lives a master by the name Hungkara."

The five lotsawas went to the place of Master Hungkara. They gave some gold to the attendant Saukhya Deva and said, "We are sent by the king of Tibet to request teachings from the master. Please help us to get an audience."

He answered, "The master remains in meditation inside a house encircled by nine rings of walls. I cannot meet him, but I will take you inside. Go directly before the master, offer him the gold, and request teachings. Then he will agree."

The attendant opened the gate to the house with nine consecutive walls, and the five Tibetan monks went before the master.[24] They prostrated, offered gold, and said, "Great master, we are sent by the Dharma king of Tibet to search for a teaching through which one can attain the supreme accomplishment of mahamudra in a single lifetime. Please bestow it upon us, master. If we do not obtain the teaching, we will be punished. Master, please accept us with your compassion."

Master Hungkara replied, "It is wonderful that the king of Tibet has the nature of a bodhisattva and gives thought to the Dharma. Also it is very good that you monks have overcome difficulties and disregarded life and limb to come meet me. Therefore, we must have a karmic link. First, you must receive empowerment. Empowerment is the root of the Secret Mantra. Without receiving empowerment, one cannot have the Secret Mantra explained and one cannot practice it."

Having said that, Hungkara opened up the mandala of the Sixty-eight Crescents, conferred the empowerment, and thereby showed them the vision of the sixty-eight herukas. Following that, he gradually opened up the mandalas of the Fifty-eight Crescents, the Nine Crescents, the Single Crescent, and the Three-Storied Three Crescents and showed the monks the vision of the deities.

Hungkara then bestowed the empowerments of Nectar Medicine and disclosed the vision of the deities based on the three mandalas of medicine sadhana: the *Fragment Sadhana of the Eight-Petaled Lotus*, the *Powder Sadhana of the Eight-Spoked Wheel*, and the *Sadhana of the Moist*

Compound of Samaya Substance of the Nine Crescents.

After that, Hungkara consecrated them with longevity in three mandalas and conferred the empowerment of immortal life: the *Longevity Sadhana within the Articles of Perfect Auspiciousness,* the *Longevity Sadhana within the Secret Space of the Consort,* and the *Longevity Sadhana within the Secret Perfect Space.*

He also offered the empowerment for the conduct of the Secret Mantra in three mandalas: the *Sadhana of Primordially Pure Innate Nature of Awakened Mind,* the *Union Bodhichitta Sadhana of Pure Space,* and the *Liberation Bodhichitta Sadhana of Pure Compassion.*

Having explained the applications of these sadhanas, he composed a daily practice of Vishuddha and said, "Now practice one-pointedly for the period of a year, show some signs, and afterwards you can return to Tibet."[25]

The five Tibetan monks discussed among themselves their different perceptions of what Humkara had said. Palgyi Yeshe of Lang said, "As I see it, the master has become afraid that the Dharma will spread to Tibet. Since the Indians are very possessive of the Buddhadharma our lives are in danger."

Namkhai Nyingpo of Nub retorted, "A mother does not poison her own child. The master does not give deceitful advice. The one who does not follow his master's word and disregards his counsel will go to hell. I am not leaving; you proceed as you please."

When the four of them made preparations to return, the master blessed a teak dagger and gave it to Palgyi Yeshe of Lang. "Keep it at your hand when you walk and plant it at your pillow before you sleep. You are in danger of obstacles."

The four monks set out to return to Tibet. When they were sleeping at the bank of a lake in Nepal, Palgyi Yeshe of Lang drove the teak dagger into the ground at his pillow. Epagsha of Drugu removed the dagger to his pillow. Because of previously not trusting their master's words, a naga-demon who was living in that lake, by the name of Lord of Black Swamp, transformed himself into a black snake and killed Palgyi Yeshe of Lang by biting his little toe.

The three monks then arrived before King Trisong Deutsen, presented the teachings, and related the story of the remaining two. The king did not believe them. The evil-minded ministers became jealous of the Buddhadharma and said, "Of the five men sent to India, you have done away with two, so now, the three of you shall be expelled." Gyalwey Lodrö of Drey was then expelled to To-yor Nagpo to the north; Epagsha of Drugu was expelled to the valley of Shangshung; and Singharaja of Ruley was expelled to Lower Dokham.

In India, the master then composed an extensive commentary, likened to a lamp for the root tantra of *Vishuddha Sadhana*, and explained it to Namkhai Nyingpo of Nub. He bestowed upon him the *Single Fire and Sole Skull* representing the scripture of Vishuddha, likened to the heart within the chest.[26] By practicing for one year in Golden Rock Garuda Forest, Namkhai Nyingpo had a vision of the Great Glorious One with consort and attained the supreme and common accomplishments. The master then told him, "Now the time has come for you to go to Tibet."

Having arrived miraculously in Tibet, Namkhai Nyingpo went before King Trisong Deutsen and said, "Your Majesty, I have a teaching for you to practice that causes a sentient being to accomplish the result of buddhahood. It is known as the glorious *Vishuddha Sadhana*." After that, he uttered:

> This single *Vishuddha Sadhana*
> Is the embodiment of the great bliss of all buddhas,
> The profound yoga that perfects the three kayas,
> The magic of the dakinis, the delightful supreme
>   bliss.

Having said this, Namkhai Nyingpo cut open his chest with a curved knife of white silver. He showed King Trisong Deutsen the vision of the forty-two peaceful deities in the upper part of his chest and the fifty-eight heruka deities in the lower part. King Trisong

Deutsen felt confidence in the words and the essential meaning, and in the deities and the master. He prostrated, bowing his head with great devotion.

Henceforth, King Trisong Deutsen regarded Namkhai Nyingpo as a supreme object of veneration. From him, the king received the glorious *Vishuddha Sadhana.* But the ministers became envious and said, "It is improper that a king should make a subject his master. That is detrimental to the royal law and is in disharmony with tradition." After this, Namkhai Nyingpo was expelled to Kharchu at Lhodrak.

Namkhai Nyingpo practiced sadhana at Iron Dagger Rock to the west. The signs of accomplishment in his practice were that a butter lamp spontaneously kindled, he left an imprint of his body, his dagger could pierce solid rock, and he could travel by riding on the rays of the sun.

After some time, King Trisong Deutsen fell sick, and no amount of healing ceremonies would help. No matter how many ransom offerings and astrological calculations were made, they did not produce any result. A divination was performed that showed that all methods were useless, except inviting back the monk Namkhai Nyingpo. Two emissaries were sent off to Lhodrak, where they made the request. Namkhai Nyingpo responded, "The two of you go ahead, I will follow." The master sent the two men ahead of himself, but arrived first by his miraculous power.

Namkhai Nyingpo was asked, "What is necessary for His Majesty's healing ceremony?"

He replied, "I do not need anything other than what the king himself eats and drinks. Just bring me that!" Master Namkhai Nyingpo then made a feast offering of the king's meal and enjoyed it himself.

When he had consumed about a third, a private attendant asked King Trisong Deutsen about his health, and the king said, "It appeared to me that a white woman arrived and hit me with a whip. I feel slightly better." This restored the breach of the samayas of body that the king had committed by expelling his vajra master.

When Namkhai Nyingpo had consumed two thirds of the meal, a valet asked King Trisong Deutsen about his health, and the king said, "It appeared to me that a brown woman came and hit me with a whip. Now I feel much better." That restored the violation of the samayas of speech.

When Namkhai Nyingpo then had finished eating the entire meal, a valet again asked King Trisong Deutsen about his health, and the king said, "It appeared to me that a black woman came and hit me with a whip. Now I do not feel even the slightest bit ill." That restored the king's violation of the samaya of mind.

The ministers then said, "This is a proof that the two of them, the king and Namkhai Nyingpo, simply wanted to meet again." The ministers wanted to punish Namkhai Nyingpo and said, "Monk, while the sun is about to set, you can bathe the king's head, but you will be punished if you are not out when the sun has set." Namkhai Nyingpo planted his teak dagger at the boundary between the sun and the shade. After that, he bathed the king's head.

Having stopped the sun for about half a day, Namkhai Nyingpo said, "Now, gather the cattle home." As he took out the dagger from the boundary of sunlight and shade, the sun went completely red and disappeared.

The ministers were terrified and said, "This monk sorcerer has come to perform black magic on us. He must be killed. King Trisong Deutsen and the master are on their way here; let's wait for them!" Having agreed on that, they laid an ambush for the king and Namkhai Nyingpo.

Namkhai Nyingpo knew this and exclaimed fiercely, "HUNG! HUNG!" A lightning bolt struck down from the sky and spun around the fingertip of his threatening hand gesture, causing some of the evil-minded ministers to faint, while others were paralyzed with fear. Even King Trisong Deutsen was scared.

The master asked, "Wasn't Your Majesty a little startled?"

The king replied, "I was completely terrified. Monk, the boom of your HUNG is more frightening than a thunder crack. This should satisfy these black-minded ministers for a while."

The monk Namkhai Nyingpo then flew up into the sky and went to Kharchu at Lhodrak.

This was the thirteenth chapter in the immaculate life story of the Lotus-Born Master, on how five Tibetan monks went to India to search for teachings and how master Namkhai Nyingpo attained accomplishment.

14

KING TRISONG DEUTSEN THEN DREAMED that glorious Vajrasattva appeared in the sky and gave this prophecy: "King, there is in the country of India a teaching known as the sacred Great Perfection that, unlike training in the teachings on causation, gives liberation simultaneous with understanding. You must send two Tibetan translators."

The king went before Master Padma in the gathering hall at Chimphu and related his dream. The master responded, "That dream is most propitious. Let two of your most intelligent subjects take ordination from Khenpo Bodhisattva and learn translation. I will teach some techniques in magical powers so they will have no obstacles on their journey."

King Trisong Deutsen was told that the two most intelligent in Tibet were Vairochana of Pagor, the son of Hedo of Pagor, and Lekdrub of Tsang, the son of Plain God of Tsang. He sent them his command, and they received ordination from Master Bodhisattva. They learned the skill of translation, and Master Padma gave instructions on magical powers.

The king furnished them each with a drey of gold dust and a gold *patra* and sent them off to bring back the sacred Great Perfection from India. The border guards tried to rob the gold, but Vairochana applied his magical skill; he transformed his gold into sand and one drey of sand into gold, which he gave to the border guards. Delighted, they allowed him free passage to India.

When the translators arrived in India they inquired about who was the most learned in the sacred Great Perfection. All the replies were in agreement that the master Shri Singha was the most learned.[27] They went before Shri Singha and made this request, offering their gold dust and the gold patra, "Great master, the king of Tibet has received the prophecy 'Bring back from India the instruction that gives enlightenment within one lifetime, known as the sacred Great Perfection.' Therefore, we were sent to search for it. We beg you wholeheartedly to bestow this teaching upon us."

In these words the master then gave his consent: "The king of Tibet has great faith, and the two of you are most diligent. Since the teaching on the sacred Great Perfection will flourish in Tibet, I shall teach it to you. The Indian king jealously guards the Buddhadharma, so we must be resourceful."

Having spoken in this way, Shri Singha took them into a house surrounded by nine walls and conferred the empowerment of direct anointment. He then placed a huge copper vessel upon a tripod, and the master sat himself upon it. He donned a cotton robe with lattice work, put a copper pipe to his mouth, and gave teachings.[28]

Shri Singha taught twenty-five tantras: First, to demonstrate in detail the major and minor points of awakened mind, he taught the *Great Extensive Space Tantra*. To put into practice the meaning of awakened mind that is difficult to comprehend, he taught the *Great Extensive Space Chiti Tantra*. To demonstrate that the nature of mind is utterly free, he taught the *Great Space Liberation Tantra*. To demonstrate that the nature of mind is unchanging, he taught the *Quintessence King Tantra*. To demonstrate that the nature of mind is embodied in the sphere of the essence, he taught the *Tantra of the Sphere of Awakened Mind*. To demonstrate that the nature of mind is self-existing wisdom, he taught the *Wisdom Essence Tantra*. To demonstrate the nature of mind in extensive stages, he taught the *Garland of Instruction Tantra*. To demonstrate that the nature of mind is general for everyone, he taught the *Secret Ocean Tantra*. To realize and comprehend that the nature of mind is one's own awareness, he taught the *Wisdom Knowledge Tantra*. To unify everything within the space of Samantabhadra, the nature of mind, he taught the *Pure Space Tantra*.

To gain confidence in the supreme suchness of the nature of mind, he taught the *Essence Chiti Tantra*. To demonstrate flawlessly the basis of the nature of mind, he taught the *Great Space Tantra of Awakened Mind*. To demonstrate that the nature of mind is the Single Sphere, he taught the *Single Mind Tantra*. To remain unmistakenly in naturalness in the nature of mind, he taught the *Single Meditation Tantra*. To demonstrate indirectly, stage-by-stage, the nature of mind, he taught the *Short Indirect Meditation Tantra*. To demonstrate that the nature of mind is vital in all scriptures, he taught the *Auspicious Lamp Tantra*. To demonstrate the nature of mind, following the steps of empowerment, he taught the *Epitomized Great Space Empowerment Tantra*. To demonstrate that the nature of mind is beyond words of expression, he taught the *Wisdom Lamp Tantra*. To demonstrate that the nature of mind, like space, is devoid of a self-nature, he taught the *Summit Tantra of Letterless Great Space*. To demonstrate how all mental phenomena originate, he taught the *Shining Jewel Tantra*. To demonstrate that all mental phenomena are devoid of an essence, he taught the *Jewel Lamp Tantra*. To demonstrate that all mental states are self-originated, he taught the *Jewel Garland Tantra*. To demonstrate that the nature of mind is manifest within the realms, he taught the *Tantra of the Lamp of the Three Realms*. To demonstrate the definite and correct meaning of the nature of mind, he taught the *Definite Essence Tantra*. To demonstrate that the nature of mind is changeless, he taught the *Most Secret Vajra Tantra*. To demonstrate that the nature of mind is present as buddhahood, right now, within sentient beings, he taught the *Primordial Buddhahood Tantra*. Thus he taught twenty-five tantras.

Following this, Shri Singha taught the Eighteen Major Scriptures. Since everything originates from awakened mind, he taught the *Awareness Cuckoo Scripture*. To outshine all effort and fabrication, he taught the *Great Strength of Awareness Scripture*. Since the nature of mind is perfected within dharmadhatu, he taught the *Great Garuda View Scripture*. Since the nature of meditation is perfected within space, he taught the *Pure Gold on Stone Scripture*. To perfect the nature of meditation, he taught the *Great Space Never-Waning Banner Scripture*.[29]

To resolve the nature of mind to be emptiness, he taught the *Wonderful Wisdom Scripture.* To demonstrate the means of meditation, he taught the *Meditation Accomplishment Scripture.* To demonstrate that the nature of mind is naturally dharmakaya, he taught the *Supreme King Scripture.* To demonstrate that the nature of mind is the Single Sphere, he taught the *Nonarising Tilaka Scripture.* To turn the wheel in the three states of existence, showing that the nature of mind is beyond birth and death, he taught the *Wheel of Life-Force Scripture.* To demonstrate that desirable qualities originate from the nature of mind, he taught the *Wish-Fulfilling Jewel Scripture.* To let all conceptual thinking rest in the state of dharmata, he taught the *All-Embodying Jewel Scripture.* To demonstrate in full detail that all the vehicles are perfected and originate in the nature of mind, he taught the *Great Space King Scripture.* To demonstrate that resting in the nature of mind, the state of Samantabhadra, is unsurpassed, the summit amongst all, he taught the *Spontaneous Summit Scripture.* To demonstrate that the meaning of the nature of mind is devoid of fabrications and naturally rests in the state of ease, he taught the *All-Encompassing Bliss Scripture.* To demonstrate that awakened mind remains untainted by the defects of emotional disturbances and is ornamented with the jewelry of qualities, he taught the *Jewel-Studded Bliss Scripture.* To demonstrate that all of samsara and nirvana originates within the expanse of awakened mind, he taught the *Variegated Great Treasury Scripture.* To demonstrate and epitomize all the vehicles within awakened mind, he taught the *Epitome of Teachings Scripture.* Thus he taught eighteen volumes of scriptures.

Master Shri Singha then said, "I have now fully expounded the teachings. The Indians are very possessive of the Dharma, so on the way back to Tibet, your lives are in danger. Practice, therefore, the art of swift feet." He then gave them the instructions on swift feet. The master gave Pagor the name Vairochana. Lekdrub of Tsang did not accomplish the art of swift feet and, desiring to impress the king, he went on ahead, but was murdered by the guards at the border.[30]

Vairochana feared that the gatekeepers would rob his teachings, so he copied all his Indian manuscripts on palm leaves with the magical writing of *arura* juice.[31]

On the evening of his departure, all the locks on the gates of Vajra Seat resounded spontaneously. The monastic guards warned the gatekeepers, "The Tibetan monk will carry off the Dharma! Don't allow him to leave." The gatekeepers locked all the gates and guarded them. The next morning Vairochana arrived and they said, "Everybody had bad dreams last night, so let's see what the Tibetan monk is carrying?" They stripped him naked, but since he had nothing more than two volumes of palm leaves they said, "This is not the man. He has nothing but blank palm leaves without any writing; let him go," and they allowed him to proceed.

Vairochana thought that he would not be able to escape the border guards, though he had accomplished the art of swift feet, so he befriended the chief border guard Youthful, gave him gold dust, and made him take an oath. The chief guard then removed many other guards, enabling Vairochana to proceed.

All the Indian panditas dreamed that the sun was carried off to Tibet by a monk and disappeared. The trees and flowers withered, and the chirping of birds lost their melodiousness.

The king of Vajra Seat inquired of the panditas, "What is the reason for this?"

"The Tibetan monk must have carried the Buddhadharma away," they replied.

Soldiers adept in the art of swift feet were dispatched, but the chief border guard said, "Nobody looking like a Tibetan monk has come by here. Only a shaven tribesman from Mön passed by, and he was not carrying anything. If he is the man, he must already have reached Tibet by now." The swift-footed soldiers returned.

Due to his accomplishment of swift feet, Vairochana reached Tibet from Vajra Seat in seven days. He went before King Trisong Deutsen and related his story, "I have returned with the teachings desired by Your Majesty. The Indians are very protective of the Dharma, the Tibetan ministers are hostile toward the Dharma, and you, Your Majesty, are easily influenced. It is possible that slander will spread. I request you to not pay heed to it." Thus he advised.

The king at Vajra Seat then said, "It is now too late to catch the Tibetan monk. Punish the master that gave him the teachings, whoever he may be!" Oracles were consulted, divinations and astrological calculations were tried, yet they were unable to determine who the master was.

An old brahman lady adept in the divination of the rishis said, "If I have a vision and it opposes my good sense, I cannot relate it to the king."

The king replied, "It will be all right, just tell!"

The lady said, "Well, I see a lake on the summit of three mountains. At the top I see a multicolored plain. There I see something whose body is full of eyes and has a red beak as big as an arm span. That is the one who gave the teachings." Everybody found this too incredible to believe.

The king then said, "We must send swift-footed soldiers to Tibet and spread some slander." Two soldiers adept in the art of fast-walking were dispatched.

Two mendicants then arrived at the top chamber of Samye where Vairochana was teaching the Dharma to the king and said, "This Tibetan monk did not bring the Dharma teachings back from India. Instead he has brought many evil mantras of the heretics with which he will destroy you. He is a heretic; you should kill him!" Having proclaimed this, they fled.

The ministers said, "This is true; he will destroy Tibet! Let him be drowned!"

King Trisong Deutsen retorted, "This is not right! It is the Indians who jealously are trying to guard the Buddhadharma!" The ministers would not listen, so the king took a beggar from a primitive tribe and made him wear Vairochana's hat and clothing. The man was placed within a copper pot, the lid was nailed on, and it was thrown into the Tsangpo river to float downstream.[32] Vairochana took hiding in the upper enclosure of the palace behind a carved out pillar. At midnight, King Trisong Deutsen served refreshments to Vairochana and received instructions.

When Vairochana had completed the teachings on the *Eighteen Marvels of Mind in Fifty Chapters*, a private attendant and Lady Margyen of Tsepang noticed what was taking place and let it be known.[33] The ministers assembled and said, "Your Majesty has made a grave mistake. You have squandered away all the gold and silver of the treasury of the ancestral kings, smearing them on clay images while claiming to make temples. Pretending to practice the Dharma, you have taken a primitive tribesman and thrown him in the river. On the sly, you are keeping a black magician who will destroy Tibet and you obey whatever he says. He must be punished. Open up the door! If he isn't punished, you destroy the law of the kingdom!"

King Trisong Deutsen despaired and asked Vairochana what to do. The master replied, "Your Majesty, in former times I was born in Gyalmo Tsawarong as a son to King Leksher and Palmo. I still have some residual karma and beings to influence there, so expel me to that place. Your Majesty, listen to me! In India lives a master by the name Vimalamitra, who is the most learned among all the Indian panditas. Invite him and establish a Dharma assembly. At that time, you should let these teachings I have given be verified, and all the ministers will gain trust. Then you and I will meet again." King Trisong Deutsen was powerless and manipulated by his ministers, so Vairochana was expelled to Gyalmo Tsawarong.

When Vairochana reached a northern place called Yakla Sewo, he looked back toward Central Tibet. It looked like dawn at sunrise. When he looked toward Kham, it seemed like darkness closing in at sunset. Tears fell from his eyes involuntarily, but he had to proceed.

Arriving in Gyalmo Tsawarong, he stayed on a mountain side. All the birds of Central Tibet gathered around the master in the air above and circumambulated him. The people of Tsawarong could not believe this. When they looked, they discovered the master. "A sophist from Tibet has come," they said and threw him into a lice pit. After that he was cast into a frog pit but he remained unharmed. They took him out and proclaimed him a holy personage.

Vairochana said, "I was sent to India in search of the Dharma by the Tibetan king and his ministers. The Indians, possessive of the Buddhadharma, accused me of being a black magician. Therefore, I was expelled by the king and the ministers. In a former life, I was born here. In the past I was Bhikshu Purna, the son of King Leksher and Palmo."

The people believed him and said, "It is marvelous that he knows the succession of former lives." They prostrated before him and expressed sincere regret. Placing his foot above their heads, they served him and paid respect.

Later Vairochana thought, "I must make the sacred Great Perfection flourish here in Gyalmo Tsawarong." He then went to a place where many children were herding the cattle and instructed them to say "Vajra Being, Great Vajra Being." Most of them could not and said, "Va-bey va-bey," but two of the children said, "Vajra Being, Great Vajra Being." The two boys called Prince Turquoise and Prince Naga could pronounce it correctly.[34]

In the evening, Master Vairochana placed the two boys on his right and left side and trained them in the general points, while during the daytime he taught them the scriptures. They learned and realized the sacred Great Perfection. Then they propagated the Dharma and made it flourish in Gyalmo Tsawarong, like the rising sun.

This was the fourteenth chapter in the immaculate life story of the Lotus-Born Master, telling how Vairochana of Pagor went to India in pursuit of the Dharma and was expelled to Tsawarong.

15

KING TRISONG DEUTSEN NOW CONTEMPLATED, "My
aspiration is to establish this kingdom of Tibet in the way
of the Dharma. I sent the most intelligent Tibetans to India
to bring wonderful teachings back to Tibet. Yet, the ministers who
are hostile toward the Dharma felt jealous and did not allow me the
freedom to practice those teachings. My ministers penalized under
the royal law and expelled the translators who were sent in search
of the Buddhadharma. Now I must invite an Indian pandita, who
is learned in both the outer and inner teachings. Of all the intelligent
Tibetan boys, I must make some train in translation, some take
ordination, and some practice the Dharma."

Having thought in this way, King Trisong Deutsen brought all
the four districts of Tibet under his command and proclaimed this
new law: "I am a king who upholds the Dharma, so from this day
on I shall instigate religious law. I will take a pebble from below the
feet of whomever can take ordination, learn translation, or practice
the Dharma. I will make this pebble an object of veneration above
my head."

Then Master Padmakara, the knower of past, present, and future,
felt moved to speak to King Trisong Deutsen and his ministers and
proclaimed these words:

> Your Majesty, Dharma king,
> It is most excellent that you establish religious law.
> I, the Lotus-Born One,

Perceive the three poisons as enlightened body,
   speech, and mind.
I realize thoughts to be the space of dharmata.
All my disturbing emotions have naturally subsided.
I am spontaneously freed from the chains of fix-
   ation.
Natural wisdom dawns continually.

As proof of that, through my quality of super-
   knowledge,
I perceive right now what will happen in the future.
In the same way, I see what took place in the past.

Prior to this life, the three of us,
Padmakara, Khenpo Bodhisattva,
And you, King Trisong Deutsen,
Were born as bastard brothers
In the land of Magadha.
Our mother was a poor poultry woman.
As a virtuous deed, we built a stupa for our
   mother.

In front of that stupa, the Jarung Khashor,
We made offerings and this aspiration:
"May we establish the teachings of the Dharma
In the border land that is frozen with ice!"

Because of making such an aspiration,
In the following life,
We were born as sons of a rakshasa, a rishi, and a
   brahman.
We made huge and extensive offerings
In front of the same stupa,
And each formed an aspiration.

The aspiration of the rishi son was as follows:
"May I be born as a Dharma king
In Tibet, the land frozen with ice,
And may I establish the doctrine of the Buddha!"

By the power of making that aspiration,
You are now born as the monarch
And are worthy of being called a Dharma king.

The aspiration of the brahman son was as follows:
"When you are a Dharma king,
May I be a learned pandita
And uphold the doctrine of the Buddha!"

By the power of making that aspiration,
We could meet here, although you were born in
     Sahor.
You are an abbot qualified to give ordination.

I, Padma, the son of the rakshasa aspired thus:
"When you are born as a Dharma king,
May I be a siddha endowed with magical powers,
Who can protect the doctrine of the Buddha!"

By the power of making that aspiration,
Although born in Uddiyana, we have met here,
And I shall protect the teachings of the Buddha.

When, in the Indian land of Magadha,
The son of the rishi Shriman
And his wife Kramati,
Called Asamaru, passed away,
He was reborn as the ruling king of Tibet.
Everything that people may want or cherish
And all the teachings of the Tripitaka
Will appear during the reign of this king.

When, in the Indian land of Kushaka,
The son born to the courtesan
Named Pramani Lata passed away,
He became the minister Trisang Yablhag.
Dharmashila, having passed away,
Is now the minister Gyalto Rami.
Dharmaprajna, having passed away,
Is now the minister Trisang Lhalö.

Dharmakaya, having passed away,
Is now Palgyi Senge of Shübu.
Dharmasukha, having passed away,
Is now the minister Dosher Trelchung.
Dharmamitra, having passed away,
Is now the one called Tara Lugong.

These six ministers
Have made the aspiration to meet together
In this primitive region, the land frozen with ice.
Their karmic residue from the country of India
Has ripened now in the land of Tibet.
They have become ministers of the present ruler
And have appeared during his reign.

These six ministers, who are hostile toward the
     Dharma,
Long ago, in their former lifetimes,
Took rebirth as various animals.
Now, in this life, they have the mark
Of the animal as which they were formerly born.

Gyatsa Lhanang, the pig,
Who comes from the central land of Nairanjara,
Now, has a black mole on the tip of his nose,
As proof that he was formerly a pig.

Tara Lugong, the ploughing ox,

Who comes from the northern district of that
     central land,
Now has a mole above his neck,
As proof that he was formerly an ox

Yablhag, the watchdog,
Who was a dog in that same land,
Now has a mole in the center of his forehead,
As proof that he was formerly a watchdog.

A cock in that same country
Is now the minister Dosher Trelchung.

He now has a feather in his bellybutton,
As proof that he was formerly born as a cock.

A jackal in that country
Is now the one named Gyalto Rami.
He now has a skull resembling a jackal,
As proof that he was formerly a jackal.

After dying, these six animals
Were born as six sons of a prostitute
And they made the wish to meet together in Tibet.
They now are born as the king's ministers.

The ministers who support a religious kingdom
Will proceed to the higher realms in future lives,
While those without interest in the Dharma will go
    to the lower realms.

The son of the brahman Purna Surya
Is reborn as the one named Bodhisattva.
He attained excellence, having been the preceptor
For a countless number of monks.

When the rishi of Dragyur Forest,
The monk Singha, passed away,
He was reborn as the monk called Pal-yang.

In the central land of Nairanjara,
The monk Gyalbu Nyingpo kept his monastic
    vows.
When this son of the courtesan Essence of
    Discipline
And the rishi Kamaraja passed away,
He was reborn as the one called Gyalwa Cho-yang.

When the monk Jeta,
The son of the brahman Gunasiddhi
And Queen Leksher Palmo,
Passed away in the Indian country Mutra,
He was reborn as the one named Namkhai
    Nyingpo.

When the monk Manjushri,
The son of the brahman Wisdom Wealth
And the courtesan Kumari Toruna,
Passed away at Vajra Seat,
He was reborn as the one called Lui Gyaltsen.

When the son of Gau Nyijor Tita
And the courtesan maiden Naraya
Passed away in the country of India,
He was reborn as the one called Kawa Paltsek.

When a naga girl passed away
On the great continent of Iron Tree,
She was reborn as the one called Drenpa Namkha.

When five rishi daughters from Vaishali
Passed away in the land of India,
They were reborn as five monks.[35]

When the two princes Righteous and Joyful
Passed away in the country of India,
They became Yeshe Yang and Drenka.

The two daughters of the layman Ananda
Were reborn as Lekdrub and Darma.

When the prince of Tsawarong
Called Bhikshu Purna passed away,
He was reborn as the one known as Vairochana.

Someone like me, the Lotus-Born One,
In the present knows whatever happened in the
    past.
The law of the Buddhadharma will flourish
    tremendously
During the reign of Your Majesty.

Thus he sang. King Trisong Deutsen, the ministers, the disciples, and everyone in the four districts of Tibet under the domain of the king rejoiced therein.

King Trisong Deutsen then made the law of the Buddhadharma as tight as a silk string. He made everyone who had taken ordination his object of respect and established a community of venerable monks. He encouraged the tantric laymen to practice sadhana and established a community of ngakpas. The king permitted all his subjects to practice the teaching of their liking. He gave the title "object of respect" to whoever copied and recited the words of the sugata. He sent the most intelligent and eloquent to India to learn the art of translation.

Khenpo Bodhisattva taught Dharma terminology and the colloquial languages. He gave the laymen instructions in writing, divination, and astrology and acted as both preceptor and master for those taking ordination. Master Padmakara performed all the Dharma rituals of Secret Mantra, such as the conferring of empowerment and consecration.

This was the fifteenth chapter in the immaculate life story of the Lotus-Born Master, telling how the king established the law of the Buddhadharma.

16

K ING TRISONG DEUTSEN THEN REFLECTED DEEPLY
and formed this intention, "Here in Tibet I will make the
sacred Dharma shine like the rising sun. Therefore I must
invite the great master Vimalamitra, who is reputed to be the most
learned among the five hundred panditas in India."[36]

The master Vimalamitra was an emanation of the Great Compassionate One. The Indian King Dharma Ashoka had a daughter
named Dharmabodhi, whose ravishing beauty resembled a divine
maiden. Once, while sleeping in a flower garden, she dreamed that
an extremely handsome white man came and anointed her with a full
vase of nectar. As the liquid passed down through the crown of her
head, her whole body was filled with bliss.

After twenty-one days, without any physical discomfort, she gave
birth to a baby boy. Thinking that it was dreadfully shameful to
have given birth to a child without a father, she took the baby and
abandoned him in the desert. When later she looked for the child,
he was sitting with his eyes wide open and wakeful. Feeling pity for
the baby, she took him home and nurtured him.

Monthly and yearly the boy grew up much faster than other
children. When five years had passed, he went to the monastery of
Nalanda. From the panditas there, he studied the five sciences and
the Tripitaka. In particular, he became learned in all the tantras.

He took ordination from the master Shri Singha and was given
the name Vimalamitra, Immaculate Friend. Following that, he became the most eminent among the learned ones. He acted as the
officiating priest for the Dharma king Dharmachakra and resided in

the monastery of Vikramashila with five hundred panditas.

King Trisong Deutsen gave the translators Kawa Paltsek, Chokro Lui Gyaltsen, and Rinchen Chok of Ma each one drey of gold dust. He sent them off with this order, "Offer some gold to the Dharma king Dharmachakra at the Indian temple of Vikramashila. Beseech the king to send me the gift of a pandita who is learned in all the outer and inner teachings. You three translators shall then invite the pandita and return!"

The three translators presented the gold to the king of Vikramashila and said, "Since you are a monarch who sustains the Dharma, King Trisong Deutsen, the Dharma king of Tibet, requests you to give him the gift of a pandita who is expert in all the outer and inner teachings."

King Dharmachakra replied, "Well, we must ask my court assembly of five hundred panditas, who will congregate tomorrow at noon."

The next day at noon the king called upon the five hundred panditas, presented each of them with a mandala offering of gold, and said, "The Dharma king of Tibet has presented me with a gift of gold and has requested me to send a pandita who is learned in all the outer and inner teachings. He has furnished these three translators as escorts, so I beseech the most learned of you to go."

Master Vimalamitra, the most learned among the five hundred panditas, was seated in the middle row. All the five hundred panditas—the two hundred and fifty to his right and the two hundred and fifty to his left—looked toward Vimalamitra, and the king said, "This means that you must go."

Vimalamitra reflected, "The king of Tibet may have great faith in the Dharma, but his ministers are antagonistic toward the teachings of the Buddha. It is well known that they had the translator Vairochana expelled. It is not sure whether I can tame them. I should not, however, turn my back on the Tibetan king's faith. In order not to transgress the command of the king of India, I must go!" Having reflected in this way, he stood up and exclaimed "Bodhisattva dathim!" three times.

The three translators interpreted that in different ways. Kawa Paltsek understood it to mean that he agreed to go, saying:

> When the arrow supported by the bow
> Is sent off by the strength of the man's finger,
> The arrow can reach the target.

Rinchen Chok of Ma understood it to mean that he agreed to go, saying:

> When the boat supported by the ocean
> Is rowed by the strength of the man with oars,
> The boat can cross the waters.

According to the understanding of Chokro Lui Gyaltsen, it meant:

> In a place that is not his own country,
> The person endowed with qualities
> Will pour the river of his mind
> From the full vase of his body.

Having obtained permission from the king and all the panditas, the translators invited Master Vimalamitra. He went to Samye holding a *kapali* the size of four fingers, on which was written eight Indian characters. King Trisong Deutsen and all the subjects formed a welcome party. When Vimalamitra arrived at Samye, they escorted him to Khorsa Chenmo. The master neither bowed to the king nor paid homage before the divinities. Because of this, the ministers said, "In the past we have invited many panditas here to our temple. In the future we also will invite them. Why is it that you, a pandita, neither bow to the king nor pay homage in the shrine hall?"

Vimalamitra replied, "Do you, king and ministers, know the meaning of homage?"

"I don't know the meaning of homage," the king answered.

107

Vimalamitra responded, "I pay homage by being indivisible from the deity. Due to this fact, the symbolic deities cannot bear my gesture of respect. I therefore do not bow down to the statue of a deity. Also, I do not bow down to a king."

King Trisong Deutsen then thought, "I wonder if he is really a Buddhist or a heretic."

Vimalamitra knew his thought and said, "Are you displeased, king?"

Vimalamitra then put on his Dharma robes and made a gesture of homage to the statue of Buddha Vairochana, the image of the personal practice of the king, saying:

> To Vairochana, the form body of the supreme
>   deity,
> Vimalamitra, the wisdom deity, bows down
> Within the relative state of illusion.

By making this gesture of homage, the image of Vairochana split apart from the top of its head down to the base of its throne. King Trisong Deutsen thought, "He really is a heretic," and showed an utterly depressed face.

Again Vimalamitra inquired, "Your Majesty, are you displeased?"

"I am not pleased," the king responded.

Making another gesture of homage, Vimalamitra uttered:

> To Vairochana, the supreme wisdom deity,
> The form aggregate of Vimalamitra
> Confers the true empowerment endowed with the
>   five wisdoms.

Placing his hands at the top of the head of the Vairochana image, it became even more splendid than before. Countless rays of light issued forth, filling the Three-Storied Central Temple with light. Vimalamitra performed next a consecration by permeating all the divine images at Samye with rays of light.

King Trisong Deutsen then exclaimed, "I bow down to you!" He prostrated himself and said, "Outwardly, you wear the dress of a monk, but within you are a yogi who has attained accomplishment of Secret Mantra. Henceforth I beg you not to pay homage to me!"

Vimalamitra replied, "Since you are a king who upholds the Dharma in Tibet, I surely must show you respect." He made the gesture of joining his palms and the light rays from his hands scorched the king's garment. The king then again prostrated himself.

King Trisong Deutsen requested the great master Vimalamitra to sit upon a lion throne with nine layers of cushions and offered him a huge brocade cape, numerous kinds of food, and a silver vase filled with three drey of gold dust. The master looked extremely displeased and did not utter anything, so the king thought, "This covetous man from south of Nepal is still not satisfied!"

The master perceived this and said, "King, hold up your sleeve!" The king did that and Vimalamitra filled three drey of sand into his sleeve and said, "Keep this for a moment!" King Trisong Deutsen couldn't hold it and let it slip. The sand then turned into gold and Vimalamitra said, "Great king, for me all appearances are gold. But to fulfill the aspirations of Your Majesty, just for now, I shall accept your gift."

On the meadow in front of the central temple, a Dharma throne was erected, and Vimalamitra was requested to teach the Dharma. The master reflected, "Formerly Vairochana taught the resultant vehicle, but it did not tame the Tibetans and he was expelled. Therefore, I must now teach gradually, beginning with the causal vehicles."

While he was expounding the causal vehicles of philosophy[37] to King Trisong Deutsen and the ministers, the king sent for tea from the area of Shangpo. On their way, the traders reached Gyalmo Rongkhar, where Vairochana asked them, "Where do you come from?"

The traders answered, "We come from Central Tibet. We are sent by our king to fetch tea."

Vairochana said, "Well, is the king's health good? Is the yoke of the royal law steadfast? Is the silk knot of the Dharma law tight? Who is the court priest? What are the titles of the teachings being translated?"

In reply, they said, "The king is in good health. The royal law is strict. The Dharma law is also tight. The court priest is Vimalamitra, who was invited from India. They are translating the teachings known as the causal vehicles."

Master Vairochana then said, "I was expelled when translating the resultant vehicle, such as the sacred Great Perfection, but now they are listening to the causal vehicles. Yudra Nyingpo, go there and do something to satisfy these Tibetan ministers who hate the Dharma."

Yudra Nyingpo put on a coat of woven cloth, a sorcerer crown of canvas, and took a wooden sword in his hand. The Early and Later Translation of the Great Perfection he made into two scrolls on which he wrote the Six Vajra Lines. He placed them behind his left and right ears and went to Tibet.

Yudra Nyingpo arrived at Samye, where Vimalamitra was teaching the causal vehicles to King Trisong Deutsen and the ministers. Stripping naked, he mounted the wooden sword as if it were a horse and rode in using a whip on his rear end shouting, "Kakapari, kakapari!"

Due to the ministers' hostility toward the Dharma, Vimalamitra, afraid to be punished under the law, had never been seen to smile even once since he arrived in Tibet. But when he saw this yogi, he smiled and said, "Dathim, dathim!"

Vimalamitra was later invited to the palace. After food was offered, King Trisong Deutsen asked, "Since you have arrived in Tibet, master, you have not been seen to smile even once, but today you smiled. Why was that?"

Vimalamitra replied, "That I never smiled in the past was because it depresses me that the Tibetan ministers revile the Dharma. I smiled today because I was delighted that such a yogi lives in Tibet."

"Well," the king said, "What did it mean when the yogi said, 'Kakapari, kakapari'?"

Vimalamitra replied, "He was talking about the teachings saying:

> Buddhahood is not attained through the immature
>   teachings of the shravakas.
> A great distance is not traversed by the gait of a
>   crow.
> Without teaching the resultant vajra vehicle,
> What is the use of teaching the vehicle of cause?

"Well," King Trisong Deutsen asked, "Why did you say, 'Dathim, dathim,' master?"

Vimalamitra replied, "It meant that all the teachings are the realization of the victorious ones and are without duality. Just like the nature of molasses or salt, all the Buddhadharma is devoid of duality."[38]

The king sent someone to find the yogi saying, "Find out who that yogi is!"

The yogi was found sitting and drinking while flirting with a *chang* lady. When asked, "What is your name? Who is your teacher? What is the name of your teaching?" he answered, "I am Yudra Nyingpo. My teacher is Vairochana. My teaching is the sacred Great Perfection."

This was reported to King Trisong Deutsen, who declared, "Invite him here! I must ask him for teachings!" Yudra Nyingpo was then placed on a throne of precious substances and offered a mandala of gold. The king and the close disciples received teachings from Master Vimalamitra in the morning and from Yudra Nyingpo in the afternoon. Thus they received the Five Early and Thirteen Later Translations of the Great Perfection. As the teachings of the two masters turned out to be identical, the Tibetan ministers felt regret for having expelled Vairochana. Three emissaries were sent off with a gold patra as a gift and invited Vairochana back from

Tsawarong. King Trisong Deutsen and the ministers placed his feet above their heads and venerated him as a supreme object of respect.

This was the sixteenth chapter in the immaculate life story of the Lotus-Born Master, on how Master Vimalamitra was invited and Vairochana's expulsion regretted.

17

KING TRISONG DEUTSEN NOW INVITED the great learned master Danashila from the land of Singala and the great learned master Kamalashila from the land of China. He had previously invited Master Bodhisattva of Sahor, Vimalamitra of Kashmir, and Master Padmakara of Uddiyana. Thus he had invited five great learned and accomplished masters.

The translators present were Kawa Paltsek, Chokro Lui Gyaltsen, Yeshe Dey of Nanam, Rinchen Chok of Ma, and Jnana Kumara of Nyag. The minor translators were Tsemang of Denma, Namkhai Nyingpo of Nub, Atsara Yeshe Yang of Ba, Gobum Yujin, Loki Chung, and others. Having in this way extended invitations to numerous translators and panditas, King Trisong Deutsen presented a request for the Dharma to be taught.

Master Padmakara was not born from a womb, but from a lotus flower. In general, since he brought the beings of the three realms under his sway and possessed the power of outshining the three levels of existence, all the gods and demons of India and Uddiyana offered him the core of their life-force. In particular, he bound under oath all the gods, demons, and yakshas of Tibet. Especially, since he tamed the building site of Samye, he sat on a three-layered lion throne.

Master Vimalamitra had presided as the most eminent scholar among five hundred panditas. He functioned as a bridge for all the Buddhadharma to be translated into the Tibetan language and had comprehension of an ocean of instructions; all the teachings of outer and inner Vajrayana as well as of Vinaya, Sutra, and Abhidharma.

Since he had attained perfect recall and knew all the Dharma without any trace of ignorance, he sat on a two-layered lion throne.

Khenpo Bodhisattva was adorned with the precious three trainings and comprehended all the Dharma without the slightest failing. But, especially since he had been the first master at the court, he sat on a lion throne with three padded cushions.

The two masters Danashila and Kamalashila were adorned with numerous qualities of learning and therefore each sat on a lion throne.

The translator Vairochana had been sent to India to request teachings and had met with numerous learned and accomplished masters. He had gained comprehension of all the Buddhadharma and reached the ultimate point of accomplishment. His ambitious companion, Lekdrub, returned earlier than Vairochana and was murdered by the border guards. Vairochana, after having attained the art of swift feet, returned later. He was pursued by swift-footed soldiers from India, but avoided getting caught and, in addition, fooled the border guards with unreal gold. Due to Vairochana's ingenuity no other swift-footed soldiers or border guards turned up. Vairochana could translate from twenty-one languages and was therefore superior to the other translators. He had been expelled to Gyalmo Tsawarong and had not died, although he was thrown into pits with lice and frogs. Since he was a bodhisattva abiding on the levels, he sat on a lion throne. All the other translators sat upon silken cushions.[39]

King Trisong Deutsen presented each translator and pandita with a mandala of gold. He gave them Chinese tea, Nepalese *gola*, Tibetan grain wine, Indian rice wine, and so forth, each according to his liking. He also offered them innumerable mundane gifts. The king prostrated himself, circumambulated them, and finally said:

> EMAHO, Master Padmakara of Uddiyana,
> Master Bodhisattva of Sahor,
> Master Vimalamitra of Kashmir,

Master Danashila of Singala,
Master Kamalashila of China,
Great translator Vairochana,
You other translators and panditas,
My supreme objects of veneration,
Since I have pledged to be a king who upholds the
    Dharma,
I request you to translate into Tibetan, without
    exclusion,
All the Buddha's words and commentaries, and the
    tantras, scriptures, and instructions.
Turn the wheel of the sacred teachings!
Kindle the torch of the sacred teachings!
Shower down the rain of the sacred teachings!
Blow the great conch of the sacred teachings!
Beat the drum of the sacred teachings!

King Trisong Deutsen then invited all the translators and panditas to the Exalted Palo Temple. In the Bodhi Temple they made aspirations, in the Temple of Purification they took baths, in the Maitreya Temple they made predictions, in the Meditation Temple they established a meditation center, in the Translation Temple they did translations, and in the Vishva Temple they expounded the vehicles. Thus they established a Dharma assembly for the duration of thirteen years. They expounded the Buddhadharma, translating from the languages of India, Uddiyana, Sahor, Kashmir, Singala, and China.

The masters Jnanamitra, Danashila, and Kamalashila and the translators Kawa Paltsek, Chokro Lui Gyaltsen, and Yeshe Dey of Nanam translated all the sutras. They rendered the *Jewel Mound*, *Buddha Avatamsaka*, and the three extensive and medium length versions of the Prajnaparamita scriptures.

Khenpo Bodhisattva, the minor translators, and Tsemang of Denma translated all the root texts for the Vinaya, Sutra, and Abhidharma. Master Kamalashila and Rinchen Chok of Ma translated many sutras from the Chinese versions, including the *Hundred-fold Homage for Amending Breaches*. Master Vimalamitra and the translator Jnana Kumara of Nyag translated many outer and inner teachings of Secret Mantra. Master Padma and the translators Namkhai Nyingpo and Vairochana translated many tantras of Secret Mantra belonging to the Eight Sadhana Teachings. In particular, Vairochana asked Master Padma many questions about Secret Mantra and composed numerous teachings on questions and answers from the replies.

This was the seventeenth chapter in the immaculate life story of the Lotus-Born Master, telling how the Dharma teachings were translated and established at Samye.

18

❋

KING TRISONG DEUTSEN now said to Master Padmakara, "Due to my excellent merit, all my aspirations have been fulfilled. Especially, it is an extremely great fortune that the sacred Dharma has been translated and taught, spreading its light like the rising sun. Now I implore you to grant me a teaching to make my life span most excellent."

He made this request while performing a feast gathering. Master Padma replied, "Your Majesty, someone with the most excellent merit cannot also have the longest life. Yet, Your Majesty, since I have reached the vidyadhara level of longevity, I shall perform the life-sadhana and confer upon you the empowerment of longevity."

Thus, Padmakara practiced the sadhana of longevity, having opened up the mandala for accomplishing indestructible life. Signs of accomplishment appeared, and he sent this message to King Trisong Deutsen: "Come and I shall give you the empowerment of longevity and pour the nectar of immortality from the vase of life!"

The ministers protested, "Your Majesty, since you have such great merit you also will have a full life span. Do not drink that water from the vase of longevity! The master is nothing but an evil-minded Nepalese with great appetite for wealth. It is possible that he has put poison in the life-vase to kill Your Majesty and seize the kingdom."

King Trisong Deutsen retorted, "The great master nirmanakaya does not make mistakes!" But it was of no avail. Thus the ministers prevented the king from receiving the empowerment.

Master Padma snapped his fingers once, revealed the mandala of

Buddha Amitayus within the vase to the king and ministers, and then the mandala dissolved into space. Master Padma himself drank the water of longevity, by which all the pores of his body became completely filled with golden vajras the size of rice grains. King Trisong Deutsen felt regret and said, "Now I will not listen to the evil words of the ministers. Please kindly accept me, master!"

Master Padma again disclosed the mandala of longevity and performed the practice. When the time came for conferring the empowerment, the ministers said to the king, "The master did not die because he has knowledge of poison-spells. King, you do not have that knowledge, so you will certainly die." Again the ministers dissuaded the king from receiving the empowerment.

After that, Master Padma concealed the vase of longevity with a miraculous terma instruction and a skull cup as a terma treasure at the Crystal Cave of Drag Yangdzong. He concealed it making this aspiration: "When the time of the last five-hundred-year period arrives, my emanation will appear, who will be wrathful, fierce, powerful, and have a black mole at his heart center in the shape of a vajra. He will open the door to this treasure of my heart. He will take out this life-vase and the miraculous terma instruction and, having attained the vidyadhara level of longevity, he will subdue all demons and heretics with magical armies."

King Trisong Deutsen then said to Master Padma, "Although I have no doubt about you conferring the empowerment of longevity upon me, the ministers who are hostile toward the Dharma would not allow me. Please now give me a method for prolonging my life span!"

Master Padma replied with this song.

> Since the king has great power,
> And since the Tibetan people have great faith,
> It is possible that the kingdom will flourish a little.
> If you would have received my life-empowerment,
> You could have lived until one hundred and eight
> years of age.

The ministers did not allow Your Majesty,
So, in the beginning of the Year of the Ox,
When you have reached fifty-six,
The time for your death will arrive.

If longevity ceremonies can be performed for you,
Your life span can be extended for thirteen years.
After Your Majesty passes away,
The power of the kingdom will wane.

Following that, when three generations have passed,
An emanation of Vajrapani will appear
With the name King Ralpachen.
He will make the Buddhadharma flourish.

In the later part of that king's life,
An emanation of Mara with evil conduct
Will appear having the name "Lang."[40]
He will make the sacred Buddhadharma decline.

There is no doubt that dreadful times will come.
The royal law will be destroyed, and the king will
        wage war.
The people of Tibet will despair.
Tibet will be split and its districts divided.

An emanation of the Lord of Secrets
Named Lhalung Palgyi Dorje
Will then subdue that evil king.
An emanation of Manjushri
Known by the name of Gongpa Sal
Will then rekindle the embers of the Buddha-
        dharma,
And the teachings and the law will flourish for
        a while.
King, you must have ceremonies of longevity
        performed.

After Padmakara had spoken in this way, all the translators and
panditas discussed which long-life ceremony would bring the great-

est benefit to King Trisong Deutsen. As the outer fulfillment ritual, they translated the following ten sutras for the king's daily practice: the *Essence of Knowledge* as the sutra of the view, the *Wisdom of Passing* as the sutra of meditation, the *Excellent Conduct* as the sutra of aspiration, the *Vajra Subjugator* as the sutra of purification, the *Confession of Downfalls from Bodhichitta* as the sutra of confession, the *White Ushnisha* as the sutra of exorcism, the *Blue-Clad One* as the sutra of protection, the *Boundless Life* as the sutra of longevity, the *Stream of Wealth Goddess* as the sutra of prosperity, and the *Single Syllable* as the sutra of quintessence. After these scriptures were translated, they were given to the king for his daily practice.

As the inner fulfillment ritual, they translated the *Amendment of Breaches of Secret Mantra* with its liturgical application. In the past, a sentient being with the body of a *sülpo* had killed his master and committed the action without intermediate. He fell into the hells and was purified by a confession made by Samantabhadra. In the same way, Master Padma mended all the king's breaches of the sacred commitments and thus purified his obscurations.

As confessional liturgies for the secret fulfillment ritual, Padmasambhava composed the following four confessions for the four aspects of approach and accomplishment: the *Confession of the Supreme Wisdom Body*, the *Confession of Twenty-eight Points for Adopting and Avoiding*, the *Secret Confession of the Four Classes of Dakinis*, and the *Confession of the Expanse of the View*, also known as the *Natural Confession*. Just as Vajrasattva in the past had taught the brahman named Human Skull and purified his obscurations, in the same way, Master Padma mended all the king's breaches of sacred commitment and thus purified his obscurations.

Furthermore, as antidotes to the combinations of diseases resulting from imbalances of the four elements, the Chinese doctor Hashang Tetsa and the court physician Nyang Tsen composed many teachings on the tantras of healing. Additionally they made many medicinal concoctions and preparations of essence-extracts.

As the remedy against the external haughty spirits of the world,

Master Padmakara translated a thousand chapters on types of thread-crosses based on the *Net of One Thousand Gods and Demons,* as well as the *Four Oceans of the Universal Mother Deities,* such as the outer thread-cross, the inner thread-cross, the male thread-cross, and the female thread-cross, and so on. In particular, since nagas govern the country of Tibet, Master Padma composed many rituals for them, such as the *Propitiation of Nagas, Hiding the Naga Treasure, Binding the Entrustment to Nagas, Restoring the Naga Castle, Relinquishing Harmful Influences,* and numerous other ritual texts. He also composed many Vajrayana practices such as the *Garuda Remedy Sadhana,* the *Hayagriva Subjugation of Nagas,* and the *Combined Sadhana of the Three Wrathful Ones.*

Master Padma also translated one hundred subsidiary protective rituals including the *Protective Ritual of the Highly Proficient King,* the *Protective Ritual of the Invisibility Wand Against One Thousand Gods and Demons,* as well as the sadhanas of rituals for protective charms to wear or hang above doors.

Having made these supportive rituals, Padmasambhava extended King Trisong Deutsen's life thirteen years beyond the age of fifty-six, when formerly he was supposed to pass away. Thus the king was able to live for sixty-nine years.

Master Padma then said, "Due to your extremely great merit, Your Majesty, you can reach the full measure of your life span and henceforth have no obstacles. You now possess both qualities."

> This was the eighteenth chapter in the immaculate life story of the Lotus-Born Master, on how he performed supportive rituals for the king and extended his life span.

19

❀

Next, King Trisong Deutsen presented all the panditas he had invited from India with a mandala of three drey of gold. He offered garments, food, and drink and sponsored an extensive thanksgiving. The king gave presents to all the lotsawas for translating the Buddhadharma and proclaimed them to be worthy of venerating above the crown of his head.

The Indian panditas, including Master Vimalamitra, were permitted to return to their countries. The translators and many disciples escorted them to India. Thus, due to the extreme merit and generosity of King Trisong Deutsen, the Dharma kings of India permitted the panditas to teach the Dharma in Tibet.

Masters Padmakara and Khenpo Bodhisattva had been repeatedly connected as brothers in former lives. So the king did not permit them to leave. The two masters promised to stay, and Master Bodhisattva remained in meditation in the Bodhi Temple.

Master Padmakara took as his consort and support for sadhana the sixteen-year-old goddesslike daughter of Palgyi Wangchuk of Kharchen with the name Lady Tsogyal of Kharchen. She was endowed with the nature of a wisdom dakini. They remained in the profound meditation practice of Secret Mantra in the gathering hall of dakinis at the Tregu Cave of Chimphu.

King Trisong Deutsen then thought, "The teachings will be of no benefit unless they are applied in practice. I must therefore request instructions on the sadhanas of Secret Mantra!" Having considered this, he went before Master Padma in glorious Chimphu and laid out a seat of silk brocade. He offered Master Padma a coat of white wolf skin and a maroon cape of brocade. Having filled silver vessels with various kinds of wine made from rice and grapes, he presented them, holding them in his right and left hands. Having offered innumerable mundane presents, he uttered this request in the manner of praising the body, speech, and mind of the master:

OM

Great Compassionate One, lord who tames sentient
    beings,
Your blazing bodily form subdues mundane spirits.
Having achieved the levels, your body is beyond
    decline.
I salute and praise your form which equals
    dharmakaya.

AH

From the center of the lotus crescent of your vajra
    tongue,
Your perfect and splendorous voice emanates and
    absorbs the subjugating mantras,
Pacifying, increasing, magnetizing, and subjugating.
Supreme king of Secret Mantra,
I salute and praise your speech, which equals the
    voice of Hayagriva.

HUNG

The various shrine objects of body, speech, and
    mind[41]
And glorious Samye, my sacred aspiration,
Were built and consecrated by you, master.
I devotedly bow before you who equal a
    nirmanakaya.

Though I am not worthy of requesting and
    beseeching you,
I beg you kindly to pay heed to me.
Please think of us with compassion and bestow
    upon us

The sadhanas of Secret Mantra that give
enlightenment within one lifetime.

Saying this, he humbly prostrated himself. Master Padma then
said this reply to King Trisong Deutsen:

EMAHO
King and benefactor of the doctrine, upholder of
the Dharma,
I have accomplished the vidyadhara level of im-
mortal life.
I have achieved the supreme accomplishment of
mahamudra.
I have received the empowerment of the expression
of awareness in the supreme Secret Mantra.
I will completely fulfill your wishes.

Vairochana, who could translate from twenty-one languages;
Lekjin Nyima, who knew twenty-one kinds of scripts of India and
Tibet; Tsemang of Denma, who was the most eminent in fast
writing; the lotsawa Namkhai Nyingpo; and Atsara Yeshe Yang of
Ba—these five were the lotsawas and assistants who translated sa-
dhana texts from the languages of Uddiyana, India, and other
countries into Tibetan.[42]
Guru Padma composed the Nine Sadhana Sections based on the
Nine Root Tantras. Based on the *Yama Display Root Tantra* and the
Dark Red Yama Tantra, he composed the sadhanas of Manjushri Body.
Based on the *Steed Display Root Tantra* and the *Mighty Lotus Tantra,* he
composed the sadhanas of Lotus Speech. Based on *Heruka Galpoche*
and the *Supramundane Scripture,* he composed the sadhanas of Vishuddha Mind. Based on the *Most Supreme Display Root Tantra* and the
Eightfold Volume, he composed the sadhanas of Nectar Quality. Based
on the *Kilaya Display Root Tantra* and the *Twelve Kilaya Tantras,* he
composed the sadhanas of Kilaya Activity. Based on the *Mother Deities*

Display Root Tantra and the *Mother Deities Assemblage Tantra,* he composed the sadhanas of Liberating Sorcery of Mother Deities. Based on the *Vidyadhara Display Root Tantra* and the *Vidyadhara Accomplishment Tantra,* he composed the *Hundred and Eight Sadhanas of Guru Vidyadhara.* Based on the *Tantra of Taming Haughty Spirits,* he composed the general and specific sadhanas of Mundane Worship. Based on the *Wrathful Mantra Tantra,* he composed the general and specific sadhanas of Maledictory Fierce Mantra.

Following that, he composed the Four Particularly Important Instructions. Since the *Wheel of Yama* is difficult to understand, he composed the *Keylike Wheel of Magic;* since Kilaya is difficult to accomplish, he compsed the *Unified Basic Essence Sadhana.* Since the Mother Deities, even when accomplished, are difficult to enjoin to activities, he composed the *World-Wheel of the Mother Deities to Show the Place of Death.* Moreover, since the spirits of the male class, though swift to act, are obstinate and very distrusting, he composed the *Wheel of Bonds and Suppression.*

Master Padmakara then composed the extremely profound and most eminent sadhana of the glorious Assemblage of Sugatas, a sadhana that condenses the Eight Sadhana Teachings into one. Based on the tantras of the *Root Tantra of the Assemblage of Sugatas,* the *Subsequent True Enlightenment Tantra,* the *Final Subsequent Mantra Tantra,* the *Tantra of Amending Incompleteness,* and the *Opening Key Tantra,* he composed the following sadhanas: the peaceful sadhana of the *Supreme Hundred Families,* the *Five Families,* the *Single Family of the Great Secret,* the *Single Form,* and others. To practice the mandala of the wrathful deities with seven hundred twenty-five herukas as a single mandala, he composed major, medium, and lesser texts for the stages of development and completion, the *Continuous Mantra Practice,* and others.[43]

Eight disciples, headed by King Trisong Deutsen, then received the complete teachings on these stages at the hermitage of the Cave of Chimphu. Master Padma opened the mandala of the peaceful and wrathful buddhas and performed the recitation for the empowerment. First he conferred in full all the general empowerments for the mandala of peaceful deities. Following that, when initiating them into the mandala of wrathful deities, the eight disciples each threw a flower made of a drey of gold. Master Padma gave each disciple the teaching corresponding to the deity upon which their flower fell.[44]

King Trisong Deutsen's flower fell in the center, on the mandala of the Most Supreme, so he was given the tantras and sadhanas of Assemblage of Sugatas. The flower of Namkhai Nyingpo of Nub fell on the mandala of Vishuddha Mind, so he was given the tantras and sadhanas of Vishuddha Mind. Sangye Yeshe of Nub threw his on the mandala of Manjushri, so he was given the tantras and sadhanas of Manjushri Body. Gyalwa Cho-yang of Ngenlam threw his on the mandala of Lotus Speech, so he was given the tantras and sadhanas of Lotus Speech. Lady Kharchen's fell on the mandala of Vajra Kilaya, so she was given the tantras and sadhanas of Kilaya Activity. Palgyi Yeshe of Drogmi's fell on the mandala of Mother Deities, so he was given the tantras and sadhanas of Liberating Sorcery of Mother Deities. Palgyi Senge of Lang threw his on the mandala of Tamer of All Haughty Spirits, so he was given the tantras and sadhanas of Mundane Worship. Vairochana's fell on the mandala of the Black Powerful One, so he was given the tantras and sadhanas of Maledictory Fierce Mantra.

Master Padma then fully transmitted all the stages of empowerment with their oral instructions. He thus ripened and freed the king and the disciples. The eight disciples then practiced their various sadhanas, and each of them had a certain sign of accomplishment.

King Trisong Deutsen, although he was supposed to die at the age of fifty-six, extended his life span thirteen years and became sixty-nine. He realized his physical body to be a mandala of deities and could journey through all buddhafields.

Also, the other of the eight disciples reached accomplishment: Namkhai Nyingpo could travel by riding on the rays of the sun, Sangye Yeshe could stab his dagger into rock, Gyalwa Cho-yang of

Ngenlam could emit the neigh of glorious Hayagriva, Lady Tsogyal could resurrect the dead, Palgyi Yeshe could perceive the dakinis and order the Mother Deities to carry out activities, Palgyi Senge of Lang could employ the eight classes of gods and demons as servants, and Vairochana could command the mundane haughty spirits to accomplish the activities. In this way they reached countless attainments.

This was the nineteenth chapter in the immaculate life story of the Lotus-Born Master, telling how Master Padma transmitted the sadhanas of Secret Mantra and how the king and the disciples engaged in sadhana practice.

20

KING TRISONG DEUTSEN NOW REASONED, "In the five-hundred-year period of degeneration, a protector must guard my temple." He presented a feast offering to Padmasambhava and said:

EMAHO, gracious master,
From now until the last five-hundred-year period
There will never be a king with a merit like mine.
The ministers will be evil, and Tibet will break
    into pieces.
Who will protect all the temples in Central Tibet,
In the four districts and the Border Temples?
Master, to safeguard the Buddhadharma,
Please be kind enough to bestow the subjugating
    mantras of life-force, hail, and spells.

Master Padma replied, "In the final five-hundred-year period of the dark age, the need for a Dharma protector to guard Your Majesty's temples and for subjugating mantras to safeguard the Buddhadharma will be extremely great. I shall therefore bind under oath any particular god or demon Your Majesty may favor and place him as your temple guardian."

King Trisong Deutsen then made this request: "In general, the nagas govern the four districts of Tibet. In particular, they are my friends and they have great abilities and miraculous powers. Moreover, they are the custodians of the treasures of wealth. So I beseech you to place the nagas as the temple guardians."

Master Padma, the king, and the close disciples went to the bank of the splendorous Lake Maldro where they placed a bowl made of zi stone with a water offering. Master Padma entered the samadhi that subjugates and magnetizes the nagas. He inserted the big toe of his left foot into the lake, made the hook gesture, and said, "NAGARAJA ANGKUSHA JAH." Immediately the lake became wild and turbulent. The king of the nagas with his whole retinue appeared from within the lake, upside down, and remained on the surface. Master Padma said, "Why are you coming in this disrespectful way with your head pointing downwards?"

The naga king retorted, "We are not showing disrespect. If we were to come in our normal way, although we are incapable of causing the master harm, since our appearance, touch, and breath are poisonous, your reverend entourage would be injured. We were afraid to make the master so angry as to destroy all the cities of the nagas."

Master Padma said, "Very well! Now you must be the guardians of the temple of Samye!"

The naga replied, "Please do not say that. When the final five-hundred-year period arrives, people will be poor and destitute. They will dig into sacred land, split open sacred rocks, and cut down sacred trees. We naga kings will not transgress the master's command, but our subjects will wreak havoc."

At this King Trisong Deutsen said, "Great master, if they feel incapable of promising to be temple guardians, since the nagas are the custodians of wealth, please ask them to bestow a boon of their opulence since my treasuries are depleted."

Master Padma told the naga king, "Well, if you cannot be temple guardians, then fill King Trisong Deutsen's treasuries with precious jewels."

The naga replied, "I will bestow wealth on the master and the king! Seven days from now, leave the doors to your treasuries open. King and subjects, keep your backs turned and do not look, no matter what sounds you may hear." Having said this, all the nagas of the lake disappeared.

Master Padma and King Trisong Deutsen and the close disciples returned. On the morning of the seventh day they left the doors to the treasury open. At first, Samye became totally enveloped in mist, then loud sounds, cries, and noises were heard. The palace and all the temples trembled, so the king became apprehensive and sent a minister to look. The minister said, "The whole plain around Samye is crawling with snakes." After that he suddenly vomited blood and died.

When the noise disappeared and the mist dispersed, Master Padma told King Trisong Deutsen to look in the treasuries. The king had one hundred and eight treasuries with precious possessions, but they had all been emptied by his virtuous deeds. Now they were just as full as before. The king was overjoyed and sang:

> EMAHO
> Wish-granting jewel, source of fulfilling all
>   needs and desires,
> You free all the beings to be tamed
> From the misery of poverty and want.
> I bow down with praise to the precious
>   nirmanakaya.

King Trisong Deutsen then asked Master Padma:

> Omniscient and precious nirmanakaya,
> All-knowing guru, please tell me
> Who shall be the Dharma protector to guard
>   the temples
> Of glorious Samye, my noble aspiration?

Master Padma replied:

Alas, great king,
The times will get worse and worse.
Even Samye, your noble aspiration,
Will suddenly be destroyed by sand.

The ruler's heart will be possessed by an evil spirit.
The royalty will be upset by internal discord.
The temples will be arenas for strife
And be destroyed by explosives, fire, and meteors.

The temples in central and outlying districts
Will be occupied by criminals.
The centers of learning will turn into armories,
And the practitioners will destroy the Buddha-
     dharma.

Mantrikas will die at the knife blade,
And the king's advisors will lack success in
     upholding his reign.
People will carry knives under Dharma robes,
And rulers will be murdered with poison.

Lay people will have family disputes and die by
     weapons.
Mantrikas will have family disputes and resort to
     black magic.
People will wear armor their entire life,
And soldiers will be guarding the outer doors.

Sons will fight against their fathers,
And the age of weaponry will advance.
Dharma practitioners will not render service,
But will trust in charlatans and frauds.

People will wear the evil clothing of coats of dog
     skin and pointed helmets.
They will carry the evil weapons of sticks and
     walking staffs
And preach evil Dharma, the emptiness of nihilism.

The talk of Dharma will be heard in the beer
houses.

These are the omens that the Buddhadharma is
about to perish.
At such a time, the warrior spirit King Pekar
Is needed as the guardian of the temples.
He now resides in the land of Mongolia.

Your Majesty, give the decree for war
And conquer the Gomdra district of Bhata
Mongolia.
He will come here, giving chase to the valuables.
Then I shall appoint him as temple guardian.

King Trisong Deutsen then prepared for war and defeated the
district of Bhata Mongolia. After that, the one known as King
Shingja Chen, as Düpo Yabje Nagpo, and as King Pekar of the
warrior spirits arrived, chasing after the valuables. His right brigade
was one hundred warriors dressed in tiger skins. His left brigade was
one hundred arhat monks. His following was one hundred mendicants dressed in black. His trail blazers were one hundred women
dressed in black. His outer ministers were one hundred horsemen.
His inner ministers were one hundred savage warriors. His entertainment was one hundred tigers and lions. His emanations and reema-
nations were one hundred monkeys and apes and one hundred
peacocks and cats.

Master Padma then gave his command and bound King Pekar
under oath. At Pekar Temple, he established a shrine and appointed
Pekar as the temple guardian of glorious Samye and of the whole
temple complex.

Following this, Master Padma, Vairochana of Pagor, Namkhai
Nyingpo of Nub, Yeshe Yang of Ba, and several others gathered the
subjugating mantras for protecting the Buddhadharma. They composed and translated an infinite number of tantras and sadhanas
connected to the eight classes of gods and demons: white gings,
black maras, red tsens, murderous yakshas, slaughter rakshasas, pes-

tilent mamos, wrathful rahulas, and vicious nagas.

Additionally, they translated countless tantras and sadhanas connected to the protectors of the Buddhadharma, such as the Glorious Black Protector, the Glorious Black Goddess, the Dark Blue Guardian of Mantra, and many others. Shenpa Pekar, Gingchen Sogdak, and Tsangtsen Dorje Lekpa were the three leaders of these eight classes of gods and demons, so many tantras and sadhanas connected to them were translated. For the rahulas who govern the heavens, freeze the waters, and send hail storms and bolts of lightning and for the vicious nagas who govern the subterrestrial regions and cause various types of leprosy, they translated an immense number of subjugating and fierce mantras. These guardians of the Buddhadharma were entrusted to King Trisong Deutsen.

When Master Padma, Vairochana, and the others gave the king these subjugating mantras for protecting the Buddhadharma, the master said, "Trisong Deutsen, fortunate ruler of Tibet, we entrust you and fully authorize you with these profound drops of nectar, the extract of the heart of the panditas and translators. Retain them; retain them in your mind!"

> At best, when a person is a suitable recipient,
> Next best, when he has great compassion,
> Or at least, when devotedly he offers material
>   wealth,
> Apart from these three cases,
> If the fierce mantras are promulgated without
>   proper entrustment,
> The male and female lords of Secret Mantra
> Will inflict a severe punishment.
> King, it will cost you your life
> And you will fall into the lower realms.
> So guard these fierce mantras as dearly as your life.

Having said this, they fully entrusted the fierce mantras to King Trisong Deutsen's safekeeping. Delighted, the king presented Master Padma with six horses from the royal stables, headed by the steed Tsalu Jadong. The horses were adorned with gold bits, head gear with inlaid turquoise, and saddles of teak. The king also offered silk brocade with Mongolian designs, six drey of gold, and his personal necklace of turquoise called Radiant Lake. Having made these offerings, he bowed down and circumambulated the master.

Master Padma responded, "It is wonderful that you can offer your illusory wealth free from attachment. It is an excellent deed!"

At this, King Trisong Deutsen thought, "The master may be a siddha, but since he comes from the south of Nepal, he seems most fond of wealth."

Master Padma read his mind and said, "Your Majesty, hold up your sleeve." The master then poured three drey of sand and three drey of pebbles into the king's sleeve and said, "Keep this for a moment." The king was unable to hold his sleeve. When it fell, the king saw that all the sand had turned into gold and the pebbles had become turquoise.

Master Padma said, "Your Majesty, I only accepted your gifts so you could purify your obscurations and gather merit. For me all appearances are gold. As I have no need for wealth, you can do with it as you please." Thus he returned all the offerings to the king.

Struck with embarrassment, King Trisong Deutsen felt deep remorse and said, "Great master, I am the king of this primitive border tribe and due to my dense obscuration I gave rise to doubt. I feel shame and regret, nirmanakaya. Please kindly accept me with your compassion. I beg you to grant me a method to mend my breaches of the sacred commitments."

Saying this, King Trisong Deutsen threw himself prostrate to the ground, respectfully bowed his head at Master Padma's feet, and cried tearfully.

Master Padma replied, "Your Majesty, as you are just a sentient being you will give rise to conceptual thinking, but that itself is not breaking the sacred commitment. Since we are yogis, that is nothing to be upset about. King, apply the view and meditation as your confession! Do not harbor the defilement of concepts in your mind! Most importantly, practice the ten virtues, forsake the ten nonvirtues, be in accord with the Dharma in whatever you do, govern the land with the law of Dharma, and do not follow the advice of evil ministers. Doubt is the enemy of Dharma, so practice free from doubt."

Having spoken in this way, Master Padma gave the king the "Ocean of Cleansing Sacred Commitment," the Hundred Syllables of Vajrasattva, the Hundred Syllables of the Herukas, and the Hundred Syllables of the Tathagatas, with their respective sadhanas, as the Daily Confession for Mending Samayas.

This was the twentieth chapter in the immaculate life story of the Lotus-Born Master, telling how he employed the guardian of the temples, translated the fierce mantras for the sake of protecting the Buddhadharma, and taught the methods for mending sacred commitments.

21

MASTER PADMAKARA then said to King Trisong Deutsen, "In order to maintain your royal law, I, Padmakara, Vairochana, Namkhai Nyingpo, Atsara Yeshe, and many others have translated the fierce mantras. We have translated the fierce and subjugating mantras collectively from the languages of Uddiyana, India, Singala, Merutsey, Nepal, Sahor, Hashang, Sangling, Serling, Bhaita, Kashmir, the sign language of dakinis, the demonic languages of yakshas and rakshasas, and from magical sounds.

"I have invited the Dharma protector Pekar from the land of Bhata Mongolia and assigned him to be the guardian of the wealth of Samye.

"For your sake, lord king, we have translated many teachings on gaining buddhahood within one lifetime. But, since Your Majesty is often swayed by distraction, you will not practice the teachings but merely retain them as a karmic residual. At the last of a string of seventeen incarnations, you will meet them again. Therefore, I have concealed them as terma treasures. Some fortunate people will reveal the treasures of these fierce mantras that can protect the Buddhadharma. People born in the four 'sturdy years' of the Ox, Sheep, Dog, and Dragon or in the 'commanding years' of the Bird or Monkey will possess the karmic potential and not meet with death if they disclose these teachings. People born in the other six[45] will lack the power to reveal the treasures and, even if they do, they will quickly die. Since the law is now strong, there is no need for the fierce means of 'life-wheel, hail and spells,' but the need will arise when evil times come, so I have concealed them in terma treasures.

"The way the treasures are buried is like this. In each treasury of the Triple-Storied Central Temple I have concealed a vital treasure for the king. Those are the treasuries of the Dharma. I have concealed vital treasures in each of the three special temples built by the three queens, the Putsab Serkhang Temple, the Khamsum Copper Temple,[46] and the Gegye Jema Temple. In each of the two Yaksha Temples I hid a terma treasure. In each of the four major and eight minor temples I have concealed a treasure. Finally, in the Pekar Temple and in each of the Four Protector Temples I buried a treasure of sorcery. Within the stupas in the four directions I concealed a Dharma treasure in the white, a sorcery treasure in the black, a treasure for arts and crafts in the red, and a medicinal treasure in the yellow.

"At the hermitage of Chimphu I concealed the great treasure of the guru's mind. At Kyerchu Temple to the south I concealed the *Tantra of Fulfilling All Needs* and the *Embodiment of the Tripitaka*. At Tsilung in Bumthang I concealed all the scriptures of the Mind Section. At Geney in Bumthang I concealed the *Assemblage of Mother Deities* and all the mother tantras. In the temple at Changtra Düntsey I concealed the Dark Red Yamantaka and all the fierce mantras. At Tra Düntsey to the north and at Kyor Düntsey I concealed one hundred and eight fierce mantras. To the right of Changdram I concealed Dharma medicine, astrological scriptures, and precious stones. In the Tsi Temple I concealed tantras, scriptures, and instructions.

"At Longthang Drönma in Kham I concealed the *Thirteen Tantras of the Goddess* and the *Razor Scriptures*. In the temple at Gampo Lha Chukhar I concealed teachings on magic, miraculous powers, and fierce mantras. At Yuru Tramdrug I concealed thirteen fierce mantras. At Lhodrak Po-ting I concealed the *Assemblage of Sugatas* and many mamo and thread-cross sadhanas. In the Lion Cave of Taktsang I concealed teachings for attaining true enlightenment. At Meadow of Mönkha I concealed the teachings on Chiti Yoga and the Four Types of Instantaneous Razor Slash. At Drag Yangdzong I concealed all the sadhanas of Kilaya and Yamantaka. At the Glorious Fortress of Lhodrak and in the Lion Cave of Taktsang I concealed one hundred subjugating and thirty fierce mantras. In the Fortress Cave at Phula I concealed the fierce mantras of the four semo sisters, the secret fierce mantras, and one secret Kilaya. At the rock of the Imprint of the Rakshasa's Claw I concealed a secret treasure of the dakinis. In the Long Cave Sky Ladder I concealed the Guru's Mind Treasure. At Glacier Rock Sky Mountain I concealed cycles of sadhanas and manuals of medicine. In Long Upper Cave I concealed the teachings on Naga Demon Razor. In the Great Cave of Tsang I concealed the teachings of Longevity Lord Yamantaka and the twenty-one Chogdungs. At the narrow defile of Shula Dragmo I concealed the three teachings concerning the ging, mara, and tsen spirits.

"Moreover, in all the sacred mountains and rocks I concealed one hundred and eight kinds of minor treasures. I hid each of them after having made an aspiration for the sake of the destined disciples. When the following occurrences take place, the time has come for these termas to be revealed:

"When people swear and wear unwholesome black garments, when the centers of learning are destroyed and the hermitages burned down, when sacred words are traded like merchandise and murder can be exonerated for a price, when people engage in battle and dress in iron coats of mail, when religious teachers become battle chiefs and monks are killed by the knife, when disputes break out at sacred places and people build their hermitages in the center of towns, when tantrikas fight among each other and put poison in food, when rulers renege on their oaths and warriors are slaughtered by the sword, when all of Tibet falls into pieces like armor breaking apart, when father fights against son and family members combat one another, when maras and tsen demons are called upon as warrior spirits and bandits guard the roads and trails, when gongpo spirits possess the hearts of men, senmo spirits possess women, theu-rang spirits take possession of children, and everyone is under the power of demonic forces, when the eight classes of gods and demons are agitated and the ages of disease and famine arrive—that is the time when three signs of incapability of containment will occur: The earth will be unable to withhold its treasures, so the wealth of Dharma treasures, wealth treasures, gold, silver, and precious stones are opened. The Dharma protectors will be unable to keep the temples entrusted to them, so the valuables of the Three Jewels are robbed and stolen. The Buddhist practitioners will be unable to uphold the practice of sadhana, so they will trade for wealth the teachings they have not accomplished and, out of desire for fame, expound to others what they have not applied themselves. When these occurrences take place, you will meet with my teachings and instructions.

"Your Majesty, in the last of your following sixteen incarnations, you will be born in a place having the shape of a fresh horse corpse split open, called Tamshul, to the southwest of here. Born in the Year of the Dragon, you will belong to a noble family and be respected by everyone. Possessing outstanding intelligence and compassion, you will be extremely diligent and put great exertion into practice. You will be able to keep your samayas correctly and have only a minor degree of craving. You will have great courage and engage little in idle talk. You will be forbearing and refrain from slandering others. You will be sharp-minded and trustworthy, fair and patient. Being born as such a personage, Your Majesty, you will take possession of all the teachings I have given you now and attain enlightenment in that very lifetime.

"Because you have the flaw of having once damaged your sacred commitments by allowing the expulsion of Vairochana, Namkhai Nyingpo of Nub, and the other lotsawas, people will disbelieve your teachings. Even the people who have the strongest link to the teachings will at one point lose faith. For that reason, you must make many confessions and purifications before your teachers, the precious ones, and the master.

"When that time arrives, if you follow my advice, accept dharmadhatu as your essential country and forsake your homeland.

"Adhere to forest retreats and remote places as your essential dwelling place and leave your house behind.

"Practice the empty and luminous dharmata as your essential meditation and remain in seclusion.

"As your essential house, dwell in the limitless dharmadhatu.

"As your essential knowledge, keep attentiveness and presence of mind and exert yourself in spiritual practice.

"As your essential treasury, gather the wealth of the three kayas in the basic nature of enlightened mind.

"As your essential merit, do not leave your body, speech, and mind in ordinariness, but practice the sublime Buddhadharma.

"As your essential advice, rely on the words of the sugata and your masters.

"As your essential fatherhood, pay respect to Samantabhadra, compassion, and be kind to all beings.

"As your essential motherhood, pay respect to Samantabhadri, loving kindness, and cherish all beings as your children.

"As your essential spouse, meditate undistractedly on the samadhi of luminosity and emptiness and keep constant company with her.

"As your essential offspring, visualize the five families of sugatas and practice the samadhis of development and completion.

"As your essential wealth, copy the scriptures of the sugatas and scrutinize and keep their meaning in mind.

"As your essential farm land, cultivate the field of faith and engage in actions that are in harmony with the Dharma.

"As your essential retinue, keep to the dakinis and protectors and present them with feast offerings and tormas.

"As your essential food, eat the nonarising nectar of dharmata and practice unchanging samadhi.

"As your essential beverages, drink the nectar of your master's oral instructions and supplicate him repeatedly.

"As your essential clothing, receive the empowerments and sacred commitments and bring them to perfection.

"As your essential entertainment, engage in the samadhi of emanating and absorbing and train in the expression of awareness.

"As your essential enjoyment, practice meditation and sadhana and bring your body, speech, and mind to maturity through the progressive stages of Dharma practice.

"As your essential spectacle, train gradually in development and completion and apply them in practice.

"As your essential warrior spirit, make constant offerings to the wisdom deity.

"As your essential court chaplain, visualize the vajra master at the crown of your head and supplicate him.

"As your essential activity, have the scriptures copied and give them to whoever has need.

"As your essential mirror, look into the sacred Dharma and exert yourself in making supplications.

"As your essential shrine room, meditate on your body being the mandala and visualize the yidam.

"As your essential ornament, train in the four immeasurables and act for the welfare of beings, without partiality or prejudice.

"As your essential Dharma practice, rest your mind in the unfabricated innate state of emptiness and luminosity.

"As your essential samaya, look constantly into your mind and reveal the purity of its nature.

"As your essential instruction, keep your character free from deceit and hypocrisy and meditate on the oral advice of the hearing lineage.

"As your essential mandala, unceasingly rest your mind in the innate state.

"As your essential view, look into the changeless dharmakaya and recognize your natural face.

"As your essential meditation, practice the yidam of nonarising and become stable in the innate state.[47]

"As your essential conduct, act without accepting or rejecting and be free from attachment.

"As your essential fruition, do not seek the result elsewhere, since the three kayas are inherent in yourself.

"If you practice like this you will attain buddhahood in Sukhavati after that life, having taken birth from within the bud of a lotus flower." Thus Padmakara gave this prophecy to King Trisong Deutsen.

Master Padma concealed the teachings as terma treasures and gave further predictions to the king.[48] King Trisong Deutsen was overjoyed and made offerings and prostrations. Master Padma then remained in meditation at Chimphu, and King Trisong Deutsen ruled according to secular and religious law.

In this way, the king laid the foundation for Samye in the Year of the Tiger and completed its building in the Year of the Horse. In the Year of the Sheep he had the Buddhadharma translated. In the Year of the Ox, at the age of fifty-six, he was supposed to pass away, but because of the healing ceremonies, he lived for another thirteen years. He passed away at sixty-nine in the Year of the Tiger, without the company of many attendants. He left a detailed will for the ministers and subjects. After passing away, he dissolved into the heart of Manjushri.

> This was the twenty-first chapter in the immaculate life story of the Lotus-Born Master, telling how Master Padma concealed the teachings and instructions as treasures and how he gave predictions to the king.

22

❀

PRINCE MUTIG TSENPO WAS ENTHRONED as king and governed according to the law of his father. He placed the foot of Master Padma above his head, laid out brocade cushions, and offered him a coat of white wolf skin to wear. Presenting drinks of grape and rice wine, he served refreshments of various kinds of food. Having offered a mandala of costly silver decorated with inlaid gold and turquoise, he requested empowerments and oral instructions.

Master Padma personally conferred upon the prince the empowerment of the mandala of the peaceful and wrathful buddhas. He gave the oral instructions on the combined sadhana of the peaceful and wrathful deities and performed the ripening and liberation in their entirety.

Following that, Master Bodhisattva dissolved his incarnated mandala in the Bodhi Temple. Master Padma and Prince Mutig wrapped the body in precious silk, sealed it with gold and turquoise within a pagoda of sandalwood, and placed it as a receptacle for worship. Master Padma then said:

> I, Padmakara,
> Was born in the land of Uddiyana due to accumulated merit.
> I remained in India for three thousand six hundred years.[49]
> Moved by karma, I went to the center of Tibet.
>
> I have now stayed here in the Land of Snow for fifty-one years.

Through the power of aspirations I have been the
    king's guru.
Having laid the foundation for Samye in the Year
    of the Tiger,
His sacred aspiration, Samye, was fulfilled in the
    Year of the Horse.
I have thus fulfilled the aspiration of the Tibetan
    king.

In the Year of the Ox, the king was fifty-six years
    of age.
Although that was the destined time for his death,
Through longevity rituals I extended his life span
    for thirteen years.
He then passed away at sixty-nine, in the Year of
    the Tiger.

Mutig Tsenpo, having enthroned you on the seat of
    power,
I have imparted to you the complete empowerments
    and oral instructions.
The monarch and the subjects expand and guard
    the kingdom
Following the law of your father, the king.

The court priest Khenpo Bodhisattva
Has dissolved his incarnated mandala in the Bodhi
    Temple.
Also I will take leave and not remain here any
    longer.
I will search for a sadhana place to do spiritual
    practice.

Having thus spoken, Padmasambhava remained in meditation for
three months and three days at the upper retreat of Chimphu. At
Drag Yangdzong he stayed for five months and five days. At White
Rock of Tidro he meditated for seven months and seven days. At
Meadow of Mönkha he meditated for one month and ten days. At

Möntha Dragtha Tramo he meditated for three months and three days. In the Mön-gong Cave he practiced for one month and seven days. At the Pearl Crystal Cave of Pama Ridge he meditated for one month and ten days. In the Crystal Cave of Yarlung he meditated for three months and three days. At Tsibri of Gyal he practiced for two months and four days. At the snow mountain of Kailash he meditated for five months and five days. At Kharchu at Lhodrak he practiced for eight months and eight days. At Tsagong of Tsari he meditated for seven months and seven days.

Master Padma consecrated these secluded locations to be sacred places for sadhana. He personally visited everywhere in the land of Tibet and concealed innumerable terma treasures for the sake of worthy people in future generations. He also buried separate location lists, guide texts, and key texts. For the sake of each destined recipient he made these aspirations, "May this meet with a person possessing the karmic destiny! May it be practiced by destined people!" He also gave these three gradual seals, "Seal of treasure, seal of entrustment, seal of concealment." As well, he gave these decrees, "Entrusted, fully entrusted! Concealed, concealed as treasure! Profound, hold it sacred!"

Master Padma then said, "May everyone who meets with my terma teachings in the future also keep this testament in mind:

"Destined people who meet with my treasure teachings in the future, if you are unable to practice my oral instructions you will have difficulties; so keep the seal of secrecy.

"If you divulge the instructions too early, other people will be jealous, covet the teachings, or slander them; so first bring forth the signs of accomplishment in your sadhana practice.

"If your desire for material gain, fame, and grandeur is too great, other people will try to harm you; so possess the teachings on magical powers.

"Keep your sacred commitments as the foundation. If you damage your samayas, you will have no auspicious circumstances in this life and in the following you will go to the hell realms.

"Keep a view that is as high as the sky. You will fall into deviations unless you resolve the view.

"Acquire a meditation that is like a gold stake driven in the ground. If your meditation is unsteady, you will not attain stability by simply pretending to practice.

"Make your conduct possess fearless confidence. With hypocrisy and pretense you cannot convert others.

"Conceal your oral instructions like a treasure. If you propagate them too openly, they will dissipate and lose value.

"Whatever meditation or sadhana you may practice, search for a master who possesses the oral instructions. If you lack the blessings of a master, there also will be no blessings from your Dharma practice.[50]

"If your view and conduct are crude, you will have obstacles in your Dharma practice. Do not let your view become mere platitude or your conduct frivolous.

"The basis for Dharma practice is samaya and compassion. Keep your sacred commitments pure and embrace others with compassion.

"Unless you have attained signs of accomplishment in a teaching yourself, do not give it to others. If you do, other people will distrust the teaching and lack appreciation.

"Do not give general teachings and oral instructions at the same time. It can happen that the link is broken after the general teachings; so first examine the recipient.

"These terma teachings are extremely profound; practice them carefully.

"If you do like this, blessings will naturally manifest. The buddha will be discovered within yourself. People will provide you with all necessities. Everyone will respect you and divine beings will give sustenance. All your wishes will be fulfilled; you will continue the lineage of the buddhas and realize the meaning of the Dharma. You will establish the congregation of the sangha and cause the Dharma to spread and flourish.

"If you fail to do so, and you do not personally apply the teachings but merely ingratiate yourself to others for the sake of food and wealth, you are selling the life-force of the buddhas and are an embarrassment to the Dharma and a bad example for the sangha. You will be a teacher of evil and a guide to the hell realms. Recklessly throwing your welfare away, you will have wasted your precious human life. My terma teachings are most sacred; treasure them dearly."[51]

This was the twenty-second chapter in the immaculate life story of the Lotus-Born Master, telling how Master Padma personally visited the sacred places for sadhana in Tibet, concealed his mind treasures, and gave oral instructions.

23

❀

Next, Master Padmakara turned his attention toward the rakshasas living on Lankapuri, the Land of Rakshasas, which is like the axe handle of the Jambu continent and lies near the country of Uddiyana.[52] He saw that the rakshasas would invade and destroy all of India, Nepal, Tibet and so forth, murdering the human race. Master Padma saw the need to guard against the rakshasas in order to bestow the gift of fearlessness to the people of the Jambu continent. He decided to leave glorious Samye and go instead to the summit of the Glorious Copper-Colored Mountain.

At this time, Prince Mutig Tsenpo and other Tibetan kings, the ministers, male and female ordained practitioners, spiritual teachers, tantrikas, meditators, yogis, healers, copyists and reciters, chieftains, women, male and female benefactors—in short, all the people of Tibet—beseeched him to remain, but he did not consent. Instead, he sang this song of feeling weariness with Tibet.

> NAMO RATNA-GURU
> Lord Amitabha and Avalokiteshvara,
> Your compassion encompasses all beings.
> Bestow your blessings so that I may be your
> disciple
> And empty samsara.
>
> Now listen here, Tibetan king and subjects.
> I, Padmakara of Uddiyana,

Arrived in Tibet due to the continuation of past
    karma
And have fulfilled the king's aspiration.

In this land of Tibet, a realm shrouded in dense
    darkness,
I have made the sun of Dharma shine
And established all beings in both happiness and
    well-being.
Since then, the king of Tibet passed away.

Now I shall not remain in Tibet.
The Tibetans and I do not agree!
I am leaving; I am going to India!

The Tibetan king and ministers and I do not agree!
They do not rule the kingdom according to the
    Dharma.
Instead the ministers control the Dharma king.
I am tired of kings who engage in evil deeds.
I am leaving; I am going to India!

The Tibetan monks and I do not agree!
They do not keep the discipline pure,
But in secret enjoy meat, wine, and women.
I am tired of hypocritical people.
I am leaving; I am going to India!

The Tibetan teachers and I do not agree!
They do not explain the Buddha's words and the
    treatises correctly,
But fool people with distorted teachings.
I am tired of people who falsify the Buddha's
    words.
I am leaving; I am going to India!

The Tibetan meditators and I do not agree!
They do not mingle the meditation state with
    postmeditation,

But make mere intellectual understanding their
    experience and realization.
I am tired of practitioners who fixate on inert
    stillness.
I am leaving; I am going to India!

The Tibetan tantrikas and I do not agree!
They do not keep the sacred commitments pure.
Instead they let both Mahayana and Secret Mantra
    stray into shamanism.
I am tired of samaya violators.
I am leaving; I am going to India!

The Tibetan yogis and I do not agree!
They do not possess the meaning of view and
    meditation in their Dharma practice,
But fool themselves with boastful platitudes.
I am tired of bragging people.
I am leaving; I am going to India!

The Tibetan chieftains and I do not agree!
They do not mingle social affairs with the divine
    Dharma,
But waste the teachings and the kingdom with evil
    intentions.
I am tired of evil-minded people with negative
    intent.
I am leaving; I am going to India!

The Tibetan benefactors and I do not agree!
They do not practice generosity free from pre-
    judice,
But always create the causes for rebirth among
    hungry ghosts.
I am tired of deceitful and tightfisted people.
I am leaving; I am going to India!

The Tibetan women and I do not agree!
They do not take faith and compassion to heart,

But follow charlatans with hollow faith.
I am tired of unfaithful, lustful women.
I am leaving; I am going to India!

Tibetan disciples, remain in peace.
I am leaving; I am going to the land of the
    rakshasas.
I pray that we may meet again in the future.

At this the Tibetan disciples all felt ashamed of themselves. With aching hearts, their eyes filled with tears and, tormented by deep despair, they made full prostrations. They placed Padmakara's feet at the crown of their heads, clutched his robe, and prayed, "Listen, great master! If you leave for India we will have no way to clear our outer and inner misconceptions. Formerly, when King Trisong Deutsen was alive, your kindness was immense. Now, please continue to care for the people of Tibet with your compassion. By all means, please stay!"

In reply to their request, Master Padma said, "During the reign of the king, I made the Buddhadharma spread and flourish. You, my followers, the king and subjects, should uphold my tradition exactly as it is, as benefactors and objects of respect. Since I am going to India, there will not be anyone to clear your outer and inner misconceptions. But unless the rakshasas are vanquished, they will overflow from their land, Lankapuri, and eat all the humans of the Jambu continent. The time has arrived for me to subjugate them so I must take leave." Having spoken, he sang this song:

Lord guru who grants the blessings,
Yidam deity who bestows the attainments,
Dakinis who dispel the obstacles,
I supplicate you; grant your blessings.

I, Padmakara of Uddiyana,
Took birth from within a lotus flower.

Untainted by the defilement of a womb,
The place of my birth is most exalted.

At first, in the realm of Uddiyana,
I became the son of King Indrabodhi
And established the kingdom in the sacred Dharma.

Next, in the different parts of India,
I met with the most eminent, learned, and accom-
	plished masters.
Diligent in learning, reflection, and meditation,
I gained mastery over mind and prana.

Finally, I came to the land of Tibet.
I tamed the mundane haughty spirits,
Fulfilled the aspiration of the king,
And brought the disciples to perfect ripening and
	liberation.

In this age that is the time of the five degen-
	erations,
The final period of the Age of Strife,
It is rare, in general, that the beings of the three
	realms
Embark on an unmistaken path.
People fall prey to the demons of wrong thinking.

In particular, the demons rob the life-force of
	beings
And later lead them to the lower realms.
Such are the rakshasas of aggression,
Who rule over the subcontinent of Chamara to the
	southwest.

Apart from me, there is no one who can subdue
	them.
My body is the indestructible vajra body
And I have attained the vidyadhara level of lon-
	gevity.

My voice has accomplished the attainment of the
    Secret Mantra teachings
With perfect powers and capabilities.
My mind has realized the state of the buddhas of
    the three times;
Thus I have actualized the mind essence of the
    nondual nature.

In order to bestow the gift of fearlessness
To the present six classes of sentient beings,
I shall go to tame the rakshasas in the southwest.

Through love, compassion, and bodhichitta,
I shall skillfully tame and establish in the Dharma
All the flesh-eating rakshasas of perverted thinking.

I am leaving to establish everyone in the twofold
    well-being,
In the pure lands of the buddhas.
All you, Tibetan king, subjects, and disciples,
Stay well and keep in good health for a long time.

I have achieved the body beyond birth and death,
So I am not subject to passing away and trans-
    migration.
I have attained mastery over the body of the four
    elements,
So I am not subject to the flaws of discomfort and
    misery.

Having fully mastered both loving kindness and
    compassion,
I feel neither tired nor weary when acting for the
    welfare of beings.
Having fully mastered the teachings of both mind
    and prana,
There is no hindrance or obstruction to my four
    activities.

King, subjects, and disciples remaining here,
Make fervent supplications with faith and devotion.
I will hold you with the hook of compassion.
Be sure never to waver in your devotion.
Then we will meet again.

Since he did not consent to stay on, King Mutig and the disciples were heartbroken and felt utter despair.

This was the twenty-third chapter in the immaculate life story of the Lotus-Born Master, telling how the Tibetan king and subjects tried to dissuade him, but were unsuccessful in obtaining Master Padma's consent when he intended to leave for the southwestern continent.

24

A T THE TIME MASTER PADMA planned to depart for the
southwestern continent to tame the rakshasas, Prince Mutig
Tsenpo and other kings entreated him in these words:
"Master, as you intend to leave for India and will not remain here
any longer, how should the Tibetan kings of future generations
behave?"

Master Padma then sang this song to the kings of Tibet:

> Kings of Tibet, possessors of merit,
> Do not equalize your royal class with your subjects.
> A king should not engage in the actions of a
>   commoner,
> But remain with a dignified and balanced poise.
>
> Benevolently, ask advice from the inner cabinet
>   ministers,
> While also being decisive in tasks and speaking
>   unrestrained.
> Do not listen to advice that will jeopardize the
>   country.
> Be gentle and cordial and never ruthless.
>
> Be wise when issuing a decree or giving gifts.
> Do not bestow too many distinctions—be
>   moderate.
> Ministers who are greedy and unintelligent
> Pose the greatest danger of destroying the fortress
>   of the country.

When the ministers take control of the country,
Be very careful with funds and avoid evil deeds.
If the country degenerates, the kingdom is lost.
Do not be gullible or easily influenced.

Ignore half of what you hear and remain un-
    daunted.
Then the kingdom will last for a long time.
If out of desire for queens and other women
You grow too fond and attached,
You will be overpowered by your emotions and
    lose control.

Do not place your trust in unreliable people.
To do so brings no success but may cost your life.
Maintain peace with your outer servants and sustain
    the inner attendants with food.
Give up prejudice; be unshakable and fair toward
    all.

Constructing temples, shrine halls, and stupas is all
    of great merit,
But in the end they become the cause for misdeeds.
It is better to pay respect to the shrines that are
    already built.

Be correct when translating the sacred Dharma.
Be decisive and hold the Buddha's words to be
    authentic.
Treasure the Three Jewels as dear as your eyes.

The different vehicles each have their own ap-
    proach,
And through any one of them the fruition can be
    attained;
Yet, give higher priority to the vajra vehicle of
    Secret Mantra.

Too many glamorous dwellings cause the risk of
    disaster.

Be very steady and scrutinize well.

Some scholars and translators will be false and lack
     discernment.
Do not trust them; there is the danger of deceit.

Attacks from gongpo spirits will threaten to destroy
     the kingdom.
Do not be fickle but remain steadfast and dignified.

Queens, you are the foundation for the heirs to the
     kingdom.
Be open-minded, generous, and patient.
Maintain a good diet and cleanliness of hands and
     face.
Keep propriety and oversee your possessions.
Avoid distraction and bridle your conduct.
Do not talk excessively but with a gentle and
     courteous manner.

Take care of your outer and inner attendants nicely
     and with grace.
Bring your children and consorts to the Dharma.
When pious in this life you will attain the realms
     of gods and humans in the following.

I, Padmakara, am now taking leave,
Whether you live in the present or will appear in
     the future,
Keep this in your hearts, kings of Tibet.

Thus he gave instructions.

This was the twenty-fourth chapter in the immaculate
life story of the Lotus-Born Master, telling how Master Padma gave his last words to the kings of Tibet.

25

THEN TRISANG YABLHAG and other ministers entreated Padmasambhava, "Master, as you intend to leave for India and will not remain here any longer, how should the ministers of future generations behave?"

In reply to this, Master Padma sang:

> Everyone who acts as the minister of a king
> Should serve the ruler with devoted body and
> speech.
> Attend the queens as your inner duty
> And rule the outer kingdom by the Dharma.
>
> Be kind to the subjects and affectionately care for
> their well-being.
> A minister's purpose is to counsel the king.
> Keep peace in the country while enforcing the law
> rigorously.
> Establish shrines for the Three Jewels and found
> Dharma centers for the Mahayana.
>
> Keeping the army on guard externally, protect the
> palace, the country, and the government.
> Recognize love and hatred and differentiate between
> good and evil.
> Never be unprepared, but anticipate and avoid
> mistakes.
> Afterward do not regret; it is too late to change.
>
> When you have acted with forethought, you can be
> free from regret even if the outcome is bad.

You are a religious minister if you abide by the
Dharma, have faith, and venerate the three
jewels.
You are a wise minister if you advise with intelligence and good judgment.
You are a brave minister if you courageously,
carefully, and adeptly overcome enmity.
You are an ingenious minister if you do not harbor
hostility, but act cleverly and skillfully in
politics.
The good and evil of the country depends upon
the quality of its ministers.
Use careful scrutiny and guard the kingdom.

I, Padmakara, am now taking leave,
Whether you live in the present or will appear in
the future,
Ministers of future generations, keep this in your
hearts.

Thus he gave instructions.

This was the twenty-fifth chapter in the immaculate
life story of the Lotus-Born Master, telling how Master Padma gave his last words to the ministers of
Tibet.

26

Jnana Kumara of Nyag and other Tibetan monks then asked, "Master, as you intend to leave for India and will not remain here any longer, how should the Tibetan monks of future generations behave?"

Master Padma sang:

> Monks of future generations who journey on the
>   path of liberation,
> Be free from selfish, temporal aims and embark on
>   the path of emancipation.
> Leave your parents, family, and friends and be free
>   from attachment.
> Shave your heads, don the robes of the Dharma,
>   and attain excellence.[53]
>
> Receive the vows and the precepts of a monk or
>   novice
> From learned monks who bear witness to the code
>   of a preceptor and teacher.
> Observe the points of the training without any
>   wrongdoing.
>
> Keep your dwelling place and begging bowl clean.
> Serve your preceptors, teachers, and elder monks.
> Wash and sweep your dwelling place nicely.
> Set out the offerings in a beautiful way.
>
> Do not sleep during dusk and dawn, but engage in
>   spiritual practice.

Apply the diverse, virtuous Dharma actions and
traverse through the stages of the path.
On the proper days, make confessions for breaches
of your precepts.
Adhere to the trainings conscientiously and avoid
severe violations.

Remain in the community of the sangha and do
not live among householders.
Do not keep company with women, even your
mother or sister.
Since you are the objects of respect for all people,
give up misdeeds.
If you act like this, you will have peace in this
world and enter the path in the following.

Pious women who abandon samsaric life and
become nuns,
Since, due to negative karma, your birth is inferior,
you may not be able to act as a learned
preceptor.
Nevertheless, cut your attachment to men and
observe the precepts with purity.
Do not frequent the dwellings of lay people, but
live in a nunnery.

Engage in teaching and study and gather as much
virtue as you can.
Recite prayers and be energetic in circumambulation
and prostration.
Keep the rules of the precepts free from deceit and
hypocrisy.
The nun who falls is despised in this life and goes
to the hells in the next.
Arouse fortitude of mind and observe pure discipline

I, Padmakara, am now taking leave,
Whether you live in the present or will appear in
the future,

Male and female monastics of Tibet, keep this in
your hearts.

This was the twenty-sixth chapter in the immaculate
life story of the Lotus-Born Master, telling how Master Padma gave his last words to the monks and nuns
of Tibet.

27

❀

Kawa Paltsek, Chokro Lui Gyaltsen, and other Tibetan Dharma teachers then asked, "Master, as you intend to leave for India and will not remain here any longer, how should the Tibetan Dharma teachers of future generations behave?"

Master Padma replied:

> Spiritual teachers of Tibet who are educated and
>   endowed with good qualities,
> You should carefully study reading and writing,
>   listen to teachings, and reflect upon them
> In the presence of a learned and accomplished
>   master.
>
> Thoroughly train in all the teachings of the
>   different vehicles,
> The Tripitaka and the outer and inner Secret
>   Mantra.
> Train also adequately in the five sciences
> In order to study all the topics of knowledge.
>
> When you become an object of other people's
>   respect
> And get involved in the distraction of meritorious
>   deeds,
> Abandon pride, conceit, and jealousy
> And do not engage in acts of self-aggrandizement.

Act according to the words that you preach.
Conduct yourself according to the Dharma and
     in harmony with all people.
Cast away the misdeed of envy,
Such as declaring "I am learned and he is not."

Teach whoever wants to learn
The particular Dharma teaching of his interest.
Serve your master and teachers
With respectful body, speech, and mind.
Offer whatever you possess, wealth, food, and
     so forth.

Do not brag about your Dharma practice,
But ask and depend on those who are learned.
Do not pretend greatness, booming like an empty
     drum.
Instead, be full of the virtues of the Dharma.

Give up rivalry with your Dharma friends.
When you have acquired even the tiniest bit of
     knowledge,
Do not be conceited and ambitious,
Since the main point is to cherish everyone with
     compassion.
Don the armor of the four immeasurables.

Unless you tame your mind with the Dharma,
How can you possibly tame the minds of others?
Be learned and control your emotions.

I, Padmakara, am now taking leave,
Whether you live in the present or will appear in
     the future,
Dharma teachers of future generations, keep this
     in your hearts.

Thus he gave instructions.

164

This was the twenty-seventh chapter in the immaculate life story of the Lotus-Born Master, telling how Master Padma gave his last words to the Dharma teachers of Tibet.

28

SANGYE YESHE and other Tibetan tantrikas then asked, "Master, as you intend to leave for India and will not remain here any longer, how should the Tibetan tantrikas of future generations behave?"

Master Padma replied:

> Tibetan tantrikas who enter the gate of Secret
>   Mantra,
> Seek an accomplished master, the root of Secret
>   Mantra.
> Through the steps of empowerments, open the
>   door to Secret Mantra.
> Observe correctly your sacred commitments, the
>   life-force of Secret Mantra.
>
> Regard the vajra master as precious as your head.
> Possess the yidam deity like the heart in your chest.
> Keep constant company with dakinis and protectors
>   like the shadow of your body.
> Guard the profound Secret Mantra like your eyes.
>
> Retain the profound essence mantra like your
>   breath.
> Value the profound development and completion as
>   dearly as your body and life.
> Soar through the view, meditation, conduct, and
>   fruition.
> Forsake the ten nonvirtues and cultivate the ten
>   virtues.

Be ready to sacrifice your life for the sake of the
    Dharma.
As most vital, endeavor in approach and
    accomplishment.
At the new and full moon, the eighth and the
    twenty-third,
Perform feast and torma offerings, do fulfillment
    rituals and petitions to the protectors.

Do not be frivolous and presumptuous, but follow
    an excellent master.
Do not let your sadhana become shamanism, but
    chant according to the meditation.
Pursue the approach and accomplishment and the
    four activities in the correct manner.
Give up doubt and hesitation about the Secret
    Mantra.
Neither trade the Secret Mantra for wealth nor
    proliferate it.
Once you reach accomplishment, the powers
    spontaneously appear.

I, Padmakara, am now taking leave,
Whether you live in the present or will appear in
    the future,
Tibetan tantrikas of future generations, keep this
    in your hearts.

Thus he gave instructions.

This was the twenty-eighth chapter in the immaculate
life story of the Lotus-Born Master, telling how Master Padma gave his last words to the tantrikas of Tibet.

29

❀

KYEMEY TOKDRÖL OF SHANG and other Tibetan
meditators then asked, "Master, as you intend to leave for
India and will not remain here any longer, how should the
Tibetan meditators of future generations behave?"

Master Padma replied:

> Meditators of Tibet who practice samadhi as most
>   important,
> To resolve the view, ask those who have realization.
> To practice meditation, listen to those who have
>   experience and understanding.
> To engage in conduct, mingle meditation and post-
>   meditation.
> Realize the fruition of the three kayas to be your
>   own awareness.
>
> As a reminder, read the Buddha's words and the
>   tantras, scriptures, and instructions.
> Do not get entranced by words; instead, scrutinize
>   their meaning.
> Follow an eminent master who possesses the oral
>   instructions.
> The meditator with vast learning will not go astray.
>
> While lacking true confidence, do not exhibit the
>   guise of a meditator.
> To cut through doubt, depend upon accomplished
>   masters.
> While ignorant, do not act with hypocrisy.

When abiding in the equanimity of dharmata,
Do not succumb to the flaws of dullness and
     agitation.
Throughout day and night, meditate in the state of
     empty cognizance.

When insight into the nature of dharmata dawns in
     your being,
Turn all pleasure and pain into support for
     spiritual practice.

No matter how loving a spouse may be, a
     meditator should not employ her as a servant.
Though female disciples may offer pleasurable
     service and have strong devotion,
They also may become a cause for disgrace.
Followers and attendants can serve you well, but
     keep them far away.

Business and meritorious activities are severe
     obstacles.
Take your mind as witness and avoid distractions.
The meditator who follows this advice is the heart
     of the victorious ones in human form.

I, Padmakara, am now taking leave,
Whether you live in the present or will appear in
     the future,
Tibetan meditators of future generations, keep this
     in your hearts.

Thus he gave instructions.

This was the twenty-ninth chapter in the immaculate
life story of the Lotus-Born Master, telling how Master Padma gave his last words to the meditators of
Tibet.

30

TRÜLSHIG OF NYANG and other Tibetan yogis then
asked, "Master, as you intend to leave for India and will not
remain here any longer, how should the Tibetan yogis of
future generations behave?"

Master Padma replied:

> Listen here, Tibetan yogis endowed with the
> confidence of view and meditation.
> The real yogi is your unfabricated innate nature.
> "Yogi" means to realize the wisdom of pure
> awareness.
> That is how you truly obtain the name yogi.
>
> Be free from ambition in the view; do not indulge
> in partiality.
> Be free from reference point in the meditation; do
> not indulge in fixating your mind.
> Be free from accepting and rejecting in the conduct;
> do not indulge in clinging to a self.
> Be free from abandonment and attainment in the
> fruition; do not indulge in grasping to things
> as real.
>
> Be free from limitation in keeping samaya; do not
> indulge in fraud and pretense.
> Be free from bias toward the Buddhadharma; do
> not indulge in scholastic sectarianism.
> Appearances are delusion; do not indulge in
> ordinariness.

Food is merely to sustain your life-force; do not
grovel for food.

Wealth is illusory; do not indulge in craving.
Clothes are to protect you from cold; do not
indulge in opulent fashions.
Equality is nondual; do not indulge in intimate
companions.
Be free from preference to country; do not indulge
in a homeland.

Make your dwelling an empty cave; do not indulge
in monastic life.
Do your practice in solitude; do not indulge in
social gatherings.
Be detached and free from clinging; do not indulge
in attachment.
Be a self-liberated yogi; do not indulge in charla-
tanism.

I, Padmakara, am now taking leave,
Whether you live in the present or will appear
in the future,
Tibetan yogis of future generations, keep this in
your hearts.

Thus he gave instructions.

This was the thirtieth chapter in the immaculate life
story of the Lotus-Born Master, telling how Master
Padma gave his last words to the yogis of Tibet.

31

RINCHEN DRAG OF NYO and other Tibetan laymen then asked, "Master, as you intend to leave for India and will not remain here any longer, how should the Tibetan men of future generations behave?"

Master Padma replied:

Old and young Tibetan men of future generations,
Keep the laws of the king sacrosanct.
Keep the decrees of the ruler inviolate.
Without losing your individual needs,
Guard the general welfare of others with your lives.

Do not take an oath in vain.
Be strict about what is prohibited.
Be in agreement when you assemble.
Do not show disdain for the destitute.

Discuss in groups to avoid future regrets.
First, let the wise people give advise.
Keep integrity and be dependable.
Follow the advice of those who can think well.

Let the courageous lead the army.
Furnish the soldiers with weaponry.
Let attendants keep guard at night.
Appoint your servants by turn.

When people trust you, do not disappoint them.
Since men are more wise,
They will achieve wealth, property, and fame.

If you allow your offspring to be learned in
    Dharma,
Wealth will always increase.
Whatever you do, first think well.
To act without forethought creates many problems.

When something can be corrected,
What is the use of remaining displeased?
When something cannot be changed,
Why harbor ill-will?

If you progress slowly, at some point you will
    arrive.
If you circumvent places of danger, you will not be
    harmed by enemies.
If you speak gently, everyone will understand.
Loud and harsh orders have only short term effect.

If you act diligently anything can be accomplished.
Being rash and inconstant only makes you tired.
Practice the sublime Dharma for the sake of this
    life and the next.
That will engender permanent benefit.

I, Padmakara, am now taking leave,
Whether you live in the present or will appear
    in the future,
Tibetan men of future generations, keep this in
    your hearts.

Thus he gave instructions.

This was the thirty-first chapter in the immaculate life
story of the Lotus-Born Master, telling how Master
Padma gave his last words to the men of Tibet.

Lady Jangchubma of Drom and other Tibetan women then asked, "Master, as you intend to leave for India and will not remain here any longer, how should the Tibetan women of future generations behave?"

Master Padma replied:

> Women, source of existence,
> You are the basis for the home, so keep the house
>   tidy.
> You are the origin of life, so let your offspring
>   embrace the Dharma.
> You are the support for the body, so appreciate
>   your husbands.
>
> A good husband is like one's heart, so respect what
>   he says.
> A bad husband is your karmic residual, so give him
>   what he wishes and do not be contemptuous.
> In-laws are like your parents, so offer them respect.
> Your husband's male relatives are like your father
>   and brothers, so rear them with food and
>   modesty.
>
> Sisters-in-law are only with you briefly, so serve
>   them well.
> The scorn of others will be upon yourself, so face
>   everyone with a smile.
> If you are short-tempered or arrogant, servants will
>   always be few.

Appearances may arise as enemies, so always remain
cheerful.

A talkative woman is a nuisance, so do not be too
fond of gossip.
Praise and respect your father and brothers and be
modest and noble-minded.
You provide the provisions for sons and husbands,
so be generous to travelers.
Sustain servants and family with meals and be
affectionate.

Do not be too miserly with your wealth; instead
share the food generously.
Show a clear and smiling face and keep strict
cleanliness.
Go to sleep late at night and rise early in the
morning.
Be diligent at the seasonal farm work and do not
procrastinate.

Foster cattle, watchdogs, and servants with compassion.
Spend as much as you can on virtue.
Thus you will be blessed in this life and have
happiness in the following.

I, Padmakara, am now taking leave,
Whether you live in the present or will appear in
the future,
Tibetan women of future generations, keep this
in your hearts.

Thus he gave instructions.

This was the thirty-second chapter in the immaculate
life story of the Lotus-Born Master, telling how Master Padma gave his last words to the women of Tibet.

33

LOGYE NYITRI BUM and other Tibetan benefactors then asked, "Master, as you intend to leave for India and will not remain here any longer, how should the Tibetan benefactors of future generations behave?"

Master Padma replied:

Tibetan benefactors who have the Dharma read
    aloud and recited
Should encourage the clergy to learn correctly to
    read and write.

First the scribes should properly learn
The shape and proportion of the letters,
The balance between what is white and what is
    black,
And to copy diligently with neither omission nor
    duplication.

The benefactors should be free from desire for
    prestige
And they should satisfy those worthy of respect
    with rewards.
The gifts should be offered with a spirit of faith
And accepted without ambitious greed.

Both benefactor and recipient should in unison
Dedicate the merit toward the attainment of perfect
    enlightenment.
When acting in this way, they will both achieve
    perfect merit.

If the benefactor has an impure motivation
And the object of respect is unsatisfied,
The virtuous action will become a misdeed.

The object of respect who engages in reading aloud
and chanting
At first should train in language and grammar;
Next he should read the words with the correct
emphasis,
And finally avoid omitting or duplicating words.

Avoid conversations with others while chanting.
Recite respectfully without omissions or dup-
lications.
Be free from ingratitude regarding the Dharma.
Give up the disrespect of carelessly stepping over
the scriptures.

Imagine that you are the master and lord of the
doctrine,
Who sounds the great drum of the Dharma,
And, while reciting, that the six classes of beings
Are liberated upon hearing the teachings.

When pausing for a session break,
The sponsor and the object of respect
Should together dedicate the virtue toward attaining
enlightenment.
The benefactor should, with a faithful frame of
mind
And with an attitude dedicated to pleasing the
object of respect,
Gratify the receiver with excellent gifts,
Such as the best food and drink.
If you act like this, both benefactor and recipient,
You will have happiness in this life and attain
enlightenment in the next.

For benefactors and recipients who do not behave
like this,

The sponsor may be stingy and count only what is
    completed;
Since the sponsor is more interested in speed,
    learnedness will not help.
The learned ones will be careless, leaving out parts
    in chanting.
While the ignorant will simply try to finish quickly.

The benefactor who does not give supplies and
    service
Will not satisfy the recipient with gifts, but will
    create resentment.
Thus the link between sponsor and object of
    respect results in misdeed.
Though the benefactor wished for merit, he only
    increased his evil karma.
At the end of this age such benefactors and
    recipients will appear.
Do not act like that, but make everything you do
    become the Dharma.

I, Padmakara, am now taking leave,
Whether you live in the present or will appear in
    the future,
Tibetan benefactors and recipients of future
    generations, keep this in your hearts.

Thus he gave instructions.

This was the thirty-third chapter in the immaculate
life story of the Lotus-Born Master, telling how Master Padma gave his last words to the benefactors and
reverend recipients of Tibet.

34

❀

THE COURT PHYSICIAN MERUTSEY and other Tibetan
healers then asked, "Master, as you intend to leave for India
and will not remain here any longer, how should the Tibetan healers of future generations behave?"

Master Padma replied:

Noble court physicians, doctors, and healers,
At first, in the presence of a master skilled in
      healing,
Carefully study the basic treatises for applying and
      preparing medicines.
Next, please your teacher and receive his oral
      instructions.
Finally, have compassion when trying to cure the
      sick.

To diagnose the illness examine the pulse, urine,
      and body surface.
To prepare a medication without identifying the
      sickness
Will only turn medicine into poison.
To give treatment after diagnosing the disease
Is like pacifying fire with the remedy of water.

At first, without practical experience, you lack the
      power of healing.
Next, without oral instructions, you cannot identify
      the disease.
Finally, without the application of treatment, the
      medicine turns into poison.

Thus the doctor becomes the sick person's
    executioner, with the murder weapon in hand.

Do not act like that, but train to become an expert.
Learned healers should treat others with kindness
    and compassion.
Curtail your craving for wealth,
Since someone healed quickly may fall sick again.

Do not give treatment according to the quality of
    the food and drink you receive,
Since someone cured now may again fall ill.
Adjust the fee of medication to the type of person.
You may cure the sick, but wrong livelihood will
    weigh heavily later.

Embrace everyone with bodhichitta and com-
    passion.
Free from craving in your heart, give immediate
    treatment.
Sick people are objects of compassion, so alleviate
    their pain.

It is excellent if you can be satisfied with whatever
    reward or fee you receive for the treatment.
Your next life will be a rebirth as the eminent king
    of the gods,
While in this life you will enjoy good health and
    happiness.

All sick people should respectfully please
The life-saving master physician with food, drink,
    and enjoyments.
Adjust the fee for treatment and the reward to the
    degree of importance.

If the sick person fails to respect the healer,
He will be despised in this life and go to the hells
    in the next,
Where he will be reborn in the hell of repeated
    death and revival.

I, Padmakara, am now taking leave,
Whether you live in the present or will appear in
    the future,
Healers and sick people of future generations, keep
    this in your hearts.

Thus he gave instructions.

This was the thirty-fourth chapter in the immaculate
life story of the Lotus-Born Master, telling how Master Padma gave his last words to the healers and sick
people of Tibet.

35

VAIROCHANA and other masters and disciples then asked, "Master, as you intend to leave for India and will not remain here any longer, how should the Tibetan masters of future generations behave?"

Master Padma replied:

> Listen, Tibetan masters and disciples who form a
>   dharmic link.
> At first, the masters should train in reaching
>   perfection in learning.
> Next, they should bring forth signs of
>   accomplishment by being diligent in practice.
> Finally, with bodhichitta, they should act
>   impartially for the welfare of beings.
>
> Masters, possess the confidence of having resolved
>   the view.
> Lay the basis of never violating your sacred com-
>   mitments
> And obtain the empowerments and reading trans-
>   missions as well as teachings on the two
>   stages.
>
> Practice while uniting samadhi and discriminating
>   knowledge.
> Conclude your sessions by implementing skillful
>   action.[54]
> Be a master who has perfected the six limits of
>   Secret Mantra.

The disciples who seek a master
Should examine the master and search for someone
    endowed with the qualities of learning and
    accomplishment.
Offer pleasing gifts and respectfully request the
    instructions.
Be persevering in the Dharma practices of learning,
    reflection, and meditation.

Receive empowerments and reading transmissions
    and request the complete teachings on the two
    stages.
By exerting yourself in practice, accomplish your
    own welfare.[55]
Once you manifest signs of accomplishment, then
    undertake benefiting others.

When the master neglects examining the disciple,
    he forms dharmic links with unworthy people.
The disciple who fails to examine the master forms
    a dharmic link of no substance.
Even practicing will yield no result, when lacking
    the blessings of the Dharma.

The master and the disciple who do not keep the
    samayas are like calves yoked together falling
    into an abyss.
Reaping the reward of the hells, there will be no
    chance for liberation.
Masters and disciples, do not act like this but
    examine each other!

The disciples should have strong faith, devotion,
    and possess compassion.
Regarding your master as a buddha, keep pure
    perception.
Engender a respectful attitude and be free from
    arrogance and conceit.

Be most generous and diligent without
    procrastination.
Master, to such disciples teach the complete oral
    instructions.

Some people grovel for teachings with flattery and
    ingratiation.
Inflated and self-aggrandizing, they act with con-
    ceited arrogance.
Unable to give, they are deceitful and hypocritical.
If you teach such unworthy people, your samayas
    will be violated.

I, Padmakara, am now taking leave,
Whether you live in the present or will appear in
    the future,
Masters and disciples, keep this in your hearts.

Thus he gave instructions.

This was the thirty-fifth chapter in the immaculate life
story of the Lotus-Born Master, telling how Master
Padma gave his last words to the Tibetan masters and
disciples who form dharmic links.

36

M ASTER PADMA THEN GAVE his general testament to
the Tibetan people of future generations.

Kings, ministers, and people of Tibet, the primitive
  borderland,
You are a race of red-faced demons lacking compassion and goodwill.
Your father's race is a monkey with little modesty
  or shame,
And your mother's race is a rock demoness,
  quarrelsome and hostile to the Dharma.
You are a race of beastly people, full of craving
  toward wealth.
Unless you practice virtue you will fall to the lower
  realms in the next life.

Do not forget that life flickers by and then you die.
What meets must part, so do not fight and cause
  strife.
What is gathered must be abandoned, so do not
  crave intemperately for wealth.
Attachment is bondage, so do not harbor unbridled
  clinging.
What is born must die, so think of your next life.

The most sinful goes to hell; who can bear that?
Through greed you are reborn a hungry ghost and
  will suffer hunger and thirst.
By rejecting the Dharma you become an animal;
  keep that in mind.

This life is only on loan; no one knows when it
will be lost.

Appearances are illusory, understand their impermanence.

Food and wealth are like dew drops; it is uncertain
when they disappear.

Remember that servants are like travelers you meet
on the road.

Enmity is delusion; understand it to be mistaken.

Keep in mind that family ties are the guide to
samsara.

Understand that offspring are only karmic creditors
claiming their due.

Your life runs out while spending it on idle talk;

Do you not notice the arrival of King Yama's
scouts?

Listen to me, Tibetan people, you red-faced
demons,

Seek the three jewels as escorts against the three
lower realms.

Take the guru, yidam, and dakini as your support
in both this and future lives.

As the road to freedom, practice the view, meditation, and conduct.

Accept the Great Compassionate One as the
destined deity of Tibet.

Forsake the ten nonvirtues and adopt the ten
virtues.

If you act like this you will have happiness in this
life and further happiness in the next.

I, Padmakara, am now taking leave,

Whether you live in the present or will appear in
the future,

All people of Tibet in general, keep this in your
hearts.

Thus he gave instructions.

This was the thirty-sixth chapter in the immaculate life story of the Lotus-Born Master, telling how Master Padma gave his last words to the Tibetan people in general.

37

THE TIBETAN KING and the disciples then all prostrated before Master Padma and circumambulated him. In particular, Prince Mutig Tsenpo said:

"EMAHO! Supreme nirmanakaya, great master, as we, the primitive tribal people of Tibet, are an irreligious race of barbarians, there is not even one of us who engages in the ten virtuous actions. In the past, King Songtsen Gampo, who was an emanation of the Great Compassionate One, built one hundred and eight major and minor temples including the Trülnang and Ramochey temples in Lhasa. He invited several panditas from India, who translated numerous sacred teachings. His kindness to Tibet was tremendous.

"Later King Trisong Deutsen invited you and many other Indian panditas. he built Samye and numerous other temples. Moreover he established religious law and made peace in Tibet with great compassion.

"King Trisong Deutsen has now passed away and you, master, are about to depart for the land of India. The country of Tibet will be shrouded in darkness, and everyone will be unprotected. This is an extremely great loss.

"The bodhisattva Avalokiteshvara, the Great Compassionate One, is destined to be the deity for the people in these snowy ranges of Tibet. Since this is his realm of conversion, master, I beg you to kindly consider us. Please grant the instruction of the Great Compassionate One that closes the doors of rebirth among the six classes of beings and leads us along the path to perfect buddhahood."

Master Padmakara replied, "Noble Prince, Tibetan kings, ministers, and all people, listen to me. This snowy land of Tibet was not personally visited in the past by the truly and completely enlightened Shakyamuni. Tibet was not within his domain of conversion. At that time it was a country inhabited by animals.

"When the Blessed One was about to pass into parinirvana, he gave a prophecy to the bodhisattva Avalokiteshvara and blessed him. Avalokiteshvara then sent an emanation of his mind, a monkey bodhisattva, to Tibet. Simultaneously Tara Goddess sent an emanation of herself as a rock demoness to Tibet. These two became the father and mother, whose offspring multiplied into the Tibetan race.

"Since the father of Tibetans was a monkey, they are restless and gullible. Since their mother was a rock demoness, they have little compassion, are fond of misdeeds, and dislike the Dharma.

"Fortunately, their parents were emanations of the Great Compassionate One and Tara. Otherwise Tibetans would be incorrigible. Therefore, it is extremely good that you have asked for the instruction on the Great Compassionate One. I shall now explain the teaching of Avalokiteshvara, the Great Compassionate One."

Having said this, Master Padma taught the king and the ministers the tantras, scriptures, sadhanas, and applications of the activities of the Great Compassionate One. He did so after dividing the instructions into two parts, the general and the specific.

> This was the thirty-seventh chapter in the immaculate life story of the Lotus-Born Master, telling how the king and the ministers requested Master Padma to teach the instructions of the bodhisattva Avalokiteshvara.

38

MASTER PADMAKARA THEN TOLD the Tibetan prince and the ministers, "The Lord of Great Compassion, Avalokiteshvara, continuously looks upon the six classes of beings with compassion. Compassion means affection, and the compassion that has sentient beings as its focus is directed toward the six classes of beings, like the affection of a mother toward her only child. Avalokiteshvara gazes with overwhelming compassion toward all the six classes of sentient beings, who are tormented by misery.

The compassion that has the Dharma as its focus is the six syllables of OM MANI PADME HUNG.

OM pacifies the suffering of the transmigration that the gods experience and makes them attain happiness.

MA pacifies the suffering caused by fighting that demigods perpetuate and makes them attain happiness.

NI pacifies the suffering of serfdom and poverty that human beings undergo and makes them attain happiness.

PAD pacifies the suffering of stupidity that animals endure and makes them attain happiness.

ME pacifies the suffering of hunger and thirst that hungry ghosts experience and makes them attain happiness.

HUNG pacifies the suffering of heat and cold that hell beings perceive and makes them attain happiness.

If all of you, headed by the king, practice the ten virtues, you will achieve the state of a god in the higher realms. But, although you attain godhood, you have not transcended suffering. When the life span of a god finishes, he experiences the misery of falling and transmigration. His body begins to emit unpleasant odors, and the radiance of his form fades away. His crops that previously grew without cultivation wither, and his bathing pools dry up. His precious steeds and wish-granting cattle run away. The Lord of Great Compassion sees this overwhelming suffering of the god, who, through his superknowledge, perceives that his divine merit is exhausted and that he is about to fall down into the lower realms.

By chiefly engaging in nonvirtues such as hatred and envy, you will be born as demigods. When the gods and demigods fight, since the gods have greater merit, the demigods lose. The demigods are cut, wounded, killed, and struck down by the wheel-like weapons of the gods. In addition, they fight and argue amongst themselves, undergoing intense and overwhelming misery. They are also aware that when they die they will go to the lower realms. Their suffering is immense.

Though you are born as a human being you are not beyond suffering. To begin with, before birth there is the suffering of being inside your mother's womb, where is it like being thrown into an abyss when your mother is lifting; like being squashed between cliffs when your mother is full of food; like fluttering in the wind when your mother is standing up; like being suppressed by a mountain when your mother is lying down; like being torn apart when your mother is working hard, gets up, or sits down; like being strangled when taking birth; like being thrown into a heap of thorns when laid down; and like a bird being carried off by a hawk when your mother takes you up again.

As you grow older there are an inconceivable number of sufferings, such as cultivating fields, working, striving, trying to accomplish something, traveling, living, being unfree and destitute, and so forth.

For the suffering of old age, the bodily elements become depleted, your complexion fades away, and the sense faculties degenerate. Your eyesight grows dim and your ears deaf; your nose dribbles, your teeth fall out, and your tongue stutters; you cannot support yourself when standing and sink down when sitting; you are repulsive to your children and to other people. You agonize in the misery of thinking "I am getting old!"

For the suffering of death, your body, cherished so dearly, is left behind. You are separated from companions and friends. No matter how much wealth or how many possessions you had, you cannot take them along. Literally thrown out by your children and servants, your body will be cast away like a stone. Then follows the misery of thinking "My consciousness must now go to the lower realms!"

Before dying, there is the distress of not achieving what you have been striving for and the pain of feeling hungry and exhausted, the misery of being unable to maintain and protect what you already possess, the all-consuming fear of being unable to face your enemies, the immense worry of being unable to take care of your family, the worry of not being able to support your son, the worry of being unable to marry off your daughter, and the pain of being busy and exhausted by constant field work.

By engaging in the ten nonvirtues, you will go to the lower realms, where you will be enmeshed in intense misery. Animals certainly have not gone beyond suffering; they are enslaved by the humans, put to plow, carry loads, and be slaughtered. Among the animals without an owner, deer get killed by hunters, fish by the fishermen, and the weak and timid are devoured by carnivorous animals, who also murder each other. In particular, the animals in the great oceans live as close together as particles of mash in rice beer; they eat one another; even the small insects eat larger animals, like bees feeding off horses and donkeys or flesh-eating insects. There is an inconceivable number of miseries.

The sentient beings reborn as hungry ghosts also are not beyond suffering. They perceive food as burning iron and drink as pus and blood. Their body gets scorched when they do try to eat something. Moreover, they have the misery of not finding food or drink and, even if they do find it, they are unable to swallow. If they succeed in forcing it down their throats, their bellies do not become full. Furthermore, there is guarded food that they have no power to eat or that somebody else comes to claim even if they do find. The hungry ghosts who live in the air have no power over themselves and inflict harm on humans. The types called *shin* and *serak* die of their own sickness. Unable to find a cure, they pass their sickness on to humans. When others beat the drum and throw the grains of exorcism, they go through tremendous suffering.

The sentient beings who are reborn in the hells suffer heat and cold that surpass the imagination. As to the eight hot hells, in the Hell of Revival you die and are revived again one hundred times a day. In the Black Line Hell your body is marked with a measuring string after which the infernal workmen cut you in half with a saw. In the Hell of Crushing you are smashed with a pestle inside an iron mortar. In the Hell of Crying one cries out after being tied with a rope around your neck. In the Hell of Loud Crying one howls after being put inside a burning iron box. In the Hell of Heat you are boiled after being put into a copper pot that is the size of the sky. In the Hell of Intense Heat you are burned and boiled while being held with iron thongs. In the Unceasing Hell you are pressed down by the wind of karma so that there is not even an instant without unbearable pain.

As to the eight cold hells, in the Hell of Whimpering you freeze and make miserable noises. In the Hell of Blisters the wind of karma makes blisters spring forth. In the Hell of Oozing Blisters the blisters burst open and ooze pus. In the Hell of Chattering Teeth you freeze so much that your teeth chatter. In the Hell of Splitting Like a Blue Lotus you freeze so much that you split into four pieces. In the Hell of Splitting Like a Big Blue Lotus your body splits into eight pieces. In the Hell of Splitting Like a Red Lotus your body splits into sixteen pieces, and in the Hell of Splitting Like a Big Red Lotus you freeze so much that your body splits into thirty-two pieces.

In the Temporary Hells you suffer at day and die at nighttime.

In the Neighboring Hells you die one hundred times a day. As to the common sufferings, you have to walk knee deep in the Pit of Embers and have to go through the Swamp of Festering Corpses. Your flesh and bones are cut asunder on the Road of Razors, and swords shower down in the Rain of Swords. On the Shalmali of Iron your body is ripped and shreaded while you try to crawl up and down a mountain that has iron spikes the size of sixteen fingers. There are an inconceivable number of hellish sufferings.

In this way the Lord of Great Compassion, noble lord Avalokiteshvara, continuously perceives that sentient beings never transcend suffering.

The compassion that is beyond a focus is to perceive the interruption of the samsaric sufferings of the six classes of beings: OM MANI PADME HUNG. OM interrupts the abyss of rebirth as a god and empties the realm of gods. MA interrupts the abyss of rebirth as a demigod and empties the realm of demigods. NI interrupts the abyss of rebirth as a human being and empties the realm of humans. PAD interrupts the abyss of rebirth as an animal and empties the realm of animals. ME interrupts the abyss of rebirth as a hungry ghost and empties the realm of hungry ghosts. HUNG interrupts the abyss of rebirth as a hell being and empties the realm of the hells. Having emptied the abodes of the six classes of beings, the realms of samsara are emptied into primordial purity. Thus, the Six Syllables, the quintessence of the Great Compassionate One, have the power to lead sentient beings to the buddhafields.

This was the thirty-eighth chapter in the immaculate life story of the Lotus-Born Master, telling how the Lord of Great Compassion gazes upon the six classes of sentient beings with the three types of compassion.

39

MASTER PADMA TOLD King Mutig of Tibet and the close disciples, "Listen, king of Tibet, nobility and subjects! OM MANI PADME HUM is the quintessence of the Great Compassionate One, so the merit of uttering it just once is incalculable. The possible multiplication resulting from a single seed of the lotus flower lies beyond the reach of thought. But compared to that, the merit of uttering the Six Syllables just once is even greater. A single sesame seed can multiply into many, but the merit of uttering the Six Syllables just once is even greater. The four great rivers and countless other minor rivers flow into the salty ocean, but the merit of uttering the Six Syllables just once is even greater. All needs and wishes are granted when you supplicate the precious wish-fulfilling jewel, but the merit of uttering the Six Syllables just once is even greater.

OM MANI PADME HUNG. It is possible to count the number of raindrops falling during twelve years of monsoon, but the merit of uttering the Six Syllables just once cannot be counted. It is possible to count all the grains sown on the four continents, but the merit of uttering the Six Syllables just once cannot be counted. It is possible to count the drops of water in the great ocean, one by one, but the merit of uttering the Six Syllables just once cannot be counted. It is possible to count each hair on the bodies of all animals in existence, but the merit of uttering the Six Syllables just once cannot be counted.

OM MANI PADME HUNG. The Six Syllables are the quintessence of the Great Compassionate One. It is possible to wear down a mountain of meteoric iron that is eighty thousand miles high by rubbing it once every aeon with the softest cotton from Kashika, but the merit of uttering the Six Syllables just once cannot be exhausted. It is possible for the *merutsey* insect to finish eating Mount Sumeru to the core, but the merit of uttering the Six Syllables just once cannot be exhausted. It is possible for the *tito* bird to remove the sand of River Ganges with its beak, but the merit of uttering the Six Syllables just once cannot be exhausted. It is possible for a small breeze to scatter the earth of the four continents and Mount Sumeru, but the merit of uttering the Six Syllables just once cannot be exhausted.

OM MANI PADME HUNG. It is possible to calcualte the merit of creating a stupa made of the seven precious substances filled with relics of the buddhas of all the world-systems and making constant offerings to it, but the merit of uttering the Six Syllables just once cannot be calculated. It is possible to calculate the amount of merit from offering incense, lamps, perfumes, bathing water, music, and so forth to buddhas and buddha realms in a number that equals the grains of sand found in the entire world-system, but the merit of uttering the Six Syllables just once cannot be calculated.

OM MANI PADME HUNG. These six syllables are the quintessence of the mind of noble Avalokiteshvara. If you recite this mantra 108 times a day, you will not take rebirth in the three lower realms. In the following life you will attain a human body and in actuality you will have a vision of noble Avalokiteshvara. If you recite daily the mantra correctly twenty-one times, you will be intelligent and able to retain whatever you learn. You will have a melodious voice and become adept in the meaning of all the Buddhadharma. If you recite this mantra seven times daily, all your misdeeds will be purified and all your obscurations will be cleared away. In following lives, no matter where you take birth, you will never be separated from noble Avalokiteshvara.

When someone is afflicted by disease or an evil influence, compared to any mundane ritual of healing or of repelling obstacles, the merit of the Six Syllables is much more effective for warding off obstacles or disease. Compared to any medical treatment or cure, the Six Syllables are the strongest remedy against sickness and evil.

The virtues of the Six Syllables are immeasurable and cannot be fully described even by the buddhas of the three times. Why is that? It is because this mantra is the quintessence of the mind of the noble bodhisattva Avalokiteshvara, who continuously looks upon the six classes of sentient beings with compassion. Thus, recitation of this mantra liberates all beings from samsara.

> Kings and disciples of future generations,
> Take the Great Compassionate One as your yidam.
> Recite the Six Syllables as the essence mantra.
> Be free from the fear of going to the lower realms.
>
> Avalokiteshvara is the destined deity of Tibet,
> So supplicate him with faith and devotion.
> You will receive blessings and attainments
> And be free from doubt and hesitation.
>
> To the knowledge of me, Padmakara,
> A teaching more profound and more swift
> Has never been taught by the buddhas of the three
>   times.
>
> I, Padmasambhava, am now taking leave.
> Keep this in your hearts,
> Tibetan followers, kings, and disciples,
> Who are present now or will appear in the future.

Upon hearing Master Padma's words, the king of Tibet and the close disciples were all overjoyed and paid homage to the master, prostrating themselves to the ground.

> This was the thirty-ninth chapter in the immaculate
> life story of the Lotus-Born Master, explaining the
> benefits and virtues of the Six Syllables of the Great
> Compassionate One.

40

WHEN MASTER PADMA was about to depart to
subdue the rakshasas in the southwest, the Tibetan
king, close disciples, and followers all escorted him to
the pass of Mang-yul. When they paid homage to him, the master
mounted a beam of sunlight and sang this song:

Lord gurus, yidams, and dakinis,
Please be seated as the adornment of the crown of
    my head.
Having taken seat, please grant your blessings.

Now listen here, Tibetan King and disciples.
I, Padmakara of Uddiyana,
Came to this world of the Jambu continent.
Through the activity of the four means of mag-
    netizing,
I fully ripened and liberated those to be trained.
Now I journey to the land of India,
And this is the way that I journey.

I am a yogi beyond word, thought, and description,
Who journeys on the plain of the view free from
    extremes.
When I journey on the plain of this view,
I journey while regarding appearance and existence
    as dharmakaya.

I am a yogi of luminous appearance and emptiness,
Who journeys on the plain of the meditation of
    empty bliss.

When I journey on the plain of this meditation,
I journey beyond meditation and postmeditation.

I am a yogi of self-liberated perception,
Who journeys on the plain of spontaneous
    conduct.
When I journey on the plain of this conduct,
I journey in equal taste, without accepting or
    rejecting.

I am a yogi of self-existing nonfabrication,
Who journeys on the plain of spontaneously
    accomplished fruition.
When I journey on the plain of this fruition,
I journey free from hope and fear.

Listen again, Tibetan king and disciples!
I am a yogi beyond word, thought, and description,
Who journeys over the pass of the view free from
    extremes.
When I journey over the pass of this view,
I journey beyond meditation throughout day and
    night.[56]

I am a yogi of luminous appearance and emptiness,
Who journeys over the pass of the meditation of
    empty bliss.
When I journey over the pass of this meditation,
I journey free from dullness and agitation.

I am a yogi of self-liberated perception,
Who journeys over the pass of spontaneous
    conduct.
When I journey over the pass of this conduct,
I journey while sowing the seeds of omniscience.

I am a yogi of self-existing nonfabrication,
Who journeys over the pass of spontaneously
    accomplished fruition.

When I journey over the pass of this fruition,
I am the buddha of perfected realization.

Listen again, Tibetan king and disciples!
I am a yogi beyond word, thought, and description,
Who journeys down the slope of the view free
    from extremes.
When I journey down the slope of this view,
I dwell in the state of nonarising dharmata.

I am a yogi of luminous appearance and emptiness,
Who journeys down the slope of the meditation of
    empty bliss.
When I journey down the slope of this meditation,
I dwell in the state of undistracted nonmeditation.

I am a yogi of self-liberated perception,
Who journeys down the slope of spontaneous
    conduct.
When I journey down the slope of this conduct,
I act according to the words of the sugatas.

I am a yogi of self-existing nonfabrication,
Who journeys down the slope of spontaneously
    accomplished fruition.
When I journey down the slope of this fruition,
I am the buddha whose stream-of-being is purified.

Listen again, Tibetan king and disciples!
I am a yogi beyond word, thought, and description,
Who journeys to the place of the view free from
    extremes.
When I journey to the place of this view,
Samsara and nirvana are of the same nature.

I am a yogi of luminous appearance and emptiness,
Who journeys to the place of the meditation of
    empty bliss.
When I journey to the place of this meditation,
The nature of thought is wisdom.

I am a yogi of self-liberated perception,
Who journeys to the place of spontaneous conduct.
When I journey to the place of this conduct,
Appearance and existence have the nature of a
mandala.

I am a yogi of self-existing nonfabrication,
Who journeys to the place of spontaneously
accomplished fruition.
When I journey to the place of this fruition,
Everything is the nature of buddhahood.

I am leaving, I am leaving for the land of the
rakshasas.
When I arrive in the land of the rakshasas,
I will display my powers of magic and miraculous
action.

I am leaving, I am leaving to tame the rakshasas.
I am leaving to establish everyone in happiness.
I am leaving to make the rakshasas embrace the
Dharma.

King of Tibet, attendants, and disciples,
May you always remain in good health.
Since I have attained the immortal body of non-
arising,
I am beyond the suffering of discomfort.

Since my compassion is unceasing,
Supplicate me with faith and devotion.
We will meet each other again and again.

Once you realize the intent of this song,
Samsara is nothing to be rejected,
And nirvana is nothing to be accomplished.
Samsara and nirvana are indivisibly dharmakaya.
That is the realization of the buddhas.
Worthy people, realize this meaning!

When Master Padma finished singing, the king and the close disciples were all full of sorrow and shed tears.

This was the fortieth chapter in the immaculate life story of the Lotus-Born Master, telling how Master Padma sang a song in response to homage.

41

T HE KING and all the disciples then made prostrations and circumambulations and begged, "Please let us go with you as attendants!"
Master Padma, in response, sang this song of accepting them.

I take refuge in the triple refuge
Of the Buddha, Dharma, and Sangha.
I supplicate the three roots
Of the guru, yidam, and dakini.
Bestow the blessing of the three perfections
Of dharmakaya, sambhogakaya, and nirmanakaya.

Listen here, Tibetan king and subjects!
I shall sing you a song illustrating the meaning of
    the Dharma.

The vulture, who soars through the skies,
Descends for food by the power of desire.
Doesn't it notice when it is caught in a snare?

The white snow-lioness, who majestically poises on
    the glaciers,
Strays down into the woods by the power of desire.
Doesn't she notice when a blizzard has built up?

The tiger, who lives in the sandalwood forests to
    the south,
Roams through ravines by the power of desire.
Doesn't he notice when an avalanche is striking?

The big fish, who swims through the waters,
Chases bait by the power of desire.

Doesn't she notice she is caught in a net?

Your mind, the primordial buddha,
Searches elsewhere by the power of desire.
Doesn't it notice that it is wandering in samsara?

Now when you have obtained the precious human
    body,
You continuously get carried away by mundane
    actions.
Don't you notice that your life is running out?

Listen once more, Tibetan king and subjects.
When you find yourself in a noisy crowd of many
    people,
Possess the instruction of your body as the
    hermitage!
If you want to cast away distracted mind, come
    follow me.

When your attention strays outwardly,
Possess the instruction of taking perceptions as
    the path!
If you want to cast away clinging to appearances,
    come follow me.

When all kinds of thoughts well up inwardly,
Possess the instruction of encountering the three
    kayas!
If you want to let go of conceptual thinking, come
    follow me.

When drowsiness, excitement, or dullness occurs in
    your meditation,
Possess the instruction of the alchemy of trans-
    muting them into gold!
If you want to achieve strength of meditation, come
    follow me.

When you find yourself in meditation or
    postmeditation,

Possess the instruction of the lamp that illuminates
    darkness!
If you want to generate experience and samadhi,
    come follow me.

When stirred up by clinging to your body,
Possess the instruction of being unattached to your
    guest house!
If you want to abandon your homeland, come
    follow me.

When you take support of the mudra of another's
    form,
Possess the instruction of taking the *phonya* as path!
If you want to strive for the short path, come
    follow me.

When you visualize your body as the path of
    means,
Possess the instruction of immediate blissful heat!
If you want to cultivate the nature of bliss and
    emptiness, come follow me.

When weighed down by the sleep of ignorance,
Possess the instruction of the luminosity of dream!
If you want to take disturbing emotions as path,
    come follow me.

When you receive the four empowerments of the
    path of ripening,
Possess the instruction of filling the vase to its
    brim!
If you want to ripen your nature, come follow me.

When you practice the yoga of shape,
Possess the instruction of your body as the
    mandala!
If you want to cultivate the path of the develop-
    ment stage, come follow me.

When you are slandered by ordinary people,
Possess the instruction of sound being like an echo!
If you want to be fearless about the criticism of
    others, come follow me.

When you meet with your hateful enemy,
Possess the instruction of being patient in the face
    of blame!
If you want to be fearless when facing a hostile
    enemy, come follow me.

When you receive affection from relatives,
Possess the instruction of cutting the root of
    samsara!
If you want to be free from clinging to relatives,
    come follow me.

When you are revered by disciples and benefactors,
Possess the instruction of naturally freeing
    attachment!
If you want to hold no attachment to disciples and
    benefactors, come follow me.

When you feel attraction toward external sense
    pleasures,
Possess the instruction of the heron-fishing bird!
If you want to hold no attachment to worldly
    actions, come follow me.

When your body is afflicted by the sickness of
    the four elements,
Possess the instruction of the equal taste of the
    illusory body!
If you want to not fear physical sickness, come
    follow me.

When at the time of death your life core is cut,
Possess the instruction of unsupported awareness!
If you want to be unafraid of the bardo, come
    follow me.

When you have not cut through the causes for
    rebirth in samsara,
Possess the instruction of closing the doors to the
    six classes of beings!
If you want to cross the abyss of the six realms,
    come follow me.

Have you understood this, king and subjects?
If you do not feel sincere faith,
The wisdom of certainty will not dawn.
If the wisdom of certainty does not arise,
You will not realize the master's instruction.

Without realizing the instruction of the master,
You will not perceive your mind as the buddha.
Practice the master's instruction
With faith, devotion, and reverence.

I am beyond both birth and death
And am not subject to either going or remaining.
My wisdom and compassion are unceasing.
In the precious jewel of my mind
The concepts of pleasure or pain do not exist.

If you can visualize me at the crown of your head,
I shall be beyond being near or far.
The buddha mandala of my body possesses no
    materiality.
In this way, generate devotion in your mind.

As I now take leave in a miraculous way,
You cannot follow me with your material bodies.
Exert yourself constantly in making supplications,
And you will always be in my presence.

Having sung this, Padmasambhava mounted a beam of sunlight
and in the flicker of a moment flew away into the sky. From the
southwestern direction, he turned his face to look back and sent
forth a light ray of immeasurable loving kindness that established

the disciples in the state of nonreturn. Accompanied by a cloudlike assembly of outer and inner dakinis making musical offerings, he then went to the southwestern continent of Chamara.

King Mutig Tsenpo of Tibet and the close disciples went home, suppressed by the anguish that Master Padma had departed to the land of Uddiyana. The despair they felt was like a camel mother who had lost her calf or like a mother who had lost her only child. The king assembled his ministers and the close disciples and said, "Trisong Deutsen, our king, has passed away. Master Padma has departed to the land of the rakshasas. All I can do now is govern the land following the law as exemplified by King Trisong Deutsen and rule the kingdom according to the Dharma as Master Padma directed. All you people should now practice whatever teaching toward which you feel inclined."

Padmasambhava's retinue of close disciples followed the king's command and everyone, reaching the state of nonreturn, attained the fruition of a vidyadhara.

This was the forty-first chapter in the immaculate life story of the Lotus-Born Master, telling how Master Padma departed to subdue the rakshasas in the southwest and sang songs to his attendants and escorts.

Epilogue

This *Jewel Garland Dharma History and Biography*

Of the great master Padmasambhava

Was written down and concealed as a precious
terma treasure

By Lady Tsogyal, who had attained perfect recall,

For the sake of inspiring faith in future disciples

And to bestow upon them the eye of the Dharma
that dispels the darkness of ignorance.

May it meet with worthy people endowed with the
karmic connection!

THIS BIOGRAPHY and Dharma history of Master
Padmakara, entitled *The Jewel Garland*, is an extraordinary
and special teaching. Seal of treasure, seal of concealment,
seal of profundity. SAMAYA. Seal seal seal!

This biography and Dharma history of the precious
Master Padmakara, entitled *The Jewel Garland*, was re-
vealed from a terma treasure by Lord Ralpachen of
Nyang.

The Abbreviated Chronicle

From whichever supreme buddhafield you remain,
Lord of beings, nirmanakaya of Uddiyana,
Rescue all your disciples and myself
With the hook of your swift-acting compassion
From the immense ocean of samsara,
And lead us to the celestial abode of Uddiyana.

Repeating this just once yields a benefit that is equal to reading the extensive chronicles.

This is a terma treasure of Lord Nyang.

Notes

1. A collection of advice by Padmasambhava to his close student Yeshe Tsogyal, published in 1990 by Shambhala Publications in Boston.

2. Throughout this book, Padmasambhava is referred to as Guru Rinpoche, Padmakara, the Precious Master, the Lotus-Born, Master Padma, and other names. The names Padmasambhava and Padmakara mean roughly the same thing: "lotus-born."

3. According to *The Golden Garland Chronicles*, the child he accidently killed was about to take rebirth in the lower realms due to immense negative actions committed in a prior life. By killing the boy, Padmakara liberated him to be reborn in a buddha realm and simultaneously manage to escape the mundane prison of a king's life.

4. For the quotation from this tantra, see note 6.

5. Tsele Natsok Rangdröl wrote this in the seventeenth century when the Nyingma School was under vicious attack due to lack of discipline.

6. In his *Pond of White Lotus Flowers* (pp. 19–20), Shechen Gyaltsab explains that Padmasambhava was predicted in the *Tantra of the Perfect Embodiment of the Unexcelled Nature:* "Eight years after I pass into nirvana, I will reappear in the country of Uddiyana bearing the name Padmasambhava. I will become the lord of the teachings of Secret Mantra." Following this prophecy, Padmasambhava appeared in this world in the following way.

   The fully perfected Buddha Amitabha, sovereign of the vajra speech of all the buddhas of the three times, resides in an immense celestial palace composed of the self-display of innate wakefulness in the center of the pure realm of Sukhavati. Inseparable from the luminous dharmakaya essence of Amitabha's mind, Padmasambhava is an unceasing miraculous display of the natural expression of compassionate energy, a manifestation of outer, inner, and secret emanations that appear according to the countless beings to be influenced and in order to accomplish their welfare. In particular, in this world Padmasambhava appeared as the regent of Buddha Shakyamuni by taking birth from a lotus flower in Lake Danakosha. Through the miraculous display of his amazing deeds, he was equivalent to a second buddha for Buddhism in both India and Tibet. On the relative level, in Maratika, he appeared to realize the vidyadhara level of longevity, the unified stage of the path of training, the realization of which is equal to that of a bodhisattva on the eighth level according to the causal vehicles. In the Cave of Yanglesho, he acted as if reaching the mahamudra level of the path of cultivation by the samadhi that illuminates the wisdom mandala of the nine divinities of Vishuddha and thus attained a state of realization corresponding to that of a bodhisattva on the tenth level according to the causal vehicles. In fact, his state of realization is indivisible from that of the buddhas of the three times and possesses the nature of wondrous manifestations that surpass the boundary of ordinary thought.

7. The clarity of the reflection of the moon on the surface of water is dependent upon the water's purity. Likewise, our perception of Padmasambhava depends upon our degree of faith.

8. Since the time of Tsele Natsok Rangdröl (b. 1608), many old manuscripts from the period of King Trisong Deutsen have been recovered from the Tun Huang caves situated five hundred miles north of Lhasa. Some of them may shed light on the early period of the transmission of Buddhism to Tibet.

9. Other sources accept that Mutig Tseypo was the youngest.

10. The venerable Thinley Norbu Rinpoche kindly added: "We should not regard Padmasambhava as an ordinary person with dualistic perception, but as a fully enlightened buddha. His action is simultaneously symbolic and miraculous in that he liberated the mind of the minister's son. Besides, this deed was skillful means enacted by Padmasambhava to create not only his expulsion, but also to prevent people from thinking that only royalty could practice Vajrayana. The activity of a buddha is difficult to understand for people whose minds are bound by nihilistic phenomena."

11. Venerable Tulku Urgyen Rinpoche deemed it necessary to explain the symbolism as follows: "The males and females are not to be regarded literally but symbolize appearance and emptiness. The term *tanagana*,

'union and liberation,' is a key word in Vajrayana practice. Using his five arrows of discriminating knowledge, Padmasambhava engaged in the act of 'liberating' the five poisons by recognizing their essence while 'uniting' with emptiness, the basic nature of all appearances."

12. These three texts appear with a variety of spellings. For instance, in *The Narration of the Precious Revelation of the Terma Treasures*, Longchen Rabjam spells them: *Yoga Jamuntaya, Tatvasamgraha*, and *Yogacharya*.

13. In *The Narration of the Precious Revelation of the Terma Treasures* (pp. 47–49), Longchen Rabjam explains that Padmasambhava received this prophecy from Vajra Varahi: "Worthy One, the true teaching on fruition within a single lifetime is unique and not realized by everyone. It abides in the vajra heart of Shri Singha. In Rugged Grove you shall attain realization!"

Through his miraculous power, Padmasambhava arrived at the marvelous charnel ground Rugged Grove in a single moment, where he bowed down before the great master Shri Singha and begged to be accepted as his disciple. Shri Singha then taught Padmakara the complete Three Sections of the Great Perfection: Mind, Space, and Instruction, including the *Tantra of the Great Perfection that is Equal to Space*. In particular, when having received all the outer, inner, and secret cycles of the Innermost Essence, Padmasambhava asked, "Great master, I beseech you to grant an instruction that enables the material body to disappear within this very lifetime, brings forth the vision of the sambhogakaya realms, and awakens one to buddhahood in the realm of dharmakaya."

Shri Singha replied, "Excellent, noble son! I have an instruction that is the pinnacle of all teachings, the innermost of all views. It transcends all the vehicles and is the heart essence of all dakinis, the subject of extreme secrecy more secret than ordinary secrets. It is the great vehicle of the Luminous Vajra Essence, beyond thinking, devoid of the intellect, and outside the domain of dualistic consciousness. It does not lie within the confines of existence or nonexistence and transcends the ranges of view and meditation, development and completion. It is the mother of all the victorious ones of the three times, the short path of all the great vidyadharas, the ultimate and unsurpassable instruction through which one can attain the enlightenment of the buddhas within three years. I shall teach it to you!"

Shri Singha then bestowed upon him the empowerments of the

Great Perfection of the Heart Essence of the Dakinis (Dzogchen Khandro Nyingtig), numerous scriptures of instructions on its application, and, as support-ive teachings, these Eighteen Dzogchen Tantras: *Dra Thalgyur Root Tantra*, the *Tantra of Graceful Auspiciousness*, the *Tantra of the Heart Mirror of Samantabhadra*, the *Blazing Lamp Tantra*, the *Tantra of the Mind Mirror of Vajrasattva*, the *Tantra of Self-Manifest Awareness*, the *Tantra of Studded Jewels*, the *Tantra of Pointing-out Instructions*, the *Tantra of the Six Spheres of Saman-tabhadra*, the *Tantra of No Letters*, the *Tantra of the Perfected Lion*, the *Pearl Garland Tantra*, the *Tantra of Self-Liberated Awareness*, the *Tantra of Piled Gems*, the *Tantra of Shining Relics*, the *Union of Sun and Moon Tantra*, the *Tantra of Self-Existing Perfection*, and the *Samantabhadri Tantra of the Sun of the Luminous Expanse*.

14. This place is believed to be Rewalsar, situated an hour's drive from Mandi in Himachal Pradesh in northern India and is now famous under the name Tso Pema, the Lotus Lake.

15. In *The White Lotus Flower*, Mipham Rinpoche describes how the dakini also taught the panditas the famous supplication to Padmasambhava known as the "Seven Line Supplication":

> HUM, orgyen yulgyi nubjang tsam
> pema gesar dongpo la
> yamtsen chog gi ngörub nyey
> pema jungney shesu drag
> khordu khandro mangpö kor
> khyekyi jeysu dagdrub kyi
> jingyi lobchir shegsu sol
> GURU-PADMA-SIDDHI HUM

> HUM, on the northwest border of the country
>   of Uddiyana,
> On the anthers of a lotus flower,
> You attained the marvelous supreme siddhi.
> Renowned as the Lotus-Born,
> Surrounded by a retinue of many dakinis,
> I will follow in your footsteps.
> Please come and bestow your blessing.
> GURU-PADMA-SIDDHI HUM

16. When taking possession of land for building a temple, the spirits, who believe the area belongs to them, must first be appeased. A torma offering is therefore consecrated and dedicated to the local deities by mudra, mantra, and samadhi.

17. *The Golden Garland Chronicles* (p. 368) adds that Padmasambhava donned ornaments of jewelry and bone, took a vajra and bell in his hands and, uttering HUNG, flew up into the sky, where he performed the consecration of the land with a vajra dance. The local spirits helped lay the foundation by placing stones on the lines where his shadow fell.

18. The entire construction took five years to complete. Begun in the Year of the Tiger (A.D. 810), it continued through the years of the Rabbit, Dragon, and Snake and was brought to completion in the Year of the Horse (A.D. 814).

19. Approximately a duration of two years.

20. *The Golden Garland Chronicles* cites these as the Eighteen Mahayoga Tantras. Another system is listed in the glossary.

21. Both the Six Secret Sections and the Eight Maya Sections belong to the category of Mahayoga and are sometimes counted among the Eighteen Mahayoga Tantras. Still, since the view in these tantras is Ati Yoga, while their conduct is Mahayoga, there is nothing wrong with classifying them in between, as belonging to the category of Anu Yoga scriptures.

22. When the great Indian master Atisha Dipamkara arrived at Samye several centuries later, he expressed deep amazement at the wealth of Vajrayana literature preserved in Tibet, since most of these scriptures had disappeared in India by that time.

23. Padmasambhava left them, saying that in the future many panditas and translators would appear and translate them (*The Golden Garland Chronicles*, p. 401).

24. *The Golden Garland Chronicles* (p. 406) includes that at first Hungkara acted displeased, exclaiming, "Some Tibetan evil spirits have arrived. HUNG HUNG!" Simultaneously he issued dazzling rays of light from his mouth, and the five Tibetan translators fainted with fear.

25. *The Golden Garland Chronicles* (p. 408) adds that the five Tibetan translators each attained some minor accomplishment: Namkhai Nyingpo, who was exceptionally intelligent, industrious, and possessed great merit, could walk with his feet the width of one hand above the ground, the twenty-eight ishvari goddesses obeyed his command, and in actuality he could unite with the seven types of wisdom goddesses. Virya of Ru-yong could display various miracles, Epagsha of Drugu was accompanied by an effulgence of wisdom light, and Gyalwey

Lodrö could revive the dead, even after seven days had passed. An additional reason that they wanted to return to Tibet was due to having received a letter from Trisong Deutsen telling them that his ministers had spread false rumors about the translators learning nothing but black magic and intending to seize the kingdom on their return. Fearing that all would be in vain unless they quickly returned, they asked permission to leave. Hungkara, on the other hand, warned them with these words, "Your lives will be in danger if you bring back to Tibet the profound Secret Mantra without having practiced more than a single mandala. Stay for another year and continue your sadhana! Bring forth some real signs of accomplishment, then you can go to Tibet."

26. This passage is elaborated upon at great length in *The Golden Garland Chronicles* (p. 411:2).

27. Shechen Gyaltsab mentions in his *Pond of White Lotus Flowers* (p. 164) that Vairochana, before meeting Shri Singha, had met the wisdom forms of the two vidyadharas Garab Dorje and Manjushrimitra in a miraculous pagoda at Dhahena. After he had presented a huge offering of gold, they conferred empowerment upon him and bestowed their blessings, with the prediction that he would receive the complete teachings from Shri Singha.

28. Because of the Indians' paranoia and jealous guarding of the sacred Great Perfection, Vairochana had to hide inside a copper pot while Shri Singha whispered the teachings to him through the pipe.

29. Among the Eighteen Major Scriptures of the Mind Section of the Great Perfection, Vairochana was only able to translate these first five scriptures into Tibetan, and they were therefore later known as the Five Early Translations of the Mind Section. During Vairochana's exile, Vimalamitra and Yudra Nyingpo later translated the following thirteen listed here.

30. According to *The Golden Garland Chronicles* (p. 423) and the *Pond of White Lotus Flowers* (p. 165), Vairochana received many further transmissions from Shri Singha of the tantras of the Mind Section and Space Section of the Great Perfection before returning to Tibet. Having attained realization through these teachings, Shri Singha told him, "Vairochana, you possess the complete tantras, scriptures, and instruction; now the time has come to proclaim the Buddhadharma in Tibet."

31. This "magical writing" is invisible ink that appears when slowly heated up over a flame. Another manuscript tells that Vairochana used an ink made of goat's milk.

32. *The Golden Garland Chronicles* (p. 433) explains further that Vairochana wept out of deep-felt pity when he heard that an innocent beggar was made to take his place and thrown into the river within a sealed copper sphere, furnished with food and drink. He made a fervent wish for the beggar's future happiness. The story continues that the beggar reached a place called Khartag where the copper pot was opened by the lord of the local fortress. The lord was so amazed that he adopted the beggar and gave him a house and a wife at a place that then prospered into a country town.

33. Other versions of the *Sanglingma* say, "When the first five parts of the *Eighteen Marvels of Mind* were completed." This seems more plausible, since Vairochana is only known to have translated five of the Eighteen Tantras of the Mind Section. See also "Five Early and Thirteen Later Translations of the Great Perfection" in the Glossary. Furthermore, *The Golden Garland Chronicles* (p. 435) narrates that Lady Margyen was holding a grudge against Vairochana who, being a monk, had refused her advances. The detailed story is found in the *Five Chronicles*.

34. Prince Turquoise later became the chief disciple of Vairochana and was known as Yudra Nyingpo, "Essence of Turquoise."

35. In *The Golden Garland Chronicles* (p. 454), the five monks are the five following translators mentioned: Yeshe Yang, Drenka, Lekdrup, Darma, and Vairochana.

36. Jamgön Kongtrül mentions in his *Encyclopedia of Knowledge* that Vimalamitra was invited to Tibet to fulfill a prophecy given to the king by Tingdzin Sangpo of Nyang, his court chaplain, who could remain in the samadhi of one-pointed meditation for seven years and possessed great clairvoyant power.

37. See the glossary entries for "Mantra and Philosophy" and the "causal" and "resultant vehicles."

38. The ultimate nature of all the Buddhadharma is the same: the realization that the innate state is nondual emptiness and luminosity, just like sugar is always sweet and salt always salty.

39. This paragraph seemed to have been corrupted in the *Sanglingma* manuscript and has been reconstructed using *The Golden Garland Chronicles* (pp. 482–483).

40. This is the later tyrant king of Tibet known as Langdarma, who was assassinated by Lhalung Palgyi Dorje. The word *lang* means "ox," referring to his former birth as a beast of burden, who was used to carrying stones and earth for the building of the great stupa of Boudhanath. Padmasambhava explained that while the brothers formed virtuous aspirations, the ox made the black wish to be able to destroy whatever the brothers could create. History shows that this negative aspiration was almost successful.

41. Statues and painted scrolls are the shrine objects of the enlightened body. The scriptures are the shrine objects of enlightened speech. Stupas and other receptacles containing sacred relics are the shrine objects of enlightened mind.

42. Also present was Yeshe Tsogyal, the female disciple who had possessed perfect recall.

43. The entire collection of the glorious Assemblage of Sugatas is found in the terma treasures revealed by Nyang Ral Nyima Öser.

44. In *The Narration of the Precious Revelation of the Terma Treasures* (pp. 81–82), Longchen Rabjam mentions that twenty-five disciples were present, including Tingdzin Sangpo of Nyang, all of whom attained accomplishment and later became renowned as the twenty-five siddhas of Chimphu.

45. The other six years are the years of the Rat, Tiger, Rabbit, Snake, Horse, and Pig.

46. The terma for the *Sanglingma Life Story* was found in this temple, the Khamsum Copper Temple, which is still well preserved.

47. In *The Golden Garland Chronicles*, Padmasambhava is instead quoted as saying: "As your essential meditation, practice the ultimate awakened mind and be stable in the innate, natural state.

48. The predictions, which are not included in the *Sanglingma*, appear in *The Golden Garland Chronicles*, (pp. 570–581). These prophecies cover the omens that portend the arrival of one hundred tertöns, the masters who are to reveal Padmasambhava's hidden teachings at their destined times. Some of the more famous are as follows: Sangye Lama, who is

considered the first tertön, Dangma Lhüngyal, Drapa Ngönshey, Nyang Ral Nyima Öser, Guru Chöwang, Sangye Lingpa, Rinchen Lingpa, Orgyen Lingpa, Drimey Öser (Longchen Rabjam), Ratna Lingpa, Chöjey Lingpa, Terdag Lingpa, Kunkyong Lingpa, Do-ngag Lingpa, Tennyi Lingpa, Dorje Lingpa, Pema Lingpa, Leytro Lingpa, Shikpo Lingpa, and Dechen Lingpa.

49. These years should be reckoned each as six months. *The Golden Cronicle* mentions that Padmakara stayed five years in the royal palace of Uddiyana, five in Cool Grove, and spent ten years studying the Dharma. In each of the following countries he stayed for two hundred years: India and China, Uddiyana and Sahor, Magadha and Tirthika, Kashmir and Singala, Li and Marutsey. In each of the following he spent ninety-eight years: Asha and Drusha, Shambhala and Shangshung, Persia and Gesar, Tokar and Rubala, Rakshasa and the Naga realm. Finally, he remained forty years in Nepal and one hundred and eleven years in Tibet.

50. *The Golden Garland Chronicles* (p. 583) contains a large number of additional teachings at this point.

51. Padmasambhava sings at this point a more lengthy song of heart advice: *The Golden Garland Chronicles* (pp. 584–588).

52. The Jambu continent is said to have the shape of the head of an axe.

53. To "attain excellence" means to become a fully ordained monk or nun.

54. The skillful actions at the end of a session of Vajrayana practice are: to dissolve the mandala in order to realize dharmakaya and avoid the view of permanence, to reemerge as the deity in order to realize sambhogakaya and avoid the view of nihilism, to dedicate the merit and make pure aspirations in order to ensure the perpetual manifestation of nirmanakaya for the welfare of all sentient beings.

55. Two types of welfare are mentioned here: The highest welfare for oneself is to realize the dharmakaya endowed with the supreme wisdom qualities. The welfare for others is to manifest the sambhogakaya in order to teach the noble bodhisattvas and the nirmanakayas who are visible to all beings.

56. The higher level of meditation transcends the need to hold a conceptual object as a reference point.

Bibliography

TIBETAN SOURCES

Chokgyur Lingpa. *Wish-Fulfilling Tree.* RNAM THAR DPAG BSAM LJON SHING. Included in the Chokling Tersar collection of rediscovered treasures. Translated by Keith Dowman (and Tulku Pema Wangyal, Taklung Tsetrül Rinpoche) in *The Legend of the Great Stupa,* Berkeley: Dharma Publishing, 1973.

Deep and Vast Chronicles. BKA' THANG ZAB RGYAS. Revealed by an unknown Bönpo tertön. Its four volumes make it the most extensive version of Guru Rinpoche's life story. Ven. Tulku Urgyen Rinpoche mentioned that he read it when he was a child and he was amazed by its richness of detail. This scripture is yet to appear outside of Tibet.

His Holiness Dudjom Rinpoche. *Nyingma Chöjung.* BOD SNGA RABS PA RNYING MA'I CHOS 'BYUNG LHA DBANG G.YUL LAS RGYAL BA'I RNGA BO CHE'I SGRA DBYANGS. A translation of this important historical work has been completed by Gyurme Dorje and Matthew Kapstein in *The Nyingma School: Its History and Fundamentals,* Boston: Wisdom Publications, 1991.

Garland of Precious Jewels: The History of the Heart Essence of the Dakinis. MKHA' 'GRO SNYING THIG GI LO RGYUS RIN PO CHE'I PHRENG BA. In *Khandro Nyingtig,* vol. 2, which is within the *Nyingtig Yabshi* collection. The history of the transmission of the Dzogchen teachings to Tibet by Padmasambhava and their subsequent concealment as terma treasures.

Göl Lotsawa Shönnu Pal (1392–1481). *The Blue Annals.* DEB THER SNGON PO. Translated by George N. Roerich. Delhi: Motilal Banaisidass, 1976.

Great Replica. RJE BTSUN THAMS CHAD MKHYEN PA VAI RO TSA NA'I RNAM THAR 'DRA 'BAG CHEN MO. Dehra Dun, India: Khochen Tulku.

Translated by Anila Jinpa Palmo and as yet unpublished. The detailed life story of the great translator Vairochana and the transmission of the Dzogchen teachings through the buddhas and vidyadharas, written by the chief disciples of Vairochana.

Guru Tashi Tobgyal (also known as Jangdag Karma Guru Chögyal Wangpo, 1550–1602). *Ocean of Perfect Wonders: A Life Story of Padmasambhava.* RIG 'DZIN GRUB PA'I DBANG PHYUG CHEN PO PAD-MA 'BYUNG GNAS KYI RNAM PAR THAR PA NGO MTSHAR PHUN SUM TSHOGS PA'I RGYA MTSHO ZHES BYA BA 'GRO BA RANG GROL. Gangtok: Sherab Gyaltsen Lama, 1976. 19 chapters, 719 pages. This detailed version of Padmakara's life story is not a terma but a condensation of many other termas and biographies. In the colophon he mentions the following: *The Ocean of Sindhura,* the *Longer and Shorter Chronicles of Ngadag Nyang,* the *Eleven Deeds of Padmakara* by Guru Chöwang (1212–1270), the chronicles of Sangye Lingpa, Dorje Lingpa (1346–1405), Ratna Lingpa, and Orgyen Lingpa, the *Longer and Shorter Nub Edition* by Nubtön and Nub Gyalseypa, the *Namthar Thorbuba* written by Pema Lingpa, and the *Secret Life Story of Guru Rinpoche* written by Yeshe Tsogyal.

————. *Ocean of Wondrous Sayings to Delight the Learned Ones.* 5 vols. BSTAN PA'I SNYING PO GSANG CHEN SNGA 'GYUR NGES DON ZAB MO'I CHOS KYI 'BYUNG BA GSAL BAR BYED PA'I LEGS BSHAD MKHAS PA DGA' BYED NGO MTSHAR GTAM GYI ROL MTSHO. New Delhi: His Holiness Dilgo Khyentse. An immensely detailed Dharma history of the transmission of the teachings in the Nyingma School.

Gyurmey Tsewang Chogdrub of Kathog (18th century). *Drum of the Gods.* 2 vols. BDE BAR GSHEGS PA'I BSTAN PA THAMS CAD KYI SNYING PO RIG PA 'DZIN PA'I SDE SNOD RDO RJE THEG PA SNGA 'GYUR RGYUD 'BUM RIN PO CHE'I RTOGS PA BRJOD PA LHA'I RNGA BO CHE LTA BU'I GTAM. This major work forms the last volumes of the Nyingma Gyübum published by His Holiness Dilgo Khyentse Rinpoche. Detailed history of the Nyingma tantras: How the teachers of the three kayas appeared, how the Buddhadharma appeared in this world, the translation of the tantras into Tibetan, a catalogue of the *Nyingma Gyübum,* and the benefits of republishing these tantras.

Jamgön Kongtrül Lodrö Thaye (1813–1899). *Encyclopedia of Knowledge.* 3 vols. SHES BYA KUN LA KHYAB PA'I GZHUNG LUGS NYUNG NGU'I TSHIG GIS

RNAM PAR 'GROL BAR LEGS BSHAD YONGS 'DUS SHES BYA MTHA' YAS PA'I RGYA MTSHO. New Delhi: His Holiness Dilgo Khyentse Rinpoche. His autocommentary on the famous *Treasury of Knowledge* (Shes bya mdzod), a literary work of amazing scope and depth. A translation of this work was initiated by the Very Venerable Kalu Rinpoche.

————. *Life Story of Padmasambhava.* A short biography of Guru Rinpoche extracted from *The Precious Garland of Lapis Lazuli,* ZAB MO'I GTER DANG GTER STON GRUB THOB JI LTAR BYON PA'I LO RGYUS RIN PO CHE BAI DUR-YA'I PHRENG BA, an explanation of termas and a collection of life stories of the 108 main tertöns written by Jamgön Kongtrül and found in his *Rinchen Terdzö,* vol. I. An English translation of this extract by Erik Pema Kunsang is included in *Dakini Teachings,* Boston: Shambhala Publications, 1990.

————. *Life Story of Vairochana.* VAI RO RNAM THAR PADMA'I DGA' TSHAL. 71 pages. Short terma in poetic verse form. Included by His Holiness Dilgo Khyentse in the *Rinchen Terdzö.*

————. *Vajra Necklace: A Life Story of Padmasambhava* GU RU'I RNAM THAR RDO RJE'I RGYAN PHRENG. Included by His Holiness Dilgo Khyentse in the *Rinchen Terdzö.* 24 pages. Short terma in poetry.

Jigmey Lingpa (1729–1798). *All-Pervading Adornment.* DE BZHIN GSHEGS PAS LEGS PAR GSUNGS PA'I GSUNG RAB RGYA MTSHO'I SNYING POR GYUR PA RIG PA 'DZIN PA'I SDE SNOD DAM SNGA 'GYUR RGYUD 'BUM RIN PO CHE'I RTOGS PA BRJOD PA 'DZAM GLING MTHA'I GRU KHYAB PA'I RGYAN. In *Nyingma Gyübum,* vol. 34, 671 pages.

Karma Chagmey (1613–1678). *History, Meditation and Benefits of the Supplication in Seven Chapters.* GSOL 'DEBS LE'U BDUN PA'I LO RGYUS DMIGS RIM PHAN YON DANG BCAS PA. 78 manuscript pages. An explanation of the seven famous supplications to Guru Rinpoche revealed by the hermit Sangpo Drakpa and given to the great tertön Rigdzin Gödem. The daily practice of these supplications embody the entire life-story of Padmasambhava, all his lineages of transmission, and all the levels of his teaching.

Kunga Dorje (1309–1364). *Red Annals.* DEB THER DMAR PO.

Lhatsün Ngönmo. *Liberating History of the Great Stupa Jarung Khashor.* MCHOD RTEN CHEN PO BYA RUNG KHA SHOR GYI LO RGYUS THOS PAS GROL BA. 59 pages. Published recently in India. Translated by Keith Dowman as *The Legend of the Great Stupa,* Berkeley: Dharma Publishing, 1973.

Longchen Rabjam (1308–1363/4). *Great History of Nyingtig.* RDZOGS PA CHEN PO SNYING THIG GI LO RGYUS CHEN MO. In *Vima Nyingtig,* which is within the *Nyingtig Yabshi* collection. Explains the transmission of the Instruction Section of the Great Perfection from Buddha Samantabhadra through the Indian vidyadhara masters to Vimalamitra and the Tibetan lineage holders, until reaching Longchen Rabjam and the third Karmapa, Rangjung Dorje.

——. *Illuminating Sunlight: A Dharma History.* 2 vols. CHOS 'BYUNG RIN PO CHE'I GTER MDZOD THUB BSTAN GSAL BAR BYED PA'I NYI 'OD. New Delhi: His Holiness Dilgo Khyentse. The author quotes his name as being Gyalsey Thugchok Tsal.

——. *Narration of the Precious Revelation of the Terma Treasures.* GTER 'BYUNG RIN PO CHE'I LO RGYUS. In Khandro Yangtig, vol. OM. 100 pages. The historical background for the Khandro Nyingtig. In this work the *Sanglingma* is quoted at great length. This history also includes the Dzogchen lineage of Padmasambhava, from Buddha Samantabhadra to Shri Singha, his transmission of the Dzogchen teachings to the close disciples headed by Yeshe Tsogyal.

Mipham Jampal Gyepey Dorje (1846–1912). *Essence of Accomplishment.* DPAL SGRUB PA CHEN PO BKA' BRGYAD KYI SPYI DON RNAM PAR BSHAD PA DNGOS GRUB SNYING PO. Published by His Holiness Dilgo Khyentse Rinpoche in the *Collected Works of Mipham Rinpoche.* A most wonderful explanation of the general meaning of the Eight Sadhana Teachings, combining the teachings transmitted through Garab Dorje, King Jah, Vimalamitra, Padmasambhava, Vairochana, and Namkhai Nyingpo.

——. *White Lotus Flower.* PADMA DKAR PO. Darjeeling: Taklung Tsetrül Rinpoche. An explanation of the famous "Seven Line Supplication" to Padmasambhava.

Namkhai Nyingpo. *Life Story of Yeshe Tsogyal.* BOD KYI JO MO YE SHES MTSHO RGYAL GYI MDZAD TSHUL RNAM PAR THAR PA GAB PA MNGON BYUNG RGYUD MANG DRI ZA'I GLU PHRENG. Woodblock of the manuscript available at Sangdog Palri Temple in Kalimpong, India. Translated by Tarthang Tulku as *Mother of Knowledge,* Berkeley: Dharma Publishing, 1983, and by Keith Dowman as *Sky Dancer,* London: Routledge and Kegan Paul, 1984.

Nyang Ral Nyima Öser (1124–1192). *Historical Origin of the Teachings of the Assemblage of Sugatas.* BDE GSHEGS 'DUS PA'I BKA'I BYUNG TSHUL.

Published by H.H. Dudjom Rinpoche in *Eight Sadhana Teachings of the Dharma Cycle of the Assemblage of Sugatas* (BKA' BRGYAD BDE GSHEGS 'DUS PA'I CHOS SKOR), vol. 1, 41 pages. This terma scripture is the detailed account of how the Eight Sadhana Teachings were transmitted from Buddha Samantabhadra to Dharmavajra, the dakini Leykyi Wangmo, the eight Indian vidyadharas and Padmasambhava, and then to the eight Tibetan disciples. Also included is a detailed list of the tantras received by the vidyadharas and the scriptures contained in the *Assemblage of Sugatas.*

————. *Honey from the Center of the Flower: A Dharma History.* CHOS 'BYUNG ME TOG SNYING PO SBRANG RTSI'I BCUD. Published by VGH Wissenschaftverlag, 1985. 459 pages. One of the oldest historical narrations of the transmission of Buddhism to Tibet, with special emphasis on the life and teachings of Padmasambhava. Two additional versions of this scripture were published by Lama Tenpa by the order of His Holiness Dilgo Khyentse.

————. *Immaculate Legacy.* SPRUL SKU MNGA' BDAG CHEN PO'I SKYES RABS RNAM THAR DRI MA MED PA'I BKA' RGYA CAN. 163 pages. Narration of fifteen former lives of Nyang Ral Nyima Öser, spoken to his chief disciples and written down by Migyur Dorje, a yogi from Central Tibet. These fifteen incarnations include King Trisong Deutsen, a son of the god Indra named Prince Boundless Radiance, the Tibetan king Ralpachen, the Indian prince Chöden, the Indian prince Mahayana, a prince in Uddiyana named Dharma Shvadha, the Nepalese prince Dharmaraja, Prince Udarphala in the country of Singala, Prince Enang-O in Lower Dokham, the Indian prince Dharimuka, Adharipa in the country of Li, Shvadha Garpa in China, Rinchen Jungney in the district of Latö Burang, Prince Shri Singha in the country of Sahor, Prince Purna Tri to the east of Bodhgaya, and finally the great tertön master Nyang Ral Nyima Öser.

————. *Sanglingma Life Story.* SLOB DPON PAD-MA 'BYUNG GNAS KYI SKYES RABS CHOS 'BYUNG NOR BU'I PHRENG BA, RNAM THAR ZANGS GLING MA'O. Included by Jamgön Kongtrül in the *Rinchen Terdzö.* 41 chapters, 202 pages. The first known terma biography. The *Sanglingma* exists also in a longer version of 286 pages. This version, also revealed by Lord Nyang, is so far unpublished, but is found at the National Archives, Kathmandu, Nepal, under the title U RGYAN GU RU PADMA 'BYUNG

GNAS KYI RNAM THAR 'BRING PO ZANGS GLING MAR GRAGS PA. The *Sanglingma* is also present in an extensive 2 vol. version, which was banned in Central Tibet due to some clear and damaging predictions about certain ministers' involvement in the decline of Buddhism in Tibet in the twentieth century. This version of 1260 pages was found in the Mustang region of Nepal and is also available at the National Archives, Kathmandu, Nepal.

Orgyen Lingpa (1329–1367 or 1360). *Concise Chronicle.* Also known as *Kathang Düpa.* O RGYAN PAD-MA'I BKA' THANG BSDUS PA. 16 chapters plus predictions, 38 small pages. Written down by Vairochana and later revealed from a terma treasure by Orgyen Lingpa at Samye Chimphu. Translated by Erik Pema Kunsang in an unpublished manuscript using a print from woodblocks kept at Thodung Gompa in the Solukhumbu region of Nepal.

————. *Five Chronicles.* BKA' THANG SDE LNGA. Five sections in 853 pages. Recently republished by the Government of His Holiness the Dalai Lama in Dharamsala. The Five Chronicles of Gods and Demons, the King, the Ministers, the Queens, and the Panditas and Translators.

————. *Padma Kathang.* O RGYAN GU RU PAD-MA 'BYUNG GNAS KYI SKYES RABS RNAM PAR THAR PA RGYAS PA BKOD PA PAD-MA BKA'I THANG YIG. Long version in poetry, 108 chapters, 721 pages. Revealed in the Crystal Cave of Yarlung in Central Tibet and therefore also known as *The Crystal Cave Biography (Namthar Sheldragma).* Originally translated into French by G.-C. Toussaint as *Le Dict de Padma* (Padma Thang Yig MS. de Lithang), Paris, 1933. Later retranslated into English by Kenneth Douglas and Gwendolyn Bays as *The Life and Liberation of Padmasambhava,* Emeryville, Calif.: Dharma Publishing.

Pema Lingpa (1445/50–1521). *Radiant Mirror: A Life Story of Padmasambhava* U RGYAN SLOB DPON PAD-MA 'BYUNG GNAS KYI 'KHRUNGS RABS CHEN MO ZHES BYA BA SANGS RGYAS BSTAN PA'I BYUNG KHUNG MUN SEL SGRON ME LAS RNAM THAR DON GSAL ME LONG. Gangtok, 1977. A terma text in two volumes, revealed at Samye by Pema Lingpa.

Ratna Lingpa (1403–1478). *Golden Garland: A Life Story of Padmasambhava.* O RGYAN GU RU PAD-MA 'BYUNG GNAS KYI RNAM THAR GSER GYI PHRENG BA. 327 pages. Included in the collection of termas of Ratna Lingpa published by Ven. Taklung Tsetrül Rinpoche. This version is quite similar in length and content to the *Sanglingma Life Story* revealed by Nyang Ral Nyima Öser.

Samten Lingpa, Taksham Nüden Dorje (b. 1655). *Flawless Adornment: A Life Story of Padmasambhava.* O RGYAN GU RU PAD-MA 'BYUNG GNAS ZHES BYA BA'I RNAM THAR BCU GNYIS DRI MA MED PA'I RGYAN ZHES BYA BA JO MO MTSHO RGYAL DANG BAI RO TSAN NA GNYIS KYI MDZAD PA.

Sangye Lingpa (1340–1396). *Bright Crystal Mirror.* BLA MA DGONGS PA 'DUS PA LAS, YID CHES SHING KHUNGS BTSUN PA'I LO RGYUS SHEL GYI ME LONG GSAL BA. 81 pages. A life story of Padmasambhava by Yeshe Tsogyal from the *Lama Gongdü* cycle of termas revealed by Sangye Lingpa.

————. *The Golden Garland Chronicles.* Also known as *Kathang Sertreng.* U RGYAN GU PAD-MA 'BYUNG GNAS KYI RNAM THAR RGYAS PA GSER GYI PHRENG BA THAR LAM GSAL BYED. PAD-MA BKA'I THANG YIG. 117 chapters, 727 pages with tiny script. With its alternating poetry and prose, this delightful biography of Padmasambhava has for centuries been and still is a contribution of major importance to Tibetan Buddhist literature. Kalimpong: His Holiness Dudjom Rinpoche, 1970. Written down by Yeshe Tsogyal, who concealed it as a terma treasure for the benefit of people in the future. Revealed from a treasure in the Crystal Cave of Puri Phugmoche (pu ri phug mo che shel gyi brag phug) by Sangye Lingpa. Excerpts from this version were included by W. Y. Evans-Wentz in *The Tibetan Book of the Great Liberation,* Oxford: Oxford University Press, 1954.

Selnang of Ba. *Bashey Annals.* SBA BZHED GTSANG MA & SBA BZHED ZHABS BRTAG MA. Dharamsala: Shes-rig Par-khang, 1968. Early chronicles from the ninth century.

Sera Khandro Dekyong Wangmo. *Immaculate White Lotus: A Life Story of Padmasambhava.* CHOS NYID MKHA' 'GRO'I GSANG MDZOD LAS: O RGYAN RNAM THAR DRI MED PADMA DKAR PO. 20 pages of beautiful devotional poetry by this female tertön. Almost identical to *Wish-Fulfilling Tree,* revealed by Chokgyur Lingpa.

Shechen Gyaltsab Pema Namgyal. *Pond of White Lotus Flowers.* SNGA 'GYUR RDO RJE'I THEG PA GTSO BOR GYUR PA'I SGRUB BRGYUD SHING RTA BRGYAD KYI BYUNG BA BRJOD PA'I GTAM RDOR BSDUS LEGS BSHAD PAD-MA DKAR PO'I RDZING BU. New Delhi: His Holiness Dilgo Khyentse. 527 pages. A major historical work on the Eight Chariots of the Practice Lineage, with predominant emphasis on the Nyingma School.

Sogdokpa Lodrö Gyaltsen (b. 1552). *Dispelling the Darkness of Mind.* Also known as *Namthar Yikyi Münsel.* SLOB DPON SANGS RGYAS GNYIS PA

PAD-MA 'BYUNG GNAS KYI RNAM PAR THAR PA YID KYI MUN SEL. 255 pages. Published in India by His Holiness Dudjom Rinpoche. An English translation is under preparation by Anila Jinpa Palmo.

Taksham Nüden Dorje. *Life Story of Dorje Drolö.* BLA MA RDO RJE GRO LOD KYI RNAM THAR. A life story of Padmasambhava focusing on the esoteric meaning of his wrathful manifestation as Dorje Drolö.

Taranatha. *Threefold Confidence: A Life Story of Padmasambhava* SLOB DPON PAD-MA'I RNAM THAR RGYA GAR LUGS YID CHES GSUM LDAN. Included by Jamgön Kongtrül in the *Rinchen Terdzö,* Vol. KA. Written in accord with Indian sources.

Tsele Natsok Rangdröl (b. 1608). *Clarifying the True Meaning.* SLOB DPON RIN PO CHE PAD-MA'I RNAM THAR CHEN MO LAS BRTSAM TE DRI BA'I LAN NGES DON GSAL BYED. Replies to 18 questions in 95 pages.

RELATED PUBLICATIONS IN ENGLISH

Ancient Tibet: Research Materials from the Yeshe De Project, Berkeley: Dharma Publishing.

Blondeau, A. M. "Analysis of the Biographies of Padmasambhava according to Tibetan tradition: classification of sources." In *Tibetan Studies in Honor of Hugh Richardson,* edited by M. Aris & A. S. Suu Kyi: New Delhi: Vikas, 1980.

Crystal Mirror. Vols. 1–7. Emeryville, Calif.: Dharma Publishing, 1971–84.

Chokgyur Lingpa, Jamyang Khyentse Wangpo, and Tulku Urgyen Rinpoche. *The Great Gate: The Heart Practice of Guru Rinpoche.* Vol. 1. Kathmandu: Rangjung Yeshe Publications, 1985.

Khetsun Sangpo Rinbochay. *Tantric Practice in the Nyingma.* Translated and edited by Jeffrey Hopkins. Ithaca: Snow Lion Publications.

Khyentse, Dilgo T. *Wish-Fulfilling Jewel.* Boston: Shambhala Publications, 1988.

The Legend of the Great Stupa. Translated by Keith Dowman. Berkeley: Dharma Publishing, 1973.

The Life and Liberation of Padmasambhava. 2 vols. Emeryville, Calif.: Dharma Publishing, 1978.

Manjusrimitra. *Primordial Experience.* Boston: Shambhala Publications, 1987.

Nam-mkha'i snying-po. *Mother of Knowledge.* Translated by Tarthang Tulku. Berkeley: Dharma Publishing, 1983.

————. *Sky Dancer.* Translated by Keith Dowman. London: Rutledge and Kegan Paul, 1984.

Orgyen Tobgyal. *The Life and Teaching of Chokgyur Lingpa.* Kathmandu: Rangjung Yeshe Publications, 1982.

Sogyal Rinpoche. *Dzogchen and Padmasambhava.* Berkeley: Rigpa Publications.

Thondup Rinpoche, Tulku. *Hidden Teachings of Tibet: An Explanation of the Terma Tradition of the Nyingma School of Buddhism.* London: Wisdom Publications, 1986.

————. *The Tantric Tradition of the Nyingmapa.* Marion, Mass.: Buddhayana, 1984.

The Tibetan Book of the Dead: The Great Liberation Through Hearing in the Bardo. Translated by Francesca Fremantle and Chögyam Trungpa. Berkeley: Shambhala Publications, 1975.

Tsele Natsok Rangdröl. *The Mirror of Mindfulness.* Boston: Shambhala Publications, 1989.

Yeshe Tsogyal. *Dakini Teachings: Padmasambhava's Oral Instructions to Lady Tsogyal.* Boston: Shambhala Publications, 1990.

Glossary

THIS GLOSSARY is a compilation of information received as oral teachings from the Venerable Tulku Urgyen Rinpoche, Chökyi Nyima Rinpoche, and other present-day Buddhist masters. In addition, I have relied on the Tibetan historical sources listed in the bibliography. Some of the entries are short and contain minimal definitions, but since the Tibetan equivalents are included, the reader can seek further clarification from other sources. Other names of people, places, and scriptures are listed with their Tibetan equivalents in the Index. Many of the English terms were coined exclusively for use in this book and may be phrased differently in another context.

Abhidharma (chos mngon pa)   One of the three parts of the Tripitaka, the words of the Buddha. Systematic teachings on metaphysics, focusing on the training of discriminating knowledge by analyzing elements of experience and investigating the nature of existing things. The chief commentaries on Abhidharma are the *Abhidharma Kosha* by Dignaga, from the Hinayana perspective, and the *Abhidharma Samucchaya* by Asanga, from the Mahayana point of view. *See also* Tripitaka.

Acceptance of the nature of nonarising (skye ba med pa'i chos la bzod pa)   An important realization gained on entry to the eighth bodhisattva stage. In this book, a synonym for complete enlightenment.

Accomplishment   (1) (dngos grub, Skt. siddhi). The attainment resulting from Dharma practice, usually referring to the "supreme accomplishment" of complete enlightenment. It can also mean the "common accomplishments," eight mundane accomplishments, such as clairvoyance, clairaudiance, flying in the sky, becoming invisible, everlasting youth, or powers of transmutation. The traditional list of the eight common accomplishments includes the accomplishment of the sword, pill, eye potion, swift feet, extraction of essences, celestial realm, invisibility, and the treasures below the earth. With the consecrated sword, you can fly through the sky or to celestial realms. When eating the consecrated pill, you become totally invisible and can assume any guise, just like a yaksha. When applying the consecrated eye potion, you can see both distant and subtle objects in the world. When smearing consecrated substance on your feet, you can travel around the world in a moment. By means of the mantra and the extracted essences of flowers and so forth, you can prolong your life span, regain youthfulness, and turn iron into gold. The accomplishment of the celestial realms is mastery of a mundane god or the ability to visit the six abodes of the gods in the realm of desire. By smearing a spot of consecrated substance on your forehead, you can become totally invisible. And, finally, by revealing buried treasures of precious gems and so forth, you can fulfill the wishes of others. The most eminent attainments on the path are, however, renunciation, compassion, unshakable faith, and realization of the correct view. (2) (sgrub pa). *See* Four aspects of approach and accomplishment.

Action without intermediate (mtshams med pa'i las)   Five actions with the most severe karmic effect: killing one's mother, one's father, or an arhat, causing schism in the sangha of monks, and drawing blood from a tathagata with evil intent. These actions can also be called "immediates" because their karmic effect will ripen immediately after death without leaving time to go through a bardo state.

Activities (las, phrin las, Skt. karma)   Usually referring to the four activities of pacifying, increasing, magnetizing, and subjugating.

Activity Garland Tantra (karma ma le 'phrin las kyi rgyud)   A Mahayoga scripture listed here as one of the Six Secret Sections. Sometimes also mentioned as one of the Eighteen Mahayoga Tantras—the tantra of enlightened activity. Texts with this name are found in the *Nyingma Gyübum*, vol. TSA and SHA.

Aeon (bskal pa, Skt. kalpa)   World-age, period, cosmic cycle.

Age of Strife (rtsod dus)   The present world-age, dominated by decline and degeneration.

Amitabha (snang ba mtha' yas)   The chief buddha of the lotus family and lord of the pure land of Sukhavati. He is also the manifestation of discriminating wisdom.

Amitayus (tshe dpag med) *See* Buddha Amitayus.

Amogha Pasha (don yod zhags pa) A tantra belonging to Kriya Yoga, also known as *Meaningful Lasso Tantra*.

Ananda (kun dga' bo) One of the ten close disciples of the Buddha and his personal attendant, who recited the sutras at the First Council and served as the second patriarch in the oral transmission of the Dharma.

Anu Yoga (rjes su rnal 'byor) The second of the three inner tantras. It emphasizes knowledge (prajna) rather than means (upaya) and the completion stage rather than the development stage. The view of Anu Yoga is that liberation is attained through growing accustomed to the insight into the nondual nature of space and wisdom. According to the *Pond of White Lotus Flowers* by Shechen Gyaltsab, the teachings of Anu Yoga appeared in this world when King Ja, a Dharma king also known as Lungten Dorje, Vajra Prophecy, received empowerment and instruction from the Lord of Secrets, through which he gained full comprehension of the meaning. The scriptural lineage he received from the human vidyadhara Vimalakirti. The major texts of Anu Yoga are the Four Scriptures and the Summation. King Ja transmitted the Anu Yoga teachings to the master Uparaja and his own sons Shakputri, Nagaputri, and Guhyaputri. Later lineage masters include Singhaputra, Kukuraja the Second, and Rolang Dewa (Garab Dorje). All the masters up to this point attained enlightenment together with their retinue and departed from this world without leaving a body behind. The dissolution of the physical body can also be attained through accomplishment in the mundane practices of essence-extract, manipulation of and control over the vital essences (bindu), or through prana mastery; but the accomplishment attained through the practice of Anu Yoga is superior because of transmuting the physical body of karmic ripening into luminosity by means of the practice connected to the nonconceptual wakefulness of the path of seeing. Subsequent masters in the transmission of Anu Yoga include Vajrahasya, Prabhahasti, Shakya Little Light, Shakyamitra, and Shakya Senge (Padmasambhava). In India, Padmasambhava transmitted the teachings to Master Hungkara. From him the lineage continued to Dewa Seldzey, Dharmabodhi, Dharma Rajapala, Vasudhara of Nepal, Tsuklag Palgey, and finally Chetsen Kye from the country of Drusha, who translated the Anu Yoga teachings into the Drusha language. This is the lineage that the translator Sangye Yeshe of Nub brought to Tibet.

Appearance and existence (snang srid)   The world and sentient beings; whatever can be experienced, the five elements, and has the possibility of existence, the five aggregates.

Approach and accomplishment (bsnyen sgrub)   *See* Four aspects of approach and accomplishment.

Arhat (dgra bcom pa)   "Foe destroyer," someone who has conquered the four maras and attained nirvana, the fourth and final result of the Hinayana path.

Arura   Medicinal plant endowed with many wonderful qualities.

Assemblage of Secrets (gsang ba 'dus pa)   A Mahayoga scripture, found in the *Nyingma Gyübum,* vol. TSA. Sometimes counted among the Eighteen Mahayoga Tantras, as the tantra of enlightened mind.

Assemblage of Sugatas (bde gshegs 'dus pa)   Important cycle of teachings connected to the Sadhana Section of Mahayoga. The tantras belonging to this cycle are found in the *Nyingma Gyübum,* vol. OM, as well as in the revelations of Nyang Ral Nyima Öser. These teachings were transmitted by Samantabhadra, who manifested in the form of the peaceful Vajrasattva and wrathful Chemchok Heruka. The Lord of Secrets compiled and entrusted them to the dakini Leykyi Wangmo. She concealed these tantras in the stupa called Enchanting Mound (bde byed brtsegs pa) and later transmitted them to the eight vidyadharas, one teaching to each master: Manjushri Body to Manjushrimitra, Lotus Speech to Nagarjuna, Vishuddha Mind to Hungkara, Nectar Quality to Vimalamitra, Kilaya Activity to Prabhahasti, Liberating Sorcery of Mother Deities to Dhana Samskrita, Maledictory Fierce Mantra to Shantigarbha, and Mundane Worship to Guhyachandra. Each of these vidyadharas later transmitted their teachings to Padmasambhava, who then became the main holder of all.

Ati Yoga (shin tu rnal 'byor)   The third of the Three Inner Tantras. According to Jamgön Kongtrül, it emphasizes the view that liberation is attained through growing accustomed to insight into the nature of primordial enlightenment, free from accepting and rejecting, hope and fear. The more common word for Ati Yoga nowadays is "Dzogchen." The Ati Yoga teachings first appeared in this world to Garab Dorje, in the country of Uddiyana, to the west of India. According to *The Narration of the Precious Revelation of the Terma Treasures* by Longchen Rabjam (pp. 87–88), the great master Padmasambhava described the teachings of Ati Yoga in the following way before imparting them to Yeshe Tsogyal:

It is an instruction unlike any I have given in the past, the summit that transcends all of the nine gradual vehicles. By seeing its vital point, mind-made views and meditations are shattered. The paths and levels are perfected with no need for struggle. Disturbing emotions are liberated into their natural state, without any need for reform or remedy. This instruction brings realization of a fruition within oneself that is not produced from causes. It instantly brings forth spontaneously present realization, liberates the material body of flesh and blood into the luminous sambhogakaya within this very lifetime, and enables you to capture the permanent abode, the precious dharmakaya realm of spontaneous presence, within three years, in the domain of Akanishtha. I possess such an instruction and I shall teach it to you!

See also Dzogchen; Great Perfection.

Atisha Dipamkara Eleventh-century Indian pandita from Vikramashila, who spent the last twelve years of his life in Tibet. Founding forefather of the Kadampa School of Tibetan Buddhism, also known as Dipamkara Shrijnana and Jowo Jey (jo bo rje).

Atsara Yeshe (a tsar ye shes) *See* Yeshe Yang.

Atsara Yeshe Yang of Ba (sba a tsar ye shes dbyangs) *See* Yeshe Yang.

Avalokiteshvara (spyan ras gzigs) The bodhisattva of boundless compassion; an emanation of Buddha Amitabha. Also known as Lord of Great Compassion or Great Compassionate One.

Avatamsaka Sutra (mdo phal po che) A sutra belonging to the third turning of the wheel of Dharma. Published as *The Flower Ornament Scripture*, 3 vols., Boston: Shambhala Publications, 1984–1987.

Awakened mind (byang chub kyi sems, Skt. bodhichitta) *See* Bodhichitta.

Awareness (rig pa, Skt. vidya)   When referring to the view of the Great Perfection, "awareness" means consciousness devoid of ignorance and dualistic fixation.

Bardo (bar do, Skt. antarabhava)   The intermediate state between death and the next rebirth.

Bashey Annals (sba bzhad)   Histories of the reigns of Trisong Deutsen and Muney Tsenpo.

Bhikshu (dge slong)   A practitioner who has renounced worldly life and taken the pledge to observe the 253 precepts of a fully ordained monk in order to attain liberation from samsara.

Bhikshu Purna (dge slong purna)   The previous life of the Tibetan translator Vairochana.

Black Powerful One (stobs ldan nag po)   The chief figure in the mandala of Maledictory Fierce Mantra from among the Eight Sadhana Teachings.

Bodhi (byang chub)   "Enlightenment," "awakening," "state of realization." *See also* Enlightenment.

Bodhichitta (byang sems, byang chub kyi sems)   "Awakened state of mind." (1) The aspiration to attain enlightenment for the sake of all beings. (2) In the context of Dzogchen, the innate wakefulness of awakened mind; synonymous with *rigpa*, awareness.

Bodhisattva (byang chub sems dpa')   Someone who has developed bodhichitta, the aspiration to attain enlightenment in order to benefit all sentient beings. A practitioner of the Mahayana path; especially a noble bodhisattva who has attained the first level.

Bönpo (bon po)   The religion prevalent in Tibet before the establishment of Buddhism in the ninth century.

Border Temples (mtha' 'dul)   "Border Subduers." Four temples built by Songtsen Gampo and his Chinese queen to subjugate evil forces in the outlying districts of Tibet.

Boundless Life (tshe dpag med pa, Skt. Amitayus)   (1) Buddha Amitayus. (2) A Mahayana sutra.

Brahma (tshangs pa)   The ruler of the gods of the realm of form.

Brahma-like voice (tshangs pa'i dbyangs)   The voice endowed with the sixteen perfect qualities of Brahma, the king of the gods. A common description of a buddha's speech.

Brahman (bram ze, Skt. brahmana)   Member of the priestly caste.

Buddha (sangs rgyas)   The "Enlightened" or "Awakened One," who has completely abandoned all obscurations and perfected every good quality. A perfected bodhisattva after attaining true and complete enlightenment is known as a buddha. The Buddha generally referred to is Shakyamuni Buddha, the buddha of this era, who lived in India during the sixth century B.C. There have been innumerable buddhas in past aeons, who manifested the way to enlightenment. In the current Good Aeon, there will be one thousand buddhas, of which Buddha Shakyamuni is the fourth.

Buddha Amitayus (tshe dpag med)   "Buddha of Boundless Life"; the sambhogakaya aspect of Amitabha. The buddha associated with the empowerment of longevity and longevity practice.

Buddha Avatamsaka (sangs rgyas phal po che)   (1) A Mahayana sutra. (2) The buddha after whom the *Avatamsaka Sutra* is named.

Buddha Unchanging Light (sangs rgyas 'od mi 'gyur ba)   The primordial buddha Samantabhadra; a synonym for the enlightened state of dharmakaya.

Buddhadharma (sangs rgyas kyi bstan pa, bstan pa, chos)   Buddhism, the teachings of the Buddha.

Buddhaguhya (sangs rgyas gsang ba)   An Indian master who visited Tibet and reamined at Mount Kailash, where he taught emissaries of King Trisong Deutsen.

Buddhahood (sangs rgyas)   The perfect and complete enlightenment, in which one dwells in neither samsara nor nirvana; the state of having eradicated all obscurations and being endowed with the wisdom of seeing the nature of things as they are and with the wisdom of perceiving all that exists.

Causal philosophical teachings (rgyu mtshan nyid kyi chos)   The teachings of Hinayana and Mahayana that regard the practices of the path as the causes for attaining the fruition of liberation and enlightenment.

Causal philosophical vehicles (rgyu mtshan nyid kyi theg pa)   The two vehicles, Hinayana and Mahayana. *See also* Resultant vehicle.

Causal vehicles (rgyu'i theg pa)   *See* Causal philosophical vehicles.

Cave of Yangleshö (yang le shod kyi brag phug)   Situated in the southern end of the Kathmandu Valley, near the village of Pharping. The Upper Cave of Yangleshö is also known as Asura Cave.

Chamara (rnga gyab)   One of the eight subcontinents surrounding Mount Sumeru as well as the support for the terrestrial pure land of Guru Rinpoche, known as the Glorious Copper-Colored Mountain.

Chang (chang)   Tibetan wine, usually made from barley grains.

Charnel ground (dur khrod)   A site where bodies are left to decompose or be eaten by wild animals. Frequented by ghosts and spirits, it is a suitable place for advanced practitioners to gain progress in their realization.

Chemchok Heruka (che mchog he ru ka)   *See* Most Supreme.

Chimphu (chims phu)   The hermitage of caves above Samye in Central Tibet. Guru Rinpoche spent several years there in retreat.

Chinese teacher Hashang (rgya nag gi ston pa hva zhang)   A certain Chinese meditation teacher, Hashang Mahayana, whose viewpoint was refuted by Kamalashila in a public debate during the early spread of the teachings.

Chiti Yoga (spyi ti'i rnal 'byor)   One of the subdivisions of the Instruction Section of Dzogchen: Ati, Chiti, and Yangti. Chiti is defined as covering the general points of Dzogchen.

Chogdung (cog brdungs)   Minor teachings associated with the deity Yamantaka, the wrathful aspect of Manjushri.

Chokro Lui Gyaltsen (cog ro klu'i rgyal mtshan)   Early Tibetan translator of great importance and one of the twenty-five disciples of Padmasambhava, who recognized him as an incarnate bodhisattva. He worked closely with Vimalamitra, Jnanagarbha, Jinamitra, and Surendrabodhi. He is vital to the continuation of the Vinaya lineage in Tibet. Having attained realization at Chuwori, he aided Padmasambhava in transcribing and concealing terma treasures. The great tertön Karma Lingpa (fourteenth century) is regarded as a reincarnation of Chokro Lui Gyaltsen.

Compassion that has the Dharma as its focus (chos la dmigs pa'i snying rje)   Compassion that arises due to understanding the causes and conditions for suffering: ignorance, delusion, disturbing emotions, and the mistaken belief in an individual self and a real self-entity in phenomena. The yogi who perceives that all sentient beings undergo such self-inflicted suffering is overcome with the deepest compassion.

Compassion that is beyond a focus (dmigs pa med pa'i snying rje) This is the ultimate form of compassion. When the practitioner recognizes and realizes the innate nature, compassion is spontaneously present as an intrinsic quality that transcends the domain of ordinary dualistic confines.

Completion stage (rdzogs rim) One of the two aspects of Vajrayana practice. The meaning and depth of this principle change while ascending through the outer and inner sections of tantra. For instance, the completion stage defined as the dissolving of the visualization of a deity corresponds to Maha Yoga; the "completion stage with marks" based on yogic practices such as tummo corresponds to Anu Yoga; and the "completion stage without marks" is the practice of Ati Yoga. See also Development stage.

Crystal Cave of Drag Yangdzong (sgrag yang rdzong shel gyi brag phug) The retreat place of Padmasambhava's body. Situated between Lhasa and Samye in Central Tibet.

Crystal Cave of Yarlung (gyar klung shel gyi brag phug) One of the five major retreat places of Guru Rinpoche; the place of enlightened qualities. It is also the site where one of his chief disciples, Kharchen Yeshe Shönnu, attained realization of Nectar Quality. Situated one day's walk above Tramdruk in the Yarlung valley, Central Tibet.

Daka (dpa' bo) (1) Emanation of the chief figure in the mandala, who fulfills the four activities; male counterpart of dakinis. (2) Male enlightened practitioner of Vajrayana.

Dakini (mkha' 'gro ma) Spiritual beings who fulfill the enlightened activities; female tantric deities who protect and serve the Buddhist doctrine and practitioners. Also one of the three roots. See also Guru, yidam, and dakini.

Damaru (da ma ru) A small hand drum used in tantric rituals.

Dark age (snyigs ma'i dus) The present age, when the five degenerations of life span, era, beings, views, and disturbing emotions are rampant.

Demigod (lha ma yin) One of the six classes of beings.

Deva (lha) "Gods," the highest of the six classes of samsaric beings. Temporarily, they enjoy a heavenly state of existence.

Devadatta (lhas byin) Opponent and competitor of the Buddha. A proud scion of the Shakya clan whose pride prevented him from appreciating the qualities of the Buddha.

Development and completion (bskyed rdzogs) The two main aspects, means and knowledge, of vajrayana practice. Briefly stated, development stage means positive mental fabrication while completion stage means resting in the unfabricated nature of mind. *See also* Completion stage; Development stage.

Development stage (bskyed rim, Skt. utpattikrama) One of the two aspects of Vajrayana practice: the mental creation of pure images in order to purify habitual tendencies. The essence of the development stage is pure perception or sacred outlook, which means to perceive sights, sounds, and thoughts as deity, mantra, and wisdom.

Dhana Sanskrita (nor gyi legs sbyar) One of the eight vidyadharas, the receiver of the transmissions of Liberating Sorcery of Mother Deities, Mamo Bötong. Not much is available about his life, except his birthplace in the Thogar area of Uddiyana.

Dharma protector (chos skyong, Skt. dharmapala) Nonhumans who vow to protect and guard the teachings of the Buddha and its followers. Dharma protectors can be either mundane, i.e., virtuous samsaric beings, or wisdom dharma protectors, who are emanations of buddhas or bodhisattvas.

Dharmadhatu (chos kyi dbyings) The "realm of phenomena"; the suchness in which emptiness and dependent origination are inseparable. The nature of mind and phenomena, which lies beyond arising, dwelling, and ceasing.

Dharmadhatu palace of Akanishtha ('og min chos kyi dbyings kyi pho brang) Figurative expression for the abode of Vajradhara or Samantabhadra, the dharmakaya buddha. *Akanishtha* means "highest" or "unsurpassed."

Dharmakaya (chos sku) The first of the three kayas, which is devoid of constructs, like space. The "body" of enlightened qualities. Should be understood individually according to ground, path, and fruition. *See also* Three kayas.

Dharmata (chos nyid) The innate nature of phenomena and mind.

Dharmic (chos kyi)   Of or pertaining to the Dharma; religious or pious.

Dilgo Khyentse (ldil mgo mkhyen brtse)   *See* His Holiness Dilgo Khyentse Rinpoche.

Divine Valley Water (gshong pa'i lha chu)   Even today, a place with clear and sweet water, situated near Lhasa in Central Tibet.

Dorje Drakpo Tsal (rdo rje drag po rtsal)   "Powerful Vajra Wrath." A wrathful form of Guru Rinpoche.

Dorje Drolö (rdo rje gro lod)   A wrathful form of Padmasambhava, especially known for subduing evil forces and concealing termas for the welfare of future generations.

Dosher Trelchung (mdo gzher sprel chung)   A minister of King Trisong Deutsen; also spelled Dershey Trelchung (sder bzhed sprel chung).

Drenpa Namkha (dran pa nam mkha')   Tibetan translator and disciple of Padmasambhava. At first, he was an influential Bönpo priest, but later he studied with Padmasambhava and also learned translation. Due to his miraculous power, he is said to have tamed a wild yak simply by a threatening gesture. He offered numerous Bönpo teachings to Padmasambhava, who then concealed them as a terma treasure.

Drey (bre)   Tibetan measure of volume, equivalent to about one liter or quart. One drey of gold would weigh about 13 kilograms.

Dzogchen (rdzogs pa chen po. Skt. mahasandhi)   Also known as Great Perfection and Ati Yoga. The highest teachings of the Nyingma School of the Early Translations. In this world, the most well-known human lineage masters are: Garab Dorje, Manjushrimitra, Shri Singha, Jnanasutra, Vimalamitra, Padmasambhava, and Vairochana. Dzogchen has two chief aspects: the lineage of scriptures and the lineage of teachings (dpe brgyud dang bka' brgyud). The scriptures are contained in the tantras of the three sections of Dzogchen: Mind Section, Space Section, and Instruction Section. The first two were brought to Tibet chiefly by Vairochana, while the Instruction Section was mainly transmitted by Vimalamitra and Padmasambhava. In addition, numerous Dzogchen termas were concealed by these masters and revealed through the following centuries. The lineage of teachings is embodied in the oral instructions one receives personally from a qualified master and holder of the Dzogchen lineage. The Tibetan historian Guru Tashi Tobgyal elaborates in his *Ocean of Wondrous Sayings* about Padmasambhava's specific lineage of Dzogchen in the following way:

> The great master is of the same nature as the infinite number of buddhas of the three kayas and does, therefore, not depend upon the concept of linear transmission. He is indivisible from the buddhas and the pure realms of the three kayas. However, in accordance with how other people perceive, Padmasambhava is not only the master of the numberless tantras of Vajrayana, but possesses a unique short lineage of mastery over the profound topics of Nyingtig, the Luminous Great Perfection of the definitive meaning, entrusted to him by the three masters Garab Dorje, Manjushrimitra, and Shri Singha. In particular, Padmasambhava acted upon a prophecy from Vajra Varahi and then received detailed teachings from Shri Singha.

Early and later translation of the Great Perfection (rdzogs pa chen po snga 'gyur phyi 'gyur) This phrase refers to the Eighteen Major Scriptures of the Mind Section, a set of Dzogchen tantras taught by Shri Singha to Vairochana and Lekdrub of Tsang, as listed in chapter 14 and found in the *Nyingma Gyübum*, vol. KA. Five of them were translated by Vairochana before his exile to Tsawarong, while the remaining thirteen were later translated by Vimalamitra and Yudra Nyingpo, hence the name. They are also known as the eighteen mothers and children of the Mind Section (sems sde ma bu bco brgyad).

Early Translations (snga 'gyur) A synonym for the Nyingma tradition, the "old school." *See also* Nyingma School.

Eight charnel grounds (dur khrod brgyad) (1) Cool Grove (bsil ba tshal, Skt. sitavana) to the east, (2) Perfected in Body (sku la rdzogs) to the south, (3) Lotus Mound (pad ma brtsegs) to the west, (4) Lanka Mound (lan ka brtsegs) to the north, (5) Spontaneously Accomplished Mound (lhun grub brtsegs) to the southeast, (6) Display of Great Secret (gsang chen rol pa) to the southwest, (7) Pervasive

Great Joy (he chen brdal ba) to the northwest, and (8) World Mound ('jig rten brtsegs) to the northeast. There are also numerous other lists of charnel grounds.

Eight classes of gods and demons (lha srin sde brgyad)   There are various enumerations, but in the sutras the most general is: devas, nagas, yakshas, gandharvas, asuras, garudas, kinnaras, and mahoragas. All of them were able to receive and practice the teachings of the Buddha. These eight classes can also refer to various types of mundane spirits, who can either help or cause harm, but remain invisible to normal human beings: ging, mara, tsen, yaksha, rakshasa, mamo, rahula, and naga. On a subtle level, they are regarded as the impure manifestation of the eight types of consciousness.

Eight disciples (rje 'bangs brgyad)   The eight chief recipients in Tibet of the Eight Sadhana Teachings transmitted by Guru Rinpoche: King Trisong Deutsen, Namkhai Nyingpo, Sangye Yeshe, Gyalwa Cho-yang, Yeshe Tsogyal, Palgyi Yeshe, Palgyi Senge, and Vairochana.

Eight Maya Sections (sgyu 'phrul sde brgyad)   The Essence of Secrets, the Forty Magical Nets, the Unsurpassable Magical Net, the Leulag Magical Net, the Eightfold Magical Net, the Magical Net of the Goddess, the Magical Net in Eighty Chapters, and the Magical Net of Manjushri. In his *Essence of Accomplishment* (p. 6A:4), Mipham Rinpoche explains that the view in the Eight Maya Sections belongs to Ati Yoga, while the conduct they teach belongs to Mahayoga. For that reason they are sometimes said to be classified in between as Anu Yoga tantras. In any case, they reveal the key points of the development stage, the completion stage, and the Great Perfection and can therefore be classified under any of the three inner tantras.

Eight Sadhana Teachings (sgrub pa bka' brgyad)   Eight chief yidam deities of Mahayoga and their corresponding tantras and sadhanas: Manjushri Body, Lotus Speech, Vishuddha Mind, Nectar Quality, Kilaya Activity, Liberating Sorcery of Mother Deities, Maledictory Fierce Mantra, and Mundane Worship. *See also* Assemblage of Suga-tas; Sadhana Section.

Eight vidyadharas (rig 'dzin brgyad)   Manjushrimitra, Nagarjuna, Hung-kara, Vimalamitra, Prabhahasti, Dhana Sanskrita, Shantigarbha, and Guhyachandra.

Eighteen inner tantras of Secret Mantra (gsang sngags nang gi rgyud sde bco brgyad)   In the context of chapter 12, the term refers chiefly to the tantras of Mahayoga. They were translated into Tibetan by Padmasambhava and Chokro Lui Gyaltsen. *See also* Eighteen Mahayoga Tantras.

Eighteen Mahayoga Tantras (ma ha yo ga'i rgyud sde bco brgyad)   Listed in chapter 12. An alternative list is given by Shechen Gyaltsab in his historical work entitled the *Pond of White Lotus Flowers* and in Guru Tashi Tobgyal's *Ocean of Wondrous Sayings to Delight the Learned Ones*: (1–5) Five basic root tantras of body, speech, mind, quality, and activity: *Sarvabuddha Samayoga, Secret Moon Essence, Assemblage of Secrets, Glorious Supreme Primal Tantra,* and *Activity Garland.* (6–10) Five display tantras functioning as the utilization of sadhana practice: *Heruka Display Tantra, Supreme Steed Display Tantra, Compassion Display Tantra, Nectar Display Tantra,* and *Twelvefold Kilaya Tantra.* (11–15) Five tantras functioning as subsidiaries to conduct: *Mountain Pile, Awesome Wisdom Lightning, Arrangement of Samaya, One-Pointed Samadhi,* and the *Rampant Elephant Tantra.* (16–17) Two subsequent tantras of amending incompleteness: *Magical Net of Vairochana* and *Skillful Lasso.* (18) The one outstanding tantra that epitomizes them all: *The Essence of Secrets,* the *Tantra of the Magical Net of Vajrasattva,* also known as *Guhyagarbha.*

Eighteen Major Scriptures (lung chen po bco brgyad)   *See* Early and later translation of the Great Perfection.

Eighteen Marvels of Mind in Fifty Chapters (sems rmad du byung ba bco brgyad kyi le'u lnga bcu)   Several tantras in the first three volumes of the *Nyingma Gyübum* bear a resembling name, although none of them have fifty chapters. A writing mistake seems to have appeared, since the *Bright Crystal Mirror* by Yeshe Tsogyal says instead: "Five first parts of the *Eighteen Marvels of Mind*" (sems smad bco brgyad kyi stod kyi lnga), referring to the first five tantras translated by Vairochana.

Eightfold Magical Net (sgyu 'phrul brgyad pa)   A Mahayoga scripture in eight chapters, found in the *Nyingma Gyübum,* vol. PHA.

Eightfold Volume (bam po brgyad pa)   Tantra belonging to the Sadhana Section of Mahayoga; focused on Nectar Quality. A tantra with a similar title is found in the *Nyingma Gyübum,* vol. LA. Possibly identical with the *Scripture in Eight Chapters.* See also *Scripture in Eight Chapters.*

EMAHO (e ma ho)   An exclamation of wonder and amazement.

Embodiment of Realization (dgongs 'dus)   Anu Yoga scripture of major importance. Abbreviation of *The Scripture of the Embodiment of the Realization of All Buddhas* (sangs rgyas thams cad kyi dgongs pa 'dus pa'i mdo).

Empowerment (dbang, Skt. abhisheka)   The conferring of power or authorization to practice the Vajrayana teachings; the indispensable entrance door to tantric practice. Empowerment gives control over one's innate vajra body, vajra speech, and vajra mind and the authority to regard forms as deity, sounds as mantra, and thoughts as wisdom. *See also* Four empowerments.

Empowerment of direct anointment (rgyal thabs spyi blugs kyi dbang)   The act of bestowing the four empowerments condensed into one, transferring the totality of blessings, just as a king would empower the crown prince to wield total authority.

Empowerment of the expression of awareness (rig pa'i rtsal gyi dbang)   The empowerment for practicing Dzogchen. Sometimes it also refers to the stage of realization achieved thorugh Dzogchen practice.

Empty and luminous dharmata (chos nyid stong gsal)   A synonym for buddha nature, the enlightened essence within all beings.

Enlightenment (byang chub, Skt. bodhi)   Usually the same as the state of buddhahood, characterized by perfection of the accumulations of merit and wisdom, and by the removal of the two obscurations, but sometimes also the lower stages of enlightenment of an arhat or a pratyekabuddha.

Epagsha of Drugu (gru gu e pag sha)   One of the first Tibetans to take ordination; received transmission from Hungkara in India, together with Namkhai Nyingpo.

Equal taste (ro mnyam)   A high level of realization; perceiving the empty nature of all things.

Essence of Secrets (gsang ba'i snying po, Skt. Guhyagarbha)   The widely renowned tantra of the Early Translations which, according to Jamgön Kongtrül, is the chief of the Eighteen Mahayoga Tantras, exalted above them all like the banner of victory. The first text in the *Nyingma Gyübum*, vol. PHA. A great number of commentaries on this tantra is found in the *Nyingma Kama* collection.

Essence-extract (bcud len, Skt. rasayana)   A practice which sustains the living body with the essences of medicinal plants, minerals, and elemental energy in order to purify the body, heighten concentration, and avoid the diversions of seeking ordinary material food.

Ever-Excellent Lady (kun tu bzang mo, Skt. Samantabhadri)   "The All-good," the mother of all the buddhas of the three times; the female counterpart of the dharmakaya buddha Samantabhadra. She symbolizes emptiness and dharmadhatu.

Expedient and definitive meaning (drang don dang nges don, Skt. neyartha, nitartha)   The "expedient meaning" refers to conventional teachings on karma, path, and result, which are designed to lead the practitioner to the "definitive meaning," the insight into emptiness, suchness, and buddha nature.

Eye of dharma (chos kyi mig)   The faculty that sees reality without obscurations.

Feast offering (tshogs kyi 'khor lo, Skt. ganachakra)   A feast assembly performed by Vajrayana practitioners to accumulate merit and purify the sacred commitments.

Fierce mantras (drag sngags)   A certain type of mantra belonging to wrathful deities. They are used to dispel demonic forces that obstruct the continuation of the Buddhadharma or the welfare of sentient beings.

Fifty-eight herukas (khrag 'thung lnga bcu nga brgyad)   The five male and female herukas, eight yoginis, eight tramen goddesses, four female gatekeepers, and twenty-eight ishvaris.

Final Subsequent Mantra Tantra (phyi ma'i phyi ma sngags kyi rgyud)   Tantra belonging to the Sadhana Section of Mahayoga, found in the *Nyingma Gyübum*, vol. OM.

Five buddha families   *See* Five families.

Five early and thirteen later translations of the Great Perfection (rdzogs pa chen po snga 'gyur lnga dang phyi 'gyur bcu gsum)   *See* Early and later translations of the Great Perfection.

Five Families (rigs lnga)   Name of a sadhana text composed by Guru Rinpoche focused on Mahayoga tantra.

Five families (rigs lnga, Skt. panchakula) The five buddha families: tathagata, vajra, ratna, padma, and karma. They represent five aspects of innate qualities of the tathagatagarbha, our enlightened essence.

Five families of sugatas (bde gshegs rigs lnga) The five families or aspects of victorious ones: Vairochana, Akshobhya, Ratnasambhava, Amitabha, and Amoghasiddhi.

Five-hundred-year period (dus lnga brgya) Periods of each five hundred years. The Buddhadharma is said to last ten such periods.

Five kayas of fruition ('bras bu'i skabs kyi sku lnga) The five aspects of perfect enlightenment are described by Padmasambhava in his *Lamrim Yeshe Nyingpo:*

> The perfection of the benefit of oneself is the peaceful dharmakaya.
> The spontaneously present benefit for others is the unified sambhogakaya.
> The manifold skillful means to tame beings is the way of nirmanakaya.
> The distinct and unmixed appearance aspect is the true bodhikaya.
> Their one taste as dharmadhatu of the emptiness aspect is the vajrakaya.

Five poisonous kleshas (nyon mongs pa dug lnga) *See* Klesha.

Five poisons (dug lnga) *See* Klesha.

Five sciences (rig pa'i gnas lnga) Grammar, dialectics, healing, arts and crafts, and religious philosophy.

Five wisdoms (ye shes lnga, Skt. panchajnana) The dharmadhatu wisdom, mirrorlike wisdom, wisdom of equality, discriminating wisdom, and all-accomplishing wisdom. They represent five distinctive functions of the tathagatagarbha, our enlightened essence.

Forty-two peaceful deities (zhi ba bzhi bcu zhe gnyis) Samantabhadra and Samantabhadri, the five male and female buddhas, the eight male and female bodhisattvas, the six munis, and the four male and female gatekeepers.

Four activities (las bzhi, Skt. karma) Pacifying, increasing, magnetizing, and subjugating.

Four aspects of approach and accomplishment (bsnyen sgrub kyi yan lag bzhi) Approach, full approach, accomplishment, and great accomplishment. Four important aspects of Vajrayana practice, especially with regard to the recitation stage of yidam practice. These four aspects, however, can apply to any level of meaning within the tantras. Their traditional analogy is to invite the ruler of a country, to present him with gifts and make a specific request, to obtain his permission to carry out one's aim, and to use one's authority to accomplish the welfare of self and others. In the context of recitation practice, "approach" is to visualize the yidam deity with the mantra in its heart center; "full approach" is the spinning garland of mantra syllables emanating light rays, making offerings to all the buddhas in the ten directions; "accomplishment" is to receive their blessings, which purify all one's obscurations; and "great accomplishment" is to transform the world into the mandala of a pure realm, the beings into male and female deities, sounds into mantra, and all thoughts and emotions into a pure display of innate wakefulness.

Four continents (gling bzhi)   The four continents surrounding Mount Sumeru: Superior Body, Jambu continent, Cow Utilizing, and Unpleasant Sound.

Four districts of Tibet (bod ru bzhi)   Four areas in Central Tibet flanking the rivers Kyichu and Tsangpo.

Four empowerments (dbang bzhi)   The vase, secret, wisdom-knowledge, and precious word empowerments. Padmasambhava says in the *Lamrim Yeshe Nyingpo*:

> The vase empowerment, which purifies the body and the nadis, is the seed of the vajra body and nirmanakaya. The secret empowerment, which purifies the speech and the pranas, is the seed of the vajra speech and sambhogakaya. The phonya empowerment, which purifies the mind and the essences, is the seed of the vajra mind and dharmakaya. The ultimate empowerment, which purifies the habitual patterns of the all-ground, is the seed of the vajra wisdom and svabhavikakaya.

Four great rivers of transmissions (bka' babs kyi chu bo chen po bzhi)   The rivers of empowerment of yidam, tantric scriptures, spiritual friend, and of the expression of awareness. These four transmissions originate from Garab Dorje, King Jah, Buddhaguhya, and Shri Singha, respectively.

Four immeasurables (tshad med bzhi) Love, compassion, joy, and impartiality. Also called the "four abodes of Brahma" because their
cultivation causes rebirth as the king of the gods in the realm of form
within samsaric existence. When embraced by the attitude of bodhichitta, the wish to attain enlightenment for the welfare of others,
their cultivation causes the attainment of unexcelled buddhahood.

Four means of magnetizing (bsdu ba'i dngos po bzhi) Being generous,
uttering kind words, giving appropriate teachings, and keeping con-
sistency between words and conduct.

Four remati sisters (re ma ti mched bzhi) Part of the group of female
protectors of the Dharma known as the twelve tenma goddesses.
They approached Padmasambhava while he was practicing in the
Asura Cave, situated between India and Nepal. He gave them the
nectar of samaya and made them take an oath. Practitioners are still
required to present these twelve guardians with a regular offering
torma to ensure that they fulfill the demanded activities.

Four results of spiritual practice (dge sbyor gyi 'bras bu bzhi) *See*
Shravaka.

Four semo sisters (bse mo mched bzhi) *See* Four remati sisters.

Four shvana sisters (shva na mched bzhi) *See* Four remati sisters.

Four vidyadhara levels (rig 'dzin rnam pa bzhi'i go 'phang) The four
stages of attainment of knowledge-holders, masters of the four stages
of the tantric path of Mahayoga. The four vidyadhara levels are the
maturation, longevity (life mastery), mahamudra, and spontaneous
perfection. *See also* Vidyadhara level of longevity, mahamudra, maturation, and spontaneous perfection.

Fruition ('bras bu, Skt. phala) The end of the path. Usually the state of
complete and perfect buddhahood. Can also refer to one of the three
levels of enlightenment—of a shravaka, pratyekabuddha, or bodhisattva. *See also* View, meditation, conduct, and fruition.

Fruition of nonreturn (phyir mi ldog pa'i 'bras bu) Liberation from
samsara or the omniscient state of buddhahood.

Fulfillment ritual (bskang ba, bskang chog) A practice to purify outer,
inner, and secret or innermost breaches and violations of a practitioner's Hinayana precepts, Mahayana vows, or Vajrayana commitments.

Gandharva (dri za)   A class of sentient beings who live on scents. Gandharvas are also a type of celestial musicians living on the rim of Mount Sumeru in cloudlike castles. Often a "city of the gandharvas" is used as an analogy for illusory phenomena, like a fairy castle in the clouds.

Garab Dorje (dga' rab rdo rje, Skt. Surativajra, Prahevajra, Pramodavajra)   The incarnation of Semlhag Chen, a god who earlier had been empowered by the buddhas. Immaculately conceived, his mother was a nun, the daughter of King Uparaja (Dhahenatalo or Indrabhuti) of Uddiyana. Garab Dorje received all the tantras, scriptures, and oral instructions of Dzogchen from Vajrasattva and Vajrapani in person and became the first human vidyadhara in the Dzogchen lineage. Having reached the state of complete enlightenment through the effortless Great Perfection, Garab Dorje transmitted the teachings to his retinue of exceptional beings. Manjushrimitra is regarded as his chief disciple. Padmasambhava is also known to have received the transmission of the Dzogchen tantras directly from Garab Dorje's wisdom form.

Garuda (mkha' lding)   The mythological bird, able to travel from one end of the universe to the other with a single movement of its wings. It is also known to hatch from the egg fully developed and ready to soar through the sky.

Gate-keeping pandita (sgo bsrung ba'i pan di ta)   At the major monastic institutions in ancient India, it was the custom to nominate competent scholars to the position of defending the view of Buddhism through debate, one at each of the gates in the four directions of the monastery.

Ging (ging)   A class of beings, both male and female, often mentioned as recipients of the residual offerings in a feast ceremony. They also appear in the retinue of Buddhist deities acting as offering servants and dancers.

Glorious Blazing Wrathful Goddess Tantra (dpal 'bar ba khro mo'i rgyud)   A Mahayoga scripture. A tantra of this name is found in the Nyingma Gyübum, vol. PA.

Glorious Copper-Colored Mountain (zangs mdog dpal ri)   The terrestrial pure land of Guru Rinpoche, situated on the subcontinent

Chamara to the southeast of the Jambu continent. Chamara is the central of a configuration of nine islands inhabited by savage rakshasas. In the middle of Chamara rises the majestic copper-colored mountain into the skies. On its summit lies the magical palace Lotus Light, manifested from the natural expression of primordial wakefulness. Here resides Padmasambhava in an indestructible bodily form, transcending birth and death, for as long as samsara continues and through which he incessantly brings benefit to beings through magical emanations of his body, speech, and mind.

Glorious Supreme Primal Tantra (dpal mchog dang po'i rgyud, Skt. Shri Paramadi Tantra)   One the four major sections of yoga tantra. A tantra of the same title is sometimes listed among the Eighteen Mahayoga Tantras as the tantra of enlightened qualities.

Gola (go la, so chang)   A drink of sugar cane or grain from Nepal.

Gongpo spirits ('gong po)   A type of evil spirit symbolizing ego-clinging, sometimes counted among the eight classes of gods and demons. When subdued by a great master, they can also act as guardians of the Buddhadharma.

Good Aeon (bskal pa bzang po, Skt. bhadrakalpa)   This present aeon, in which one thousand buddhas will appear, lasting no less than 160 million years.

Great Compassionate One (thugs rje chen po, Skt. Mahakarunika)   *See* Avalokiteshvara.

Great Garuda View Scripture (lta ba khyung chen gyi lung)   A tantra with a similar title is found in the *Nyingma Gyübum*, vol. KA.

Great Glacier Lady of Invincible Turquoise Mist (gangs kyi yum chen rdo rje g.yu bun ma)   A protector of the Dharma teachings bound under oath by Padmasambhava. She was formerly a Bönpo warrior spirit (dgra lha).

Great Glorious One (dpal chen)   Identical with Vishuddha Heruka in the case of Namkhai Nyingpo's vision.

Great Perfection (rdzogs pa chen po, Skt. mahasandhi)   The third of the three inner tantras of the Nyingma School. The Great Perfection is the ultimate of all the 84,000 profound and extensive sections of the Dharma, the realization of Buddha Samantabhadra exactly as it is. *See also* Ati Yoga; Dzogchen.

Guru, yidam, and dakini (bla ma yi dam mkha' 'gro) The three roots of Vajrayana practice: the guru is the root of blessings, the yidam is the root of accomplishments, and the dakini is the root of activities.

Guru Rinpoche (gu ru rin po che) "Precious Master," the lotus-born tantric master who established Vajrayana Buddhism in Tibet in the ninth century at the invitation of King Trisong Deutsen. He manifested the attainment of the four vidyadhara levels. He hid innumerable Dharma treasures throughout Tibet, Nepal, and Bhutan to be revealed by destined disciples in the centuries to come. Guru Rinpoche resides on the summit of the Copper-Colored Mountain on the southeastern continent. He is also known by the names Padmasambhava and Padmakara. *See also* Padmakara.

Guru Vidyadhara (bla ma rig 'dzin) A deity and set of scriptures belonging to the Nine Sadhana Sections. Often the Guru Vidyadhara and the eight herukas in the Eight Sadhana Teachings form a single mandala with nine groups of deities. The chief existing scripture for the teachings on Guru Vidyadhara is called the *Root Tantra of the Assemblage of Vidyadharas* (rig 'dzin 'dus pa rtsa ba'i rgyud) and is the fifteenth tantra within the Assemblage of Sugatas, an immensely detailed collection of teachings on the Eight Sadhana Teachings and associated Vajrayana material brought to Tibet by Padmasambhava and taught to his main disciple. The *Assemblage of Sugatas* was concealed as a terma and later revealed by Nyang Ral Nyima Öser. The practice of Guru Vidyadhara is expressed through the principle known as the four aspects of approach and accomplishment. The most detailed terma on this principle was revealed by Sangye Lingpa (1340–1396) and is still renowned as *Lama Gongdü* (bla ma dgongs 'dus) in eighteen volumes of approximately seven hundred pages each. The Guru Vidyadhara is also the basis for innumerable sadhanas propagated by other tertöns, for instance the Rigdzin Dupa cycle within the termas of Longchen Nyingtig as well as the Barchey Kunsel cycle revealed by Chokgyur Lingpa and Jamyang Khyentse Wangpo, which are both widely practiced to this day.

Gyalmo Tsawarong (rgyal mo tsha ba rong) A district between eastern Tibet and China.

Gyalpo spirits (rgyal po) A type of mischievous spirit, sometimes counted among the eight classes of gods and demons. When subdued

by a great master, they can also act as guardians of the Buddhadharma.

Gyalto Rami (rgyal to ra mi)   Minister of King Trisong Deutsen; also
spelled Gyatong Rakyim (rgya stong ra khyim).

Gyalwa Cho-yang (rgyal ba mchog dbyangs)   A close disciple of Guru
Rinpoche, who attained accomplishment through the practice of
Hayagriva and later was incarnated as the Karmapas. Born in the clan
of Ngenlam in the Phen Valley, he took ordination from Khenpo
Bodhisattva in the first group of seven Tibetan monks. It is said that
he kept his vows with utmost purity. Having received the transmission of Hayagriva from Padmasambhava, he practiced in solitude and
reached the level of a vidyadhara.

Gyalwa Cho-yang of Ngenlam (ngan lam rgyal ba mchog dbyangs)   *See*
Gyalwa Cho-yang.

Gyalwey Lodrö of Drey ('bre rgyal ba'i blo gros)   One of the first
Tibetans to take ordination as a monk. He received transmission
from Hungkara in India. At first, he was a trusted attendant of
Trisong Deutsen by the name Gönpo and, later, at the time of taking
ordination, he was given the name Gyalwey Lodrö, "Victorious
Intelligence." He became erudite in translation and attained accomplishment after receiving transmission from Humkara. It is said that
he visited the land of Yama, the Lord of Death, and saved his mother
from the hell realms. After receiving teachings from Padmasambhava,
he displayed the feat of transforming a zombie into gold. Some of
this gold has been revealed in termas in later times. He achieved the
vidyadhara level of longevity and is reputed to have lived until the
time of Rongzom Pandita Chökyi Sangpo (rong zom chos kyi bzang
po; 1012–1088), to whom he gave teachings.

Gyatsa Lhanang (rgya tsha lha snang)   A minister of King Trisong
Deutsen; also spelled Gyaltsa Lhanang (rgyal tsha lha snang).

Hashang (hva shang)   In this book, one of the construction masters of
Samye was a Chinese known as Hashang Mahayana, and a Chinese
doctor by the name of Hashang Tetsa (hva shang te tsa) also occurs
here. Finally, Hashang is mentioned as one of the countries whose
language served as a source of the Dharma, and from which
translations were made. *See also* Chinese teacher Hashang.

Haughty spirit (dregs pa)   A certain type of malevolent spirit.

Hayagriva (rta mgrin)   Tantric deity always shown with a horse's head within his flaming hair; wrathful aspect of Buddha Amitabha. Here, he is identical with Padma Heruka, Lotus Speech, from among the Eight Sadhana Teachings.

Hearing lineage (nyan brgyud)   The lineage of oral teachings from master to disciple, as distinct from the scriptural lineage of textual transmission. The hearing lineage emphasizes the key points of oral instruction rather than elaborate philosophical learning.

Hepori (has po ri)   A big hill at Samye. One of four sacred mountains in Central Tibet.

Heretic (mu stegs pa)   *See* Non-Buddhist.

Heruka (khrag 'thung)   Literally, "blood drinker." A wrathful deity; drinker of the blood of ego-clinging.

Heruka Galpo (he ru ka gal po)   One of the Eighteen Mahayoga Tantras; focused on Vishuddha Mind. Both the Galpo and the Galpoche tantras are found in the *Nyingma Gyübum*, vol. RA.

Hinayana (theg pa dman pa)   The vehicles focused on contemplation of the four noble truths and the twelve links of dependent origination for the sake of individual liberation.

His Holiness Dilgo Khyentse Rinpoche (skyabs rje ldil mgo mkhyen brtse rin po che; 1910–1991)   Regarded by followers of all four schools as one of the foremost masters of Tibetan Buddhism. Among his other names are Rabsel Dawa and Tashi Paljor, and his tertön names Ösel Trulpey Dorje and Pema Do-ngak Lingpa.

Hundred and Eight Sadhanas of Guru Vidyadhara (bla ma rig 'dzin gyi sgrub thabs brgya rtsa brgyad)   One of the Nine Sadhana Sections of Mahayoga.

Hundred peaceful and wrathful divinities (zhi khro'i lha brgya)   The forty-two peaceful and fifty-eight wrathful deities. *See* Fifty-eight herukas; forty-two peaceful deities.

Hundred Thousand Tika Scripture ('bum gyi ti ka'i rgyud lung)   One of the Eighteen Mahayoga Tantras. Found in the *Nyingma Gyübum*, vol. OM.

Hungkara   One of the eight vidyadharas; receiver of the tantras of Vishuddha Mind, including Heruka Galpo. Having taken birth in either India or Nepal, at first he was erudite in a non-Buddhist religion and gained some attainments. Later his faith awakened in the Buddhist teachings, he took ordination from Buddhajnana at Nalanda, and he studied both the outer and inner aspects of Secret Mantra. His name derives from the chief deity of the mandala into which he was first initiated. At some point he took an outcaste girl as consort and practiced the four aspects of approach and accomplishment for six months. Through that practice he had a vision of the entire mandala of Vajra Heruka and reached the attainment of the supreme accomplishment of mahamudra. He wrote the *Golden Garland of Rulu*, the *Vishuddha Accomplishment*, as well as other treatises and benefited beings with tremendous activity. Finally, he departed to the realm of Buddha Akshobhya in his very body. He was associated with Rolang Sukhasiddhi, Kukuraja, and Buddhaguhya, while his lineage was transmitted to Padmasambhava and Namkhai Nyingpo, who spread his teachings in India.

Indrabodhi (rgyal po indra bodhi)   The king of the country of Uddiyana during the appearance of Padmasambhava in this world. Sometimes his name is spelled Indrabhuti.

Innermost Essence (gsang ba snying thig)   In general identical with the Instruction Section, the third of three divisions of Dzogchen. In particular it refers to the Innermost Unexcelled Cycle of Heart Essence (yang gsang bla na med pa'i snying thig gi skor), the fourth of the four divisions of the Instruction Section according to the arrangement of Shri Singha. All lineages of the Innermost Essence passed through Shri Singha and continued in Tibet through his personal disciples, Padmasambhava and Vimalamitra. In the fourteenth century these two lineages passed through Rangjung Dorje, the third Karmapa, and his close Dharma friend Longchen Rabjam (1308–1363); the latter systematized these teachings in his great body of writings. Longchen Rabjam was an incarnation of Princess Pema Sal, the daughter of King Trisong Deutsen, to whom Padmasambhava had entrusted his own lineage of Dzogchen, known as Khandro Nyingtig. He is single-handedly regarded as the most important writer on Dzogchen teachings. His works include the *Seven Great Treasuries,* the *Three Trilogies,* and his commentaries in the Nyingtig Yabshi. The practice of the Innermost Essence is continued to this very day.

Inner tantras of Secret Mantra (gsang sngags nang gi rgyud sde) Usually this term refers to the three inner tantras of Mahayoga, Anu Yoga, and Ati Yoga, but in the specific context of the translation of the tantras in chapter 12, only Mahayoga and Anu Yoga are included. The Ati Yoga tantras are listed in chapter 14.

Instruction Section (man ngag sde) The third of the three sections of Dzogchen, as arranged by Manjushrimitra. In Tibet, three lineages are represented: through Padmasambhava and Vairochana, who both received transmission from Shri Singha, and through Vimalamitra, who received transmission partly from Shri Singha and partly from Jnanasutra. The first two lineages were continued only as termas, while Vimalamitra's was passed on both as terma and as oral transmission. In the following millennium, innumerable termas were revealed, which contain the precious instructions of these three great masters. The most important of these terma treasures are included in the *Rinchen Terdzö*, a collection of termas compiled by Jamgön Kongtrül, covering the three inner tantras.

Jambu continent ('dzam bu gling) Our known world. The southern of the four continents, so-called because it is adorned with the Jambuvriksha (rose apple) tree.

Jamgön Kongtrül ('jam mgon kong sprul, 1813–1899) Also known as Lodro Thaye, Yönten Gyamtso, Padma Garwang, and by his tertön name Padma Tennyi Yungdrung Lingpa. He was one of the most prominent Buddhist masters in the nineteenth century and placed special focus upon a nonsectarian attitude. Renowned as an accomplished master, scholar, and writer, he authored more than one hundred volumes of scriptures. The most well known are his Five Treasuries, among which are the sixty-three volumes of the Rinchen Terdzö, the terma literature of the one hundred great tertöns.

Jarung Khashor (bya rung kha shor) "Permission once given (cannot be taken back)." The great white stupa at Boudhanath in the Kathmandu Valley.

Jnana Kumara of Nyag (gnyag [Skt. jna na ku ma ra]/ye shes gzhon nu) "Youthful Wisdom." Early Tibetan monk and expert translator, who received the four great rivers of transmission from Padmasambhava, Vimalamitra, Vairochana, and Yudra Nyingpo. In particular, he worked closely with Vimalamitra in translating tantras of Mahayoga and Ati Yoga. He is also known as Nyag Lotsawa, as well as Drimey Dashar, "Flawless Moonlight," his secret initiation name. In unison with Trisong Deutsen, his initiation flower fell on Chemchok Heruka. Subsequently, he received the transmission of Nectar Medicine from Padmasambhava. He practiced in the Crystal Cave of Yarlung, where he drew water from solid rock. It is said the water still flows today. Among his later incarnations is Dazang Rinpoche, a contemporary of Jamgön Kongtrül the First in the nineteenth century.

Kailash (ti se)   Sacred mountain in western Tibet; also known as Mount Tisey.

Kalachakra (dus kyi 'khor lo)   "Wheel of Time." A tantra and a Vajrayana system taught by Buddha Shakyamuni, showing the interrelationship between the phenomenal world, the physical body, and the mind.

Kamalashila   Disciple of Shantarakshita who represented the Indian position in a decisive eighth-century debate at Samye.

Karma (las)   The unerring law that virtuous actions yield virtuous results, and so forth. Voluntary action of thought, word, and deed, the effect of which determine the rebirths and experiences of individual sentient beings.

Kathang (bka' thang)   "Chronicles." Usually refers to the biographies of Padmasambhava concealed as terma treasures.

Kawa Paltsek (ska ba dpal brtsegs)   Direct disciple of both Padmasambhava and Shantarakshita; important contributor to the translation of the Tibetan Tripitaka and the *Nyingma Gyübum*. Born in the Phen Valley, he became an eminent translator in accordance with a prophecy of Padmasambhava, and he took ordination from Khenpo Bodhisattva, being among the seven first Tibetan monks. He received Vajrayana teachings from the great master Padma and attained unimpeded clairvoyance.

Khamsum Copper Temple (khams gsum zangs khang gling)   A temple at Samye built by Lady Margyen of Tsepang, a queen of King Trisong Deutsen.

Khandro Yeshe Tsogyal (mkha' 'gro ye shes mtsho rgyal)   *See* Yeshe Tsogyal.

Kharchu at Lhodrak (lho brag mkhar chu)   The retreat place of Padmasambhava's mind. It is situated one day's walk from Lord Marpa's house in Lhodrak.

Khatvanga   A staff carried by tantric adepts, representing the secret consort and the transformation of the three poisons.

Khenpo Bodhisattva (mkhan po bo dhi sattva)   *See* Shantarakshita.

Kilaya (phur ba)   (1) Sacred dagger used in tantric rituals. (2) Same as Kilaya Activity.

Kilaya Activity (phur pa phrin las)   The heruka of the karma family or the tantric teachings connected to this deity, which are among the Eight Sadhana Teachings.

King Jah (rgyal po dzah)   The first human recipient of the Mahayoga teachings and an important figurehead in the transmission of Anu Yoga.

King Trisong Deutsen (rgyal po khri srong lde'u btsan)   *See* Trisong Deutsen.

King Yama (gshin rje rgyal po)   The Lord of Death. The terrible judge of the dead. Also, a personification of impermanence, the unfailing law of karma, and one's inevitable mortality.

Klesha (nyon mongs pa)   "Disturbing emotion." Usually the five poisons: desire, anger, delusion, pride, and envy.

Kriya Yoga (bya ba'i rnal 'byor)   The first of the three outer tantras, which places emphasis on cleanliness and pure conduct. The scriptures of Kriya Tantra appeared first in Varanasi.

Kungamo (kun dga' mo)   The wisdom dakini who conferred empowerment upon Guru Rinpoche. She is also known as the dakini Leykyi Wangmo, Nyida Ngödrub, or as Guhyajnana, the chief of wisdom dakinis. *See also* Leykyi Wangmo.

Kyeho (kye ho)   Exclamation of distress or invocation.

Lady Kharchen (mkhar chen bza')   *See* Yeshe Tsogyal.

Lady Margyen of Tsepang (tshe spang bza' dmar rgyan)   One of the queens of King Trisong Deutsen. Reputed to have been a major troublemaker.

Lady Tsogyal of Kharchen (mkhar chen bza' mtsho rgyal)   *See* Yeshe Tsogyal.

Langdarma (glang dar ma)   Brother of the great Dharma king Ralpachen and the persecutor of the sangha in Central Tibet during his five-year reign. During this brief reign, he almost succeeded in eradicating Buddhism in Tibet.

Learning, reflection, and meditation (thos bsam sgom gsum)   "Learning" means receiving oral teachings and studying scriptures, in order to clear away ignorance and wrong views. "Reflection" is to eradicate uncertainty and misunderstanding through carefully thinking over the subject. "Meditation" means to gain direct insight through applying the teachings in one's personal experience.

Lekdrub (legs grub)   *See* Lekdrub of Tsang.

Lekdrub of Tsang (gtsang legs grub)   The companion of Vairochana on his journey to India. Lekdrub received half of the transmission of Dzogchen from Shri Singha, departed early, and died on his way back to Tibet. He was reborn as Yudra Nyingpo.

Level (sa, Skt. bhumi)   The levels or stages a bodhisattva traverses on the journey to complete enlightenment.

Leykyi Wangmo (las kyi dbang mo, Skt. Karmeshvari)   Also known as Karma Indranila. The dakini who transmitted the Eight Sadhana Teachings to the eight vidyadharas and later the Assemblage of Sugatas to Padmasambhava. *See also* Kungamo.

Lhalung Palgyi Dorje (lha lung dpal gyi rdo rje)   Born in Upper Drom, he was first a border guard, but developed renunciation and received ordination from Vimalamitra, together with his two brothers. He received the bodhisattva vow from Padmasambhava as well as empowerment and oral instructions in Vajrayana. He practiced meditation in White Gorge of Tsib and at Yerpa, where he reached the accomplishment of being able to traverse freely through solid rock. Years later he assassinated the evil king Langdarma.

Lhasa (lha sa)   "Abode of the gods," the capital of Tibet and the location of the famous Jokhang temple founded by King Songtsen Gampo.

Liberating Sorcery of Mother Deities (ma mo rbod gtong)   One of the Eight Sadhana Teachings of Mahayoga.

Life-wheel, hail, and spells (srog ser gtad gsum)   Three aspects of protective tantric rituals.

Loden Chogsey (blo ldan mchog sred)   One of the eight manifestations of Padmasambhava.

Lord Nyang (mnga' bdag nyang / myang)   *See* Nyang Ral Nyima Öser.

Lord of Great Compassion (jo bo thugs rje chen po)   *See* Avalokiteshvara.

Lord of Secrets (gsang ba'i bdag po)   *See* Vajrapani.

Lord Ralpachen of Nyang (mnga' bdag nyang ral pa can)   *See* Nyang Ral Nyima Öser.

Lords of the Three Families (rigs gsum mgon po)   The three bodhisatt-vas Avalokiteshvara, Manjushri, and Vajrapani.

Lotsawa (lo tsa ba)   Tibetan translators of the canonical texts, who usually worked closely with Indian panditas. The title literally means "bilingual" (skad gnyis smra ba) or the "eyes of the world" ('jig rten mig).

Lotsawa Vairochana (lo tsa ba vai ro tsa na)   *See* Vairochana.

Lotus King (pad ma rgyal po)   One of the eight manifestations of Padmasambhava.

Lotus Speech (pad ma gsung)   The heruka of the padma family or the tantric teachings connected to this deity, which are among the Eight Sadhana Teachings.

Lower realms (ngan song)   The three abodes of hell beings, hungry ghosts, and animals. *See also* Six classes of sentient beings.

Lui Gyaltsen (klu yi rgyal mtshan)   *See* Chokro Lui Gyaltsen.

Luminosity ('od gsal, Skt. prabhasvara)   A key term in Vajrayana philosophy, signifying a departure from the Mahayana's over-emphasis on emptiness, which can lead to nihilism. According to Mipham Rinpoche, "luminosity" means "free from the darkness of unknowing and endowed with the ability to cognize."

Luminous Vajra Essence ('od gsal rdo rje snying po)   A synonym for the Great Perfection or Dzogchen.

Machen Pomra (rma chen spom ra)   A powerful local spirit from the area of Kham, the chief of twenty-one major local divinities.

Magical Net (sgyu 'phrul)   A collective term for the manifestations of enlightenment that tame whoever needs to be tamed and that do so in whichever way is necessary. In this book, the term refers to a collection of tantric scriptures belonging chiefly to Mahayoga.

Magical Net of Manjushri ('jam dpal sgyu 'phrul)   A Mahayoga scripture found in the *Nyingma Gyübum*, vol. BA.

Magical Net of the Goddess (lha mo sgyu 'phrul)   A Mahayoga scripture found in the *Nyingma Gyübum*, vol. BA.

Magical Net of Vairochana (rnam snang sgyu 'phrul drva ba)   A Mahayoga scripture, which functions as a subsidiary support for engaging in yogic activities connected to the mandala. *See also* Eighteen Mahayoga Tantras.

Mahabodhi Temple (byang chub chen po)   The enormous shrine in front of the bodhi tree at Vajra Seat, Bodhgaya. *See also* Vajra Seat.

Mahamudra (phyag chen, phyag rgya chen po)   In the context of this book, *mahamudra* refers to the "supreme attainment of mahamudra," which is synonymous with complete enlightenment or the vidyadhara level of mahamudra, the third of the four vidyadhara levels.

Mahamudra level of the path of cultivation (sgom lam phyag rgya chen po)   Same as the vidyadhara level of mahamudra.

Mahayana (theg pa chen po)   "Greater vehicle." When using the terms "greater and lesser vehicles," *Mahayana* and *Hinayana*, *Mahayana* includes the tantric vehicles, while *Hinayana* is comprised of the teachings for shravakas and pratyekabuddhas. The connotation of "greater" or "lesser" refers to the scope of aspiration, the methods applied, and the depth of insight.

Mahayoga (rnal 'byor chen po)   The first of the Three Inner Tantras. Mahayoga as scripture is divided into two parts: Tantra Section and Sadhana Section. The Tantra Section consists of the Eighteen Mahayoga Tantras, while the Sadhana Section is comprised of the Eight Sadhana Teachings. Jamgön Kongtrül says in his *Treasury of Knowledge:* "Mahayoga emphasizes *means* (Skt. upaya), the development stage, and the view that liberation is attained through growing accustomed to insight into the nature of the indivisibility of the superior two truths." The superior two truths in Mahayoga are purity and equality: The pure natures of the aggregates, elements, and sense factors are the male and female buddhas and bodhisattvas. At the same time, everything that appears and exists is of the equal nature of emptiness.

Maitreya (byams pa)   "The Loving One." The bodhisattva regent of Buddha Shakyamuni, presently residing in Tushita heaven until becoming the fifth buddha of this aeon; author of five treatises preserved by Asanga.

Major and Minor Gathering Tantra (tshogs rgyud che chung)   A Mahayoga scripture explaining the ritual of a ganachakra. *See also* Feast offering.

Maledictory Fierce Mantra (rmod pa drag sngags)   One of the Eight Sadhana Teachings.

Mamo (ma mo, Skt. matari)   (1) *See* Mundane mother deities. (2) A class of semidivine beings who sometimes act as protectors of the Dharma.

Mandala (dkyil 'khor)   (1) "Center and surrounding." Usually a deity along with its surrounding environment. A mandala is a symbolic, graphic representation of a tantric deity's realm of existence. (2) A mandala offering is an offering visualized as the entire universe, as well as the arrangement of offerings in tantric ritual.

Mandarava Flower (man da ra ba me tog)   Princess of Sahor and close disciple of Guru Rinpoche, she was one of his five main consorts. Her name refers to the coral tree, *Erythrina indica,* one of the five trees of paradise, which has brilliant scarlet flowers. She is said to be identical with the dakini Niguma and the yogini by the name of Adorned with Human Bone Ornaments. In *The Precious Garland of Lapis Lazuli* (p. 352), Jamgön Kongtrül says:

> Born as the daughter of Arshadhara, the king of Sahor, and Queen Mohauki, accompanied by miraculous signs (and because of her great beauty), many kings from India and China vied to take her as their bride. Nevertheless, she had unshakable renunciation and entered the gate of the Dharma. Padmasambhava perceived that she was to be his disciple and accepted her as his spiritual consort. But the king, fearing that his bloodline would be contaminated, had the master burned alive. When Padmasambhava showed the miracle of transforming the mass of fire into a lake, the king gained faith and without hesitation offered his entire kingdom and the princess. When the king requested teachings, Padmasambhava showered upon twenty-one disciples the great rain of the Dharma by transmitting the tantras, scriptures, and oral instructions of *Kadü Chökyi Gyamtso,* the Dharma Ocean Embodying All Teachings. Thus the master established the king and his ministers on the vidyadhara levels. Guru Rinpoche accepted her as his

consort and in Maratika, the Cave of Bringing Death to an End, both master and consort displayed the manner of achieving the unified vajra body on the vidyadhara level of life mastery. Mandarava remained in India and brought tremendous benefit to beings both directly and indirectly. In Tibet, she appeared miraculously at the great Dharma Wheel of Tramdruk, where she exchanged symbolic praises and replies with Guru Rinpoche. The details of that are recorded extensively in the *Padma Kathang.* A separate life story of Mandarava is found in the collected writings of Orgyen Lingpa. Mandarava was a wisdom dakini among whose different names and manifestations are counted the yogini Adorned with Human Bone Ornaments (Mirükyi Gyenchen) at the time of Lord Marpa, Risülkyi Naljorma at the time of Nyen Lotsawa, and Drubpey Gyalmo at the time of Rechungpa. Mandarava is also accepted as being Chushingi Nyemachen, the consort of Maitripa, as well as the dakini Niguma. Her compassionate emanations and her blessings are beyond any doubt and, since she attained the indestructible rainbow body, she is surely present (in the world) right now.

Mang-yul (mang yul)   The area north of the Kathmandu Valley, between Trisuli and the present border of Tibet.

Manjushri ('jam dpal dbyangs)   One of the eight main bodhisattvas. He is the personification of the perfection of transcendent knowledge.

Manjushri Body ('jam dpal sku)   The heruka of the Tathagata Body family or the tantric teachings connected to this deity, which are among the Eight Sadhana Teachings. Also known as Yamantaka, the wrathful form of Manjushri, representing wisdom that subdues death.

Manjushri Namasangiti Tantra Expressed in Songs of Praise ('jam dpal gyi mtshan yang dag par brjod pa bstod pa glur blangs pa'i rgyud)   A tantra belonging to Kriya Yoga, known to all Tibetan Buddhists as *Jampal Tsenjö.* Translated by Alex Wayman as *Chanting the Names of Manjushri,* Boston: Shambhala Publications, 1985.

Manjushrimitra ('jam dpal bshes gnyen, pron. Jampal Shenyen)   An Indian master in the Dzogchen lineage and the chief disciple of Garab Dorje. In his role as a master in the lineage of the Sadhana Section of Mahayoga, he received the transmission of Yamantaka in the form of the *Secret Wrathful Manjushri Tantra* and other texts. Manjushrimitra was born in the Magadha district of India and was soon an adept in the general sciences and the conventional topics of Buddhism. After having become the most eminent among five hundred panditas, he received many teachings and empowerments from Garab Dorje, Lalitavajra, and other masters and reached the unified level of enlightenment, indivisible from Manjushri. Yamantaka appeared to him in person, conferred empowerment, and transmitted the tantras and oral instructions. Among his chief recipients of this teaching were Hungkara, Padmasambhava, and Hanatela. There seem to have been several masters with this name, but Guru Tashi Tobgyal in his *Ocean of Wondrous Sayings to Delight the Learned Ones* views them as being magical emanations of the same master. *See also* Sadhana Section.

Mantra (sngags)   (1) A synonym for Vajrayana. (2) A particular combination of sounds symbolizing and communicating the nature of a deity and which lead to purification and realization, for example, OM MANI PADME HUM. There are chiefly three types of mantra: guhya mantra, vidya mantra, and dharani mantra.

Mantra and philosophy (sngags dang mtshan nyid)   "Mantra" is synonymous with Secret Mantra or Vajrayana, while "philosophy" refers to the causal philosophical vehicles: Hinayana and Mahayana.

Mantradhara (sngags 'chang)   An adept of tantric rituals.

Mantric (sngags kyi)   Of or pertaining to Vajrayana.

Mantrika (sngags pa)   *See* tantrika.

Mara (bdud)   Demon or demonic influence that creates obstacles for practice and enlightenment. Mythologically said to be a powerful god, who dwells in the highest abode in the realm of desire; the master of illusion, who attempted to prevent the Buddha from attaining enlightenment at Bodhgaya. For the Dharma practitioner, Mara symbolizes one's own ego-clinging and preoccupation with the eight worldly concerns. Generally, there are four maras or obstructions to practice of the Dharma: those of defilements, death, the aggregates, and the godly mara of seduction. Sometimes the four maras are mentioned by name: Klesha, Lord of Death, Skandha, and Godly Son.

Maratika ('chi ba mthar byed)   The sacred place in eastern Nepal where Guru Rinpoche and Mandarava were blessed with immortal life by Buddha Amitayus.

Master Bodhisattva (slob dpon bo dhi sa tva)   *See* Shantarakshita.

Meadow of Mönkha (mon kha ne'u ring)   Possibly identical with Mönkha Senge Dzong, a cave situated to the east of Bumthang in Bhutan, which was used by Padmasambhava and later by Yeshe Tsogyal as a sacred place for the sadhana of Vajra Kilaya.

Meaningful Lasso Tantra (don yod zhags pa'i rgyud)   A tantra focused on Avalokiteshvara; belongs to Kriya Yoga and is also known as *Amogha Pasha.*

Meditation and postmeditation (mnyam bzhag dang rjes thob)   *Meditation* here means resting in equanimity free from mental constructs, like pure space. *Postmeditation* is when one is distracted from that state of equanimity, and one conceptually regards appearances as an illusion, mirage, dream, and so forth.

Mighty Lotus (padma dbang chen)   Same as the tantric deity Hayagriva, the chief heruka of the padma family.

Mighty Lotus Tantra (padma dbang chen gyi rgyud)   Several Mahayoga tantras with resembling names occur in the *Nyingma Gyübum*, vol. HA.

Mind and prana (rlung sems)   *Prana* here is the "wind of karma," the current of conceptual thinking, as well as the energy-currents in the body. *Mind* is the dualistic consciousness of an unenlightened being. These two are closely related.

Mind Section (sems sde)   The first of the three sections of Dzogchen. In this book, twenty-five tantras and eighteen major scriptures are mentioned. Most are found in the first three volumes of the *Nyingma Gyübum.*

Most Supreme (che mchog)   Chemchok Heruka. Usually identical with Nectar Quality, the chief heruka of the ratna family. Sometimes, in the case of Assemblage of Sugatas, Most Supreme is the heruka who embodies all the buddha families.

Mother deities (ma mo) *See* Mamo.

Mother Deities Assemblage Tantra (ma mo 'dus pa'i rgyud)   Tantra belonging to the Sadhana Section of Mahayoga. Found in the *Nyingma Gyübum*, vol. A.

Mother tantra (ma rgyud)   One of the three aspects of Anuttara Yoga, which emphasizes the completion stage or prajna. Sometimes equivalent to Anu Yoga.

Mount Hepori (has po ri)   *See* Hepori.

Mount Sumeru (ri rab lhun po)   The mythological giant mountain at the center of our world-system, where the two lowest classes of gods of the desire realm live. It is surrounded by chains of lesser mountains, lakes, continents, and oceans and is said to rise 84,000 leagues above sea level.

Mudra (phyag rgya)   Can mean either "hand gesture," spiritual consort, or the "bodily form" of a deity.

Mundane mother deities ('jig rten ma mo)   One of the Eight Sadhana Teachings. Female divinities manifested out of dharmadhatu but appearing in ways that correspond to mundane appearances through the interrelationship between the mundane world and the channels, winds, and essences within the human body. They have both an ultimate and a relative aspect. The chief figure in this mandala is Chemchok Heruka, the wrathful form of Buddha Samantabhadra in the form known as Ngöndzok Gyalpo, the King of True Perfection.

Mundane Worship ('jig rten mchod bstod)   One of the Eight Sadhana Teachings.

Naga (klu)   Powerful long-lived serpentlike beings who inhabit bodies of water and often guard great treasure. Nagas belong half to the animal realm and half to the god realm. They generally live in the form of snakes, but many can change into human form.

NAGARAJA ANGKUSHA JAH   A mantra command that means: "King of the nagas, be summoned by the iron hook!"

Nagarjuna (klu grub)   An Indian master of philosophy and tantric siddha. One of the eight vidyadharas; receiver of the tantras of Lotus Speech such as *Supreme Steed Display.* He is said to have taken birth in the southern part of India around four hundred years after the Buddha's parinirvana. Having received ordination at Nalanda monastery, he later acted as preceptor for the monks. He knew alchemy, lived for six hundred years, and transformed ordinary materials into gold in order to sustain the sangha. At Bodhgaya he erected pillars and stone walls to protect the Bodhi Tree and constructed 108 stupas. From the realm of the nagas he brought back the extensive Prajnaparamita scriptures. He was the life pillar for the Mahayana, but specifically he was a major exponent of the unexcelled vehicle of Vajrayana. Having attained the realization of Hayagriva, he transmitted the lineage to Padmasambhava.

Nalanda   The great monastic center for Buddhist studies in ancient India, situated in the present Indian state of Bihar, a few hours drive from Bodhgaya.

Namkhai Nyingpo of Nub (gnubs nam mkha'i snying po)   Born in Lower Nyal, he was one of the first Tibetans to take ordination. An adept translator, he journeyed to India where he received transmission from Hungkara and attained the body of nondual wisdom. Namkhai Nyingpo is also counted among the twenty-five disciples of Guru Rinpoche. He received the transmission of Vishuddha Mind through the practice of which he was able to fly on the rays of the sun. When meditating in Splendid Long Cave of Kharchu at Lhodrak, he had visions of numerous yidams and attained the vidyadhara level of mahamudra. Finally, he departed for celestial realms without leaving a corpse behind.

NAMO (phyag 'tshal lo)   Expression of homage and respect; salutation.

NAMO RATNA-GURU (bla ma rin po che la phyag 'tshal lo)   "I pay homage to the precious master!"

"Natural Confession" (rang bzhin gyi bshags pa)   A synonym for the "Confession of the Expanse of the View" (Tawa Longshag).

Nectar (bdud rtsi, Skt. amrita)   (1) The "nectar of immortality," the ambrosia of the gods, which confers immortality or other powers. (2) Abbreviation of Nectar Quality, the heruka of the ratna family from among the Eight Sadhana Teachings.

Nectar Medicine (bdud rtsi sman)   (1) The nectar of immortality. (2) Same as Nectar Quality.

Nectar Quality (bdud rtsi yon tan)   One of the Eight Sadhana Teachings. The heruka of the ratna family or the tantric teachings connected with that deity.

Ngadag Nyang (mnga' bdag nyang / myang)   See Nyang Ral Nyima Öser.

Ngagyur Shechen Tennyi Dargye Ling (snga 'gyur zhe chen bstan gnyis dar rgyas gling)   The seat of His Holiness Dilgo Khyentse in Nepal, situated at the Great Stupa of Jarung Khashor in Boudhanath.

Ngakpa (sngags pa)   *See* Tantrika.

Nine Root Tantras (rtsa ba'i rgyud dgu)   The most important Mahayoga tantras of the Sadhana Section (sgrub sde). Listed in chapter 19.

Nine Sadhana Sections (sgrub pa sde dgu)   The Eight Sadhana Teachings plus the teachings connected to Guru Vidyadhara. Sometimes the Assemblage of Sugatas is counted as the ninth.

Nirmanakaya (sprul sku)   "Emanation body," "form of magical apparition." The third of the three kayas. The aspect of enlightenment that can be perceived by ordinary beings. *See also* Three kayas.

Nirmanakaya Padmasambhava (sprul sku pad ma 'byung gnas)   Same as Guru Rinpoche. A respectful way of addressing Guru Rinpoche, which expresses that he is a manifestation of an enlightened being. *See also* Guru Rinpoche.

Nirvana (mya ngan las 'das pa)   The extinguishing of the causes for samsaric existence. The lesser nirvana refers to the liberation from cyclic existence attained by a Hinayana practitioner. When referring to a buddha, *nirvana* is the great nondwelling state of enlightenment which falls neither into the extreme of samsaric existence nor into the passive state of cessation attained by an arhat.

Nonarising (skye ba med pa)   In the aspect of ultimate truth, all phenomena are devoid of an independent, concrete identity and have therefore no basis for such attributes as "arising, dwelling, or ceasing," i.e., coming into being, remaining in time and place, and ceasing to exist.

Nonarising dharmata (chos nyid skye ba med pa)   The nature of things which, like space, does not come into being as a concrete, apprehensible entity.

Non-Buddhist (mu stegs pa, Skt. tirthika)   Referring to teachers of non-Buddhist philosophy, who adhere to the extreme views of eternalism or nihilism.

Nonconceptual (rnam par mi rtog pa)   Of or pertaining to the absence of conceptual thinking or discursive thought.

Nonfabrication (bzo med, ma bcos)   The key point in the training of Mahamudra and Dzogchen—that innate wakefulness is not created through intellectual effort.

Nonhumans (mi ma yin)   Spirits, ghosts, or demons.

Nonmeditation (mi bsgom)   The state of not holding onto an object meditated upon nor a subject who meditates.

Nonreturn (phyir mi ldog pa)   *See* Fruition of nonreturn.

Nonvirtues (mi dge ba) Usually refers to the ten unvirtuous actions: The physical misdeeds of killing, taking what is not given, and engaging in sexual misconduct; the verbal misdeeds of lying, uttering divisive talk, using harsh words, and gossiping; and the mental misdeeds of harboring covetousness, ill-will, and wrong views.

Nyang Ral Nyima Öser (myang ral nyi ma 'od zer; 1124–1192)   In the district of Lhodrag situated to the south of Samye in Central Tibet, a child was born to Nyangtön Chökyi Khorlo, a renowned Nyingma yogi, and his wife, Lady Yeshe Drön. The child was named Nyima Öser, "Beam of Sunlight," an extraordinary being, who possessed eight marvelous signs, including three moles in the shapes of the syllables OM AH HUNG on his forehead, throat, and heart center. After being concealed at home until the age of twelve, unknown to other people, he was taken to a fair arranged by his uncle. At the fair he outshone everyone in the horse race and, when seated upon a small throne by his uncle, Nyima Öser expounded bodhichitta, inspiring deep faith in the whole gathering. Because of the twelve-year-old long hair that was wrapped around his head to hide his ushnisha and the OM in his forehead, he was given the name Lord Nyang Ral, the "Braided Master of Nyang." Until the age of twenty-five, he studied the prevalent tantric systems of Nyingma and Shijey with many great masters. Following directions given to him by Padmasambhava in person, Nyima Öser went to the cave named Imprint of the Rakshasa's Claw and to Pearl Crystal Cave of Pama Ridge, where he received empowerment and blessings from both Padmasambhava and Yeshe Tsogyal. During the following years, Nyima Öser revealed an incredible number of terma treasures. Without propagating a single of these teachings, he kept them secret and remained in retreat at Samye Chimphu for six years. During the retreat, Padmasambhava appeared for seven days and bestowed upon Nyima Öser whichever profound instruction he requested. Finally, Padmasambhava dissolved into Nyima Öser's heart, producing an experience of bliss, clarity, and nonthought, which lasted for six months. On another occasion, Yeshe Tsogyal commanded him to go to Lhodrak and establish a temple there for the benefit of beings. Later Nyang Ral Nyima Öser went to Lhodrak, where innumerable disciples gradually gathered around him. Due to the tremendous impact of the terma treasures he revealed, Nyima Öser is considered the first of five tertön kings.

Nyenchen Tanglha (gnyan chen thang lha)   Important protector of the Nyingma teachings, regarded as a bodhisattva on the eighth level. Also the name of a mountain range.

Nyingma Gyübum (rnying ma rgyud 'bum)   "The Hundred Thousand Tantras of the Old School." A collection of scriptures belonging to the three inner tantras, gathered by Ratna Lingpa and re-edited by Jigmey Lingpa. Various editions exist, but the numbering of the volumes used in this book are from the version in thirty-six volumes published by His Holiness Dilgo Khyentse Rinpoche, New Delhi, 1974. The structure of this edition is as follows: ten volumes of Ati Yoga, three volumes of Anu Yoga, six volumes of the Tantra Section of Mahayoga, thirteen volumes of the Sadhana Section of Mahayoga, one volume of protector tantras, and three volumes of catalogues and historical background.

Nyingma Kama (rnying ma bka' ma)   "The Oral Transmission of the Old School." Fifty-six volumes in the expanded edition published by His Holiness Dudjom Rinpoche, New Delhi.

Nyingma School (rnying ma)   The teachings brought to Tibet chiefly by the great masters Padmasambhava, Vimalamitra, Shantarakshita, and Vairochana and which were translated into Tibetan. This occurred mainly during the reign of King Trisong Deutsen and in the subsequent period, up to the translator Rinchen Sangpo in the ninth century. The two main types of transmission that developed were Kama and Terma. Practices are based on both the outer and inner tantras, with emphasis on the practice of the Inner Tantras of Mahayoga, Anu Yoga, and Ati Yoga.

Nyingma tantras (rnying rgyud)   See *Nyingma Gyübum.*

Ocean of Cleansing Sacred Commitment (dam tshig khrus lung rgya mtsho)   Name of a tantric scripture on purification of samaya, the vows of Vajrayana practice.

Orgyen (o rgyan, Skt. Uddiyana)   (1) Uddiyana, the country. (2) The master from Uddiyana, Padmasambhava. *See also* Uddiyana.

Outer and inner teachings of Secret Mantra (gsang sngags phyi nang gi chos)   The three outer are Kriya, Upa, and Yoga. The three inner are Mahayoga, Anu Yoga, and Ati Yoga.

Outer Secret Mantra (gsang sngags phyi pa)   *See* Outer Tantras of Secret Mantra.

Outer Tantras of Secret Mantra (gsang sngags phyi'i rgyud sde)   The tantras belonging to the three vehicles of Kriya, Upa, and Yoga. In the context of the Old School of the Early Translations (Ngagyur Nyingma), they were translated into Tibetan mainly by Shantarakshita and Kawa Paltsek. Listed in chapter 12.

Padma (pad ma)   "Lotus." (1) Same as Padmasambhava. (2) The lotus family, from among the five buddha families.

Padma Thötreng Tsal (padma thod phreng rtsal)   The secret name of Guru Rinpoche, which means "Powerful Lotus of the Garland of Skulls."

Padmakara (pad ma 'byung gnas)   "Lotus-born." Same as Guru Rinpoche. The Sanskrit names Padmakara and Padmasambhava are used interchangeably in Tibetan literature, and sometimes the Tibetan translation, Pema Jungney, is used. *See also* Guru Rinpoche.

Padmasambhava (pad ma 'byung gnas)   "Originated from a lotus." *See also* Guru Rinpoche; Padmakara.

Palgyi Senge of Lang (rlangs dpal gyi seng ge)   One of the eight chief disciples of Padmasambhava when the empowerment of the Assemblage of Sugatas was conferred. He attained both the common and supreme accomplishments at Paro Taktsang through the practice of the Tamer of All Haughty Spirits. His father was Amey Jangchub Drekhöl, a powerful mantrika, who could employ the eight classes of gods and demons as his servants.

Palgyi Senge of Shübu (shud bu dpal gyi seng ge)   As one of the ministers of King Trisong Deutsen, he was sent as one of the first emissaries to invite Padmasambhava to Tibet. He learned translation from Padmasambhava and rendered numerous teachings of Mamo, Yamantaka, and Kilaya into Tibetan. Having attained accomplishment through Kilaya and Mamo, he could split boulders and divide the flow of rivers with his dagger.

Palgyi Wangchuk of Kharchen (mkhar chen dpal gyi dbang phyug) Here, in the *Sanglingma*, he is described as the father of Yeshe Tsogyal, but elsewhere as her brother, who became a close disciple of Padmasambhava.

Palgyi Yeshe (dpal gyi ye shes) Born into the Drogmi clan he was also known as Palgyi Yeshe of Drogmi. He was an adept translator and rendered numerous sutras and tantras into Tibetan, including the *Tantra of the Mother Deities Mamo*. He received the transmission of the mother deities from Padmasambhava and became an accomplished mantrika.

Palgyi Yeshe of Lang (rlangs dpal gyi ye she) One of the first Tibetans to take ordination. He also received transmission from Hungkara in India, but died on the way back to Tibet.

Pal-yang (dpal dbyangs) A Tibetan translator predicted by Padmasambhava. The first monk ordained by Khenpo Bodhisattva. He is also known as Ratna of Ba (sba ratna).

Pandita (mkhas pa) A learned master, scholar, or professor of Buddhist philosophy.

Parinirvana (yongs su mya ngan las 'das pa) "Completely passing beyond suffering." (1) The final entry into nirvana. (2) Honorific term for the passing away of a buddha or a fully accomplished master.

Path of liberation (grol lam) (1) When related to the path of ripening, it refers to the practice of the oral instructions of one's personal vajra master. (2) When related to the path of means, it refers to the practice of sustaining the natural state of mind—mahamudra or Dzogchen.

Path of means (thabs lam) The stages of development and completion with attributes. *See also* Completion stage; Development stage.

Path of ripening (smin lam) The process of receiving the four empowerments.

Path of training (slob pa'i lam) The first four of the five paths. The fifth
 path is called the "path beyond training" and corresponds to perfect
 buddhahood.

Patra (pa tra) A brick ornamented with flourishes. A gold patra possibly
 weighs several kilos.

Pearl Crystal Cave of Pama Ridge (mu tig shel gyi spa ma gangs) This
 is the practice cave of Guru Rinpoche, where he gave many of the
 instructions found in *Dakini Teachings* (Boston: Shambhala Publications, 1990).

Pekar (pe kar) The particular protector of the Samye appointed and
 bound under oath by Padmasambhava.

Phonya (pho nya) (1) Messenger, emissary. (2) Spiritual consort in
 vajrayana practice.

Pointing-out instruction (ngo sprod) The direct introduction to the
 nature of mind. A root guru is the master who gives the pointing-out
 instruction so that the disciple recognizes the nature of mind.

Postmeditation (rjes thob) Generally, the period of being involved in
 sense perceptions and daily activities. Specifically, the period of being
 distracted from the natural state of mind.

Potala (gru 'dzin) The pure land of Avalokiteshvara.

Prabhahasti (glang po'i od) "Radiant Elephant." Among the eight vidyadharas, he was the receiver of the transmission of the tantras of
 Kilaya Activity. Born to a royal family in the western part of India
 and named Shakyaprabha when ordained as monk, Prabhahasti became extremely well-versed in the Tripitaka and studied Secret Mantra with Vajrahasya (rdo rje bzhad pa) and numerous other masters.
 He achieved supreme accomplishment and had, together with his
 disciple Shakyamitra, a tremendous impact on the Dharma in
 Kashmir.

Prajnaparamita (shes rab kyi pha rol tu phyin pa) "Transcendent knowledge." The Mahayana teachings on insight into emptiness, transcending the fixation on subject, object, and action. Associated with
 the second turning of the wheel of Dharma.

Prana (rlung) The "winds" or energy currents of the body.

Pratyekabuddha (rang rgyal, rang sangs rgyas) "Solitarily enlightened one." A Hinayana arhat who attains nirvana chiefly through contemplation on the twelve links of dependent origination in reverse order, without needing teachings in that lifetime. He lacks the complete realization of a buddha and so cannot benefit limitless sentient beings as a buddha does.

Prince Virtuous Protector (lha sras dge mgon) The youngest son of Trisong Deutsen, also known as Murub Tseypo.

Protectors (srung ma) *See* Dharma protector.

Rahula (gza') One of the eight classes of gods and demons.

Rakshasa (srin po) One of the eight classes of gods and demons. Also the cannibal savages inhabiting the southwestern continent of Chamara. At times rakshasa refers to the unruly and untamed expression of ignorance and disturbing emotions.

Ralpachen (ral pa can; 815–841 or 866–901) The third great Dharma king of Tibet. He supported the standardization of new grammar and vocabulary for translation and the revision of old translations. He renewed old centers for learning and practice and invited many Buddhist scholars to Tibet. He was renowned for his devotion to the Dharma and is regarded as an incarnation of Vajrapani.

Ramochey (ra mo che) One of two important temples in Lhasa, which houses the statue of Buddha Shakyamuni brought to Tibet by the queens of King Songtsen Gampo.

Rampant Elephant Tantra (glang po che rab 'bog gi rgyud) A Mahayoga scripture. A tantra of this title is found in the *Nyingma Gyübum*, vol. DZA.

Ratna (rin chen, dkon mchog) "Jewel," "precious."

Red Rock (brag dmar) The location of the temple complex of Samye. The mountain slope behind Samye is of a bright red color.

Resultant vehicle ('bras bu'i theg pa) The Vajrayana system of taking fruition as the path by regarding buddhahood as inherently present and regarding the path as the act of uncovering the basic state. This is different from the causal philosophical vehicles of Mahayana and Hinayana, which regard the path as that which leads to and produces the state of buddhahood. Ultimately, these two approaches are not in conflict. *See also* Secret Mantra.

Rinchen Chok of Ma (rma rin chen mchog)   Early Tibetan translator, who was among the first seven Tibetans to take ordination from Shantarakshita. He was the chief recipient of the Magical Net of Mahayoga. He is known for translating the *Essence of Secrets (Guhyagarbha) Tantra*, the chief tantra of Mahayoga. Through the teachings he received from Padmasambhava, he attained the level of a vidyadhara.

Rinchen Terdzö (rin chen gter mdzod chen mo)   "The Great Treasury of Precious Termas." A collection of the most important revealed termas of Padmasambhava, Vimalamitra, Vairochana, and other of their closest disciples, compiled by Jamgön Kongtrül Lodrö Thaye with the help of Jamyang Khyentse Wangpo. Originally sixty-three volumes. Published by His Holiness Dilgo Khyentse Rinpoche in New Delhi, with the addition of several more volumes of termas and commentaries.

Ripening and liberation (smin grol)   Two vital parts of Vajrayana practice: The empowerments, which ripen one's being with the capacity to realize the four kayas, and the liberating oral instructions, which enable one to actually apply the insight that was introduced through the empowerments.

Rishi (drang srong)   (1) "Seer," inspired Vedic sage, brahmanical ascetic with magical powers. (2) Title for someone who has attained the power of truthful speech, so that whatever he says comes true.

Roaring Lion (seng ge sgra grogs, pron. Senge Dradrog)   One of the eight manifestations of Padmasambhava.

Rombuguhya Devachandra (lha'i zla ba)   One of the eight vidyadharas; who received the transmission of Mundane Worship. He was born in Uddiyana.

Root Tantra of the Assemblage of Sugatas (bde gshegs 'dus pa rtsa ba'i rgyud)   Tantra belonging to the Sadhana Section of Mahayoga found in the *Nyingma Gyübum*, vols. OM and AH. *See also* Assemblage of Sugatas.

Sacred commitment (dam tshig, Skt. samaya)   *See* samaya.

Sacred Great Perfection (bka' rdzogs pa chen po)   *See* Ati Yoga; Dzogchen; Great Perfection.

Sacred incantation (gzungs, Skt. dharani)   A particular type of mantra, usually quite long.

Sacred Peace Deity Tantra (zhi ba dam pa lha'i rgyud)   One of the Eighteen
    Mahayoga Tantras. In *The Golden Garland Chronicles,* this same text is
    named *Peaceful Vajradhatu Tantra* (zhi ba rdo rje dbyings kyi rgyud).

Saddharma Pundarika Sutra (dam chos pad-ma dkar po'i mdo)   "The Sutra
    of the White Lotus of the Sacred Dharma." Famous Mahayana
    scripture.

Sadhana (sgrub thabs)   "Means of accomplishment." Tantric liturgy and
    procedure for practice, usually emphasizing the development stage.
    The typical sadhana structure involves a preliminary part, which
    includes the taking of refuge and arousing bodhichitta; a main part,
    which involves the visualization of a buddha and the recitation of
    mantra; and a concluding part, which includes the dedication of
    merit to all sentient beings.

Sadhana Section (sgrub sde)   One of the two major aspects of Mahayoga
    scriptures, the other being the Tantra Section. *See also* Assemblage of
    Sugatas; Mahayoga.

Saha world-system (mi mjed kyi 'jig rten gyi khams)   The name of our
    present world system. *Saha* means "enduring," because the sentient
    beings here endure unbearable suffering.

Sahor (za hor)   An ancient Indian kingdom believed to be situated
    around Mandir in the present state of Himachal Pradesh in north
    India.

Samadhi (ting nge 'dzin)   "Adhering to the continuity of evenness." A
    state of undistracted concentration or meditative absorption which,
    in the context of Vajrayana, can refer to either the development stage
    or the completion stage.

Samantabhadra (kun tu bzang po)   The "Ever-Excellent One." (1) The
    primordial dharmakaya buddha. (2) The bodhisattva Samantabha-
    dra, who is used as the example for the perfection of increasing an
    offering infinitely.

Samantabhadri (kun tu bzang mo)   *See* Ever-Excellent Lady.

Samaya (dam tshig) The "sacred pledges, precepts or commitments" of
    Vajrayana practice. Essentially, samayas consist of: outwardly, main-
    taining harmonious relationship with the vajra master and one's
    Dharma friends; and inwardly, not straying from the continuity of
    the practice. At the end of a chapter, the single word SAMAYA is an
    oath that confirms that what has been stated is true.

Sambhogakaya (longs spyod rdzogs pa'i sku) The "body of perfect enjoyment." In the context of the five kayas of fruition, sambhogakaya is the semimanifest form of the buddhas endowed with the five perfections of perfect teacher, retinue, place, teaching, and time, which are perceptible only to bodhisattvas on the ten levels. *See also* Three kayas.

Sambhogakaya Great Compassion (longs sku thugs rje chen po) *See* Avalokiteshvara.

Samsara ('khor ba) "Cyclic existence," "vicious circle," or "round" of birth and death and rebirth within the six realms of existence, characterized by suffering, impermanence, and ignorance. The state of ordinary sentient beings fettered by ignorance, dualistic perception, karma, and disturbing emotions. Ordinary reality, an endless cycle of frustration and suffering generated as the result of karma.

Samsaric ('khor ba'i) Of or pertaining to samsara; worldly, mundane, profane.

Samye (bsam yas) The wondrous temple complex built by King Trisong Deutsen (790–844) and consecrated by Guru Rinpoche. Situated in Central Tibet close to Lhasa, it was the center of the early transmission. It is also known as Glorious Samye, the Unchanging and Spontaneously Accomplished Temple.

Samye Chimphu (bsam yas chims phu) The sacred place of Padmasambhava's speech. A mountain retreat, situated four hours' walk above Samye. During the last twelve centuries, numerous great masters have meditated in the caves at this hermitage.

Sandal Grove charnel ground (tsan dan tshal gyi dur khrod) *The Golden Garland Chronicles* (p. 179) describes this place as: "The eminent celestial sacred place of the vidyadharas, the wild jungle which is a crossroad on the secret path of great bliss." It is also counted among the traditional eight charnel grounds.

Sangha (dge 'dun) The community of practitioners; usually the fully ordained monks and nuns. The "noble sangha" means those who have achieved the path of seeing, from among the five paths, and therefore are liberated from samsara.

Sanglingma (zangs gling ma) The name of the text used for this translation of Padmasambhava's life story. *See* Translator's Preface.

Sangye Yeshe of Nub (gnubs sangs rgyas ye shes) One of the twenty-five disciples of Padmasambhava. He was the chief recipient of the Anu

Yoga teachings, as well as the Yamantaka teachings of Mahayoga. In addition to Guru Rinpoche, his other teachers were Traktung Nagpo and Chögyal Kyong of India, Vasudhara of Nepal, and Chetsen Kye from the country of Drusha. He visited India and Nepal seven times. When the evil king Langdarma attempted to destroy Buddhism in Tibet, Sangye Yeshe put fear in the king by making an enormous scorpion, the size of nine yaks, magically appear by a single gesture of his right hand. It is through his kindness that Langdarma had no courage to persecute the Vajrayana sangha who dressed in white robes and kept long hair.

Sarma Schools (gsar ma) "New Schools." The New Schools are the Kagyü, Sakya, and Gelug as well as Shijey and Chö, Jordruk, Shangpa Kagyü, and Nyendrup (the Kalachakra system).

Sarvabuddha Samayoga (sangs rgyas mnyam sbyor) "Equalizing Buddhahood." A Mahayoga scripture. Three tantras of this name are found in the *Nyingma Gyübum*, vol. MA. Sometimes counted as the tantra of enlightened body, from among the Eighteen Mahayoga Tantras.

Scripture (mdo, lung) In the context of this book, a scripture belonging to the category of Anu Yoga or Ati Yoga.

Scripture in Eight Chapters (lung bam po brgyad pa) One of the Eighteen Mahayoga Tantras, in the *Nyingma Gyübum*, vol. LA.

Scripture of the Embodiment of the Realization of All Buddhas (sangs rgyas thams cad dgongs pa 'dus pa'i mdo) The Anu Yoga scripture renowned as *Gongdü*.

Scriptures and realization (lung dang rtogs pa) Authoritative scriptures and the realization of the Dharma in the minds of noble beings.

Secret Mantra (gsang sngags, Skt. guhyamantra) Synonymous with Vajrayana or tantric teachings. *Guhya* means "secret," both concealed and self-secret. *Mantra* in this context means eminent, excellent, or praiseworthy.

Secret Mantra of the Early Translations (gsang sngags snga 'gyur) The Vajrayana system of the Nyingma School, the emphasis of which is on the Three Inner Tantras: Mahayoga, Anu Yoga, and Ati Yoga. According to Jamgön Kongtrül, the chief scriptures are the *Magical Net* of mahayoga, the *Embodiment of Realization* of Anu Yoga, and the Dzogchen tantras of the Mind Section and Space Section. These are adorned with the Eight Sadhana Teachings, while the vital life force is the Instruction Section of Dzogchen, the extract of the realization of Padmasambhava and Vimalamitra, which is contained in the collection renowned as *Nyingtig Yabshi. See also* Nyingma School; Three inner tantras.

Secret Moon Essence (zla gsang thig le)   A Mahayoga scripture in the *Nyingma Gyübum*, vol. MA. Sometimes counted among the Eighteen Mahayoga Tantras as the tantra of enlightened speech.

Self-existing wisdom (rang byung ye shes)   Basic wakefulness that is independent of intellectual constructs.

Senmo (bsen mo)   A type of evil spirit often found in company with the gyalpo class; male and female spirits symbolizing desire and anger.

Sentient being (sems can)   Any living being in one of the six realms who has not attained liberation.

Serak (bse rag)   A type of mischievous spirit who consumes the potent essences of food and wealth. He personifies ultimate envy and miser- liness and is usually exorcized during rituals to promote wealth and prosperity.

Seven aspects of union (kha sbyor yan lag bdun)   The seven qualities of a sambhogakaya buddha: complete enjoyment, union, great bliss, absence of a self-nature, presence of compassion, being uninter- rupted, and being unceasing.

Seven golden mountains (gser ri bdun)   According to the cosmology of the Abhidharma, seven circles of mountains surrounding Mount Sumeru, which is in the center of our universe.

Seven precious substances (rin chen bdun)   Ruby, sapphire, lapis, emer- ald, diamond, pearl, and coral. Sometimes the list includes gold, silver, and crystal.

Shakputri   The son of King Jah and lineage holder of both Mahayoga and Anu Yoga. He is also known as Indrabhuti the Younger and Master Lawapa.

Shakya   The name of the family clan into which Buddha Shakyamuni was born. Practitioners are often given "Shakya" as a part of their Buddhist name.

Shakya Senge (sha kya seng ge)   One of the eight manifestations of Padmasambhava.

Shakyadevi   The daughter of the Nepalese king Punyedhara. She is one of the five chief female disciples of Padmasambhava. Since her mother died during her birth, she was abandoned in a charnel ground and brought up by monkeys. Having been accepted as Padmasambhava's worthy companion, she was his consort for the practice of the nine divinities of Vishuddha in the Cave of Yangleshö, where they displayed the manner of achieving the vidyadhara level of mahamudra. Shakyadevi attained the accomplishment of the female buddha Mamaki and finally achieved the indestructible rainbow body.

Shakyamuni (sha kya thub pa)   "The Sage of the Shakyas," Buddha Shakyamuni, the historical buddha.

Shamanism (bon 'gyer)   In this book the term has the negative connotation of rituals performed for selfish or superficial, mundane aims.

Shantarakshita (zhi ba 'tsho)   "Guardian of Peace." The Indian pandita and abbot of Vikramashila and of Samye, who ordained the first Tibetan monks. He was an incarnation of the bodhisattva Vajrapani and is also known as Khenpo or Master Bodhisattva or Bhikshu Bodhisattva Shantarakshita. He is the founder of a philosophical school combining Madhyamaka and Yogachara. This tradition was reestablished and clarified by Mipham Rinpoche in his commentary on the *Madhyamakalamkara.*

Shantigarbha (zhi ba'i snying po)   One of the eight vidyadharas, receiver of the transmission of Maledictory Fierce Mantra. Born in Uddiyana and reputed to have visited Tibet, where he participated in the consecration of the Samye Temple.

Shin (gshin)   A type of spirit; either the yama type or simply the consciousness of a human who has passed away but is still lingering in the bardo state.

Shravaka (nyan thos)   "Hearer" or "listener." Hinayana practitioner of the first turning of the wheel of the dharma concerning the four noble truths, who realizes the suffering inherent in samsara and focuses on understanding that there is no independent self. By conquering disturbing emotions, he liberates himself, attaining first the stage of stream enterer at the path of seeing, followed by the stage of once returner, who will be reborn only one more time, and the stage of nonreturner, who will no longer be reborn into samsara. The final goal is to become an arhat. These four stages are also known as the four results of spiritual practice.

Shri Singha   The chief disciple and successor of Manjushrimitra in the lineage of the Dzogchen teachings. He was born in the Chinese city of Shokyam in Khotan and studied at first with the Chinese masters Hatibhala and Bhelakirti. In his *Ocean of Wondrous Sayings*, Guru Tashi Tobgyal adds that Shri Singha received a prophecy from Avalokiteshvara while traveling to Serling, telling him to go to the Sosaling charnel ground in order to be sure of the ultimate attainment. After many years, Shri Singha met Manjushrimitra in the charnel ground of Sosaling and remained with him for twenty-five years. Having transmitted all the oral instructions, the great master Manjushrimitra dissolved his bodily form into a mass of light. When Shri Singha cried out in despair and uttered songs of deep yearning, Manjushrimitra appeared again and bestowed upon him a tiny casket of precious substance. The casket contained his master's final words, a vital instruction named Gomnyam Drugpa, the *Six Experiences of Meditation*. Having received this transmission, Shri Singha reached ultimate confidence. In Bodhgaya, he found the manuscripts of the tantras previously hidden by Manjushrimitra, which he took to China where he classified the Instruction Section into four parts: the outer, inner, secret, and the innermost unexcelled sections. Among Shri Singha's disciples were four outstanding masters: Jnanasutra, Vimalamitra, Padmasambhava, and the Tibetan translator Vairochana.

Siddha (grub thob)   "Accomplished one." Someone who has attained siddhi; an accomplished master.

Siddhi (dngos grub)   *See* Accomplishment.

Sign language of dakinis (mkha' 'gro'i brda yig)   The secret script of the female spiritual beings, which can only be decoded by accomplished masters.

Singala   The land where the Anu Yoga teachings appeared.

Singharaja of Ruley (ru le sim ha ra dza)   One of the first Tibetans to take ordination, having received transmission from Hungkara in India. Also known as Viryaraja of Ru-yong.

Single Form (phyag rgya rkyang pa)   A sadhana text of Mahayoga, composed by Padmasambhava. The title refers to the sadhana practice of a single deity without a retinue.

Single sphere (thig le nyag cig)   A symbolic description of dharmakaya being like a single sphere because it is devoid of duality and limitation and defies all edges of conceptual constructs that could be formed about it.

Single Syllable (yi ge gcig ma)   A Mahayana sutra. Refers to the letter A, the syllable symbolizing the nonarising nature of emptiness.

Six classes of sentient beings ('gro ba rigs drug, Skt. shadgat)   Gods, demigods, human beings, animals, hungry ghosts, and hell beings.

Six limits of Secret Mantra (gsang sngags kyi mtha' drug)   The views of the expedient and definitive meaning, the implied and the not implied, the literal and the not literal.

Six Sadhana Sections (sgrub pa sde drug)   The phrasing of these six types of scripture differs slightly among the various versions of chronicles of Padmasambhava's life. In his *Narration of the Precious Revelation of the Terma Treasures,* Longchen Rabjam rephrases the same sequence from the *Sanglingma* so that the Six Sadhana Sections refer to the scriptures of the Six Secret Sections (gsang ba sde drug), including the scriptures for Manjushri Body, Lotus Speech, Vishuddha Mind, Nectar Quality, Kilaya Activity, and Liberating Sorcery of Mother Deities.

Six Secret Sections (gsang ba sde drug) Listed in chapter 12. The first five are found in the most common list of the Eighteen Mahayoga Tantras.

Sixty-Eight Crescents (zla gam drug cu rtsa brgyad)   Name of a mandala connected to the teachings of Vishuddha Heruka.

Skillful Lasso (thabs kyi zhags pa)   Also known as *Concise Lotus Garland* (pad mo phreng ba'i don bsdus pa), this scripture functions as a support for rituals to attain accomplishment. *See* Eighteen Mahayoga Tantras.

Sky Treasury Consecration Tantra (nam mkha' mdzod byin rlabs kyi rgyud)   The word sky treasury has the connotation of inexhaustible wealth.

Songtsen Gampo (srong btsan sgam po; 569–650 or 617–650)   The king of Tibet in the seventh century, who prepared the way for transmission of the Buddhist teachings. He is regarded as an incarnation of Avalokiteshvara. He married Bhrikuti of Nepal and Wen Cheng of China, who each brought a sacred statue of Buddha Shakyamuni to

Lhasa. Songtsen Gampo built the first Buddhist temples in Tibet, established a code of laws based on Dharma principles, and had his minister Thönmi Sambhota develop the Tibetan script. During his reign, the translation of Buddhist texts into Tibetan began.

Stream-of-being (rgyud, sems rgyud)   The individual continuity of cognition in an individual sentient being.

Stupa (mchod rten)   A dome-shaped monument housing relics of the Buddha or an accomplished master. The shape of the stupa embodies an elaborate symbolism.

Subjugating mantras (drag snags)   Mantras of wrathful deities.

Subsequent True Enlightenment Tantra (phyi ma mngon par byang chub pa'i rgyud)   Tantra belonging to the Sadhana Section of Mahayoga, found in the *Nyingma Gyübum*, vol. OM.

Suchness (de bzhin nyid, Skt. tathata)   Synonym for emptiness or the nature of things, dharmata; it can also be used to describe the unity of dependent origination and emptiness.

Sugata (bde bar gshegs pa)   "Blissfully gone." (1) The historical Buddha Shakyamuni. (2) Any fully enlightened being.

Sukhavati (bde ba can)   "Blissful Realm." The pure realm of Buddha Amitabha.

Sülpo (srul po)   A type of hideous hungry ghost.

Superknowledge (mngon shes, Skt. abhijna)   Divine sight, divine hearing, recollection of former lives, cognition of the minds of others, capacity for performing miracles and, in the case of accomplished practitioners, the cognition of the exhaustion of defilements.

Supportive rituals (zhabs brten)   Rituals performed to remove obstacles to life and health.

Supramundane Scripture ('jig rten las 'das pa'i mdo)   One of the Eighteen Mahayoga Tantras, focused on Vishuddha Mind. Found in the *Nyingma Gyübum*, vol. RA.

Supreme Hundred Families (dam pa rigs brgya)   Name of a sadhana text composed by Guru Rinpoche, focused on the hundred peaceful and wrathful deities.

Supreme Steed Display Root Tantra (rta mchog rol pa rtsa ba'i rgyud)   Tantra belonging to the Sadhana Section of Mahayoga. Two versions are found in the *Nyingma Gyübum*, vol. HA.

Supreme vidyadhara level of mahamudra (phyag rgya chen po mchog gi rig 'dzin)   (1) Supreme enlightenment. (2) The third of the four vidyadhara levels. *See also* Vidyadhara level of mahamudra.

Sutra (mdo, mdo sde)   (1) A discourse by or inspired by the Buddha. (2) A scripture of the sutra pitaka contained within the Tripitaka. (3) All exoteric teachings of Buddhism belonging to Hinayana and Mahayana—the causal teachings that regard the path as the cause of enlightenment, as opposed to the esoteric, tantric teachings. *See also* Tripitaka.

Sutra and Mantra (mdo sngags)   *Sutra* refers to the teachings of both Hinayana and Mahayana. *Mantra* refers to Vajrayana. *Sutra* means taking the cause as path. *Tantra* means taking the result as path.

Swift feet (rkang mgyogs)   The yogic art of being able to walk extremely fast, covering a long distance in a short time through control over the inner currents of energy.

Tamer of All Haughty Spirits (dregs pa kun 'dul)   The chief figure in the mandala of Mundane Worship.

Tanagana (sbyor sgrol)   The Vajrayana practice of "union and liberation": liberating ignorance and disturbing emotions by uniting with the wisdom of the enlightened state.

Tanglha (thang lha)   *See* Nyenchen Tanglha.

Tantra (rgyud)   The Vajrayana teachings given by the Buddha in his sambhogakaya form. The real sense of tantra is "continuity," the innate buddha nature, which is known as the "tantra of the expressed meaning." The general sense of tantra is the extraordinary tantric scriptures also known as the "tantra of the expressing words." Can also refer to all the resultant teachings of Vajrayana as a whole.

Tantra of Taming Haughty Spirits (dregs pa 'dul ba'i rgyud)   A tantra belonging to the Sadhana Section of Mahayoga, focused on the section of Mundane Worship.

Tantra of Taming the Elemental Forces ('byung po 'dul byed kyi rgyud)   A tantra belonging to Kriya Yoga.

Tantra of the Four Vajra Thrones (rdo rje gdan bzhi'i rgyud)   A Mahayoga scripture. Possibly identical with the *Chatuhpitha* (gdan bzhi), which is included among the tantras in the Tripitaka.

Tantra of the General Accomplishment of Knowledge Mantras (rig sngags spyi'i sgrub lugs kyi rgyud)   One of the Eighteen Mahayoga Tantras. Also named *Galpo Düpa* (gal po bsdus pa).

Tantra of the Magical Net of Vajrasattva (rdo rje sems dpa' sgyu 'phrul dra ba'i rgyud)   See *Essence of Secrets.*

Tantra Section (rgyud sde)   One of the two divisions of Mahayoga. The Mahayoga tantras appeared in this world when revealed by Vajrasattva and the Lord of Secrets to King Jah, the ruler of Sahor, who was born 112 years after Buddha's parinirvana. Some of the contemporary lineage holders were Uparaja, Kukuraja, Vimalakirti, and Jnanamitra. Subsequent masters were Shakputri, the regent and son of King Jah, King Jah's daughter Gomadevi, Singaraja, Lilavajra, Buddhaguhya, and Vajrahasya. The following generation of lineage holders were Bhashita, Prabhahasti, and Padmasambhava, the latter of whom also received the tantras directly from King Jah.

Tantras, scriptures, and instructions (rgyud lung man ngag)   The teachings of Mahayoga, Anu Yoga, and Ati Yoga, respectively.

Tantric (rgyud kyi, sngags kyi)   Of or pertaining to Vajrayana.

Tantrika (sngags pa)   "Tantric practitioner," ngakpa. A person who has received empowerment, continues sadhana practice, and keeps the sacred commitments. In particular, an adept follower of Mahayoga Tantra.

Tara Goddess (sgrol ma lha mo)   "Divine Savioress." An important female bodhisattva of compassion, the one who takes beings across the ocean of samsara. There are twenty-one forms of Tara, the most popular being the white and green Taras.

Tathagata (de bzhin gshegs pa)   "Thus-gone." Same as a fully enlightened buddha.

Tattvasamgraha Root Tantra (rtsa ba'i rgyud de kho na nyid bsdus pa)   One of the Four Major Sections of Yoga Tantra.

Tenma goddesses (brtan ma)   *See* Twelve tenma goddesses.

Terma (gter ma)   "Treasure." (1) The transmission through concealed treasures, which were hidden mainly by Guru Rinpoche and Yeshe Tsogyal, to be discovered at the proper time by a *tertön,* a "treasure revealer," for the benefit of future disciples. It is one of the two chief traditions of the Nyingma School, the other being Kama. This tradition is said to continue even long after the Vinaya of the Buddha has disappeared. (2) Concealed treasures of many different kinds, including texts, ritual objects, relics, and natural objects.

Terma treasures (gter ma)   *See* Terma.

Tertön (gter ston)   A revealer of hidden treasures, concealed mainly by Guru Rinpoche and Yeshe Tsogyal. A tertön is the reincarnation of an accomplished student of Padmasambhava who had made the aspiration to benefit people in the future.

Theu-rang (the'u rang)   A class of spirits who ride goats and as patrons of blacksmiths carry a bellows and hammer.

Thread-cross (mdos)   A tantric ritual involving structures of sticks and colored yarn, used to appease mundane spirits.

Three Inner Tantras (nang rgyud sde gsum)   Mahayoga, Anu Yoga, and Ati Yoga. These three sections of tantra are the special characteristics of the Nyingma School of the Early Translations. According to Jamgön Kongtrül the First: "The Three Inner Tantras are also known as the vehicles of the methods of mastery, because they establish the way to experience that the world and beings are the nature of mind manifest as kayas and wisdoms, and that everything is the indivisibility of the superior two truths, hereby ensuring that the practitioner will become adept in the method of gaining mastery over all phenomena as being great equality." The Three Inner Tantras are, respectively, also renowned as "development, completion, and great perfection" or as "tantras, scriptures, and instructions." According to Mipham Rinpoche, the Three Inner Tantras reached Tibet through six different lines of transmission: (1) As perceived by ordinary people in Tibet, Padmakara, the Second Buddha, taught only the instruction on the garland of views, but bestowed both the profound and extensive empowerments and instructions of all of the Three Inner Tantras to his exceptional disciples, including Sangye Yeshe, Rinchen Chok, Lui Wangpo of Khön, and many others, the oral lineages of which have continued unbroken until this very day. Moreover, the major part of his teachings were sealed as terma treasures for the benefit of followers in future generations. (2) When the great translator Vairochana had received extensively the profound teachings of the Great Perfection from the twenty-five panditas, especially from Shri Singha, he returned to Tibet and imparted the Mind Section five times, as well as the oral lineage of the Space Section—both of which we have continued uninterruptedly. (3) The great pandita Vimalamitra arrived in Tibet and taught the Instruction Section chiefly to Tingdzin Sangpo of Nyang. This lineage was transmitted both orally and through terma treasures. (4) Sangye Yeshe of Nub received from four masters in India, Nepal, and Drusha innumerable teachings, headed by the important scriptures of Anu Yoga and Yamantaka. His lineage of the *Scripture of the Embodiment of the Realization of All Buddhas* is still unbroken. (5) Namkhai Nyingpo received the transmission of the teachings of Vishuddha from the Indian master Hungkara, which he then spread in Tibet. (6) During following generations, incarnations of the king and the close disciples of Padmasambhava have successively appeared—and still continue to do so—as great masters who, at opportune times, reveal the profound teachings that had been concealed as terma treasures in order to ensure the supreme welfare of people in Tibet and all other countries, both temporarily and ultimately.

Three jewels (dkon mchog gsum, Skt. triratna) The precious Buddha, the precious Dharma, and the precious Sangha.

Three kayas (sku gsum, Skt. trikaya) Dharmakaya, sambhogakaya, and nirmanakaya. The three kayas as ground are essence, nature, and expression; as path they are bliss, clarity, and nonthought; and as fruition they are the three kayas of buddhahood. The three kayas of buddhahood are the dharmakaya, which is free from elaborate constructs and endowed with the twenty-one sets of enlightened qualities; the sambhogakaya, which is of the nature of light and endowed with the perfect major and minor marks, which are perceptible only to bodhisattvas on the levels; and the nirmanakaya, which manifests in forms perceptible to both pure and impure beings. In the context of this book, the three kayas are sometimes Buddha Amitabha, Avalokiteshvara, and Padmasambhava. *See also* Dharmakaya; Nirmanakaya; Sambhogakaya.

Three realms (khams gsum, Skt. tridhatu) The samsaric realms of desire, form, and formlessness.

Three Sections of Dzogchen (rdzogs chen sde gsum) After Garab Dorje established the six million four hundred thousand tantras of Dzogchen in the human world, his chief disciple, Manjushrimitra, arranged these tantras into three categories: the Mind Section, emphasizing luminosity; the Space Section, emphasizing emptiness; and the Instruction Section, emphasizing their inseparability.

Three trainings (bslab pa gsum)   The trainings of discipline, concentration, and discriminating knowledge.

Tika (thig le)   Essence; sphere.

Tilaka (thig le)   Essence; sphere.

Torma (gtor ma, Skt. balim)   An implement used in tantric ceremonies. Can also refer to a food offering to protectors of the Dharma or unfortunate spirits.

Tramen (phra men)   Goddesses with human bodies and animal heads. *Tramen* means "hybrid" or "alloy."

Tri Ralpachen (khri ral pa can)   *See* Ralpachen.

Tripitaka (sde snod gsum)   The three collections of the teachings of Buddha Shakyamuni: Vinaya, Sutra, and Abhidharma. Their purpose is the development of the three trainings of discipline, concentration, and discriminating knowledge, while their function is to remedy the three poisons of desire, anger, and delusion. The Tibetan version of the Tripitaka fills more than one hundred large volumes, each with more than six hundred pages. *See also* Abhidharma; Sutra; Vinaya.

Triple-Storied Central Temple (dbu rtse rigs / rim gsum)   The central structure at the temple complex of Samye.

Trisong Deutsen (khri srong de'u btsan; 790–844)   The second great Dharma king of Tibet, who invited Guru Rinpoche, Shantarakshita, Vimalamitra, and many other Buddhist teachers to Tibet, including Jinamitra and Danashila. In *The Precious Garland of Lapis Lazuli,* Jamgön Kongtrül dates Trisong Deutsen as being born on the eighth day of the third month of spring in the year of the Male Water Horse (802). Other sources state that year as his enthronement upon the death of his father. Until the age of seventeen he was chiefly engaged in ruling the kingdom. He built Samye, the first great monastery and teaching center, which was modeled after Odantapuri. He established Buddhism as the state religion of Tibet, and during his reign the first monks were ordained. He arranged for panditas and lotsawas to translate innumerable sacred texts, and he established a large number of centers for teaching and practice.

Trülnang ('phrul snang)   One of two important temples in Lhasa built by King Songtsen Gampo, which houses a statue of Buddha Shakyamuni.

Tsangpo (gtsang po, Skt. Brahmaputra)   The river flowing by Samye.

Tsele Natsok Rangdröl (rtse le sna tshogs rang grol; b. 1608)   Important master of the Kagyü and Nyingma schools. He is also the author of *The Mirror of Mindfulness* and *Lamp of Mahamudra,* both published by Shambhala Publications.

Tsemang of Denma (ldan ma rtse mang)   Important early Tibetan translator of the Tripitaka. Extremely well-versed in writing, his style of calligraphy is continued to the present day. Having received transmission of Vajrayana from Padmasambhava, he had realization and achieved perfect recall. He is said to be the chief scribe, who wrote down many termas, including the Assemblage of Sugatas connected to the Eight Sadhana Teachings.

Tsogyal (mtsho rgyal)   *See* Yeshe Tsogyal.

Tulku Urgyen Rinpoche (sprul sku u rgyan rin po che)   A contemporary master of the Kagyü and Nyingma lineages, who lives at Nagi Gompa in Nepal.

Twelve kyongma goddesses (skyong ma bcu gnyis)   Retinue of the twelve tenma goddesses.

Twelve tenma goddesses (brtan ma bcu gnyis)   Important female protectors of the Nyingma lineage, semimundane, semiwisdom protectors.

Twelve yama goddesses (ya ma bcu gnyis)   Retinue of the twelve tenma goddesses.

Twelvefold Kilaya Tantra (ki la ya bcu gnyis)   Tantra belonging to the Sadhana Section of Mahayoga. Tantras with similar titles are found in the *Nyingma Gyübum,* vols. DZA and HA.

Twenty-eight ishvari goddesses (dbang phyug ma nyer brgyad)   Wrathful emanations of the four female gatekeepers from among the forty-two peaceful deities in the mandala of Magical Net—seven for each of the four activities.

Twenty-five tantras (rgyud nyi shu rtsa lnga)   Dzogchen tantras belonging to the Mind Section and possibly also the Space Section, which were taught by Shri Singha to Vairochana and Lekdrub. Listed in chapter 14.

Twenty-one genyen (dge bsnyen nyi shu rtsa gcig) A group of powerful
spirits indigenous to Tibet. They were converted by Padmasambhava
and commanded to serve Buddhism. Today, they are still called upon
along with Nyenchen Tanglha and Machen Pomra during Vajrayana
rituals in order to guard the doctrine of the Buddha, elevate the status
of the Precious Ones, expand the community of the Sangha, increase
the life and splendor of the practitioners, raise the banner of fame,
blow the conch of renown, and increase our following and prosperity.

Two stages (rim gnyis) *See* Completion stage; Development stage.

Ubhaya (gnyis ka) "Both" or "twin." The second of the three outer
sections of tantra, usually known as Upa Yoga. The scriptures
appeared first in Mount Jakang Chen and Cool Grove. The name
refers to a combination of two aspects: the conduct of Kriya Yoga
and the view of Yoga Tantra.

Uddiyana (u rgyan, o rgyan) The country to the northwest of ancient
India, where Guru Rinpoche was born on a lotus flower. The literal
meaning of Uddiyana is "vehicle of flying" or "going above and far."
See also Orgyen, which is a corruption of the Indian word.

Unified stage of the path of training (slob pa'i zung 'jug) A high level
of accomplishment. Same as the vidyadhara level of mahamudra.

Unsurpassable Magical Net (sgyu 'phrul bla ma) A Mahayoga scripture,
found in the *Nyingma Gyübum*, vol. PHA.

Upa Yoga *See* Ubhaya.

Ushnisha (gtsug thor) A protuberance that raises infinitely into space
from the top of a buddha's head. It can be seen only by a bodhisattva
who has attained the first bhumi.

Vairochana (rnam par snang mdzad) (1) One of the five families; the chief
buddha of the tathagata family. (2) The great and unequalled
translator who lived during the reign of King Trisong Deutsen.
Vairochana (also pronounced bey-ro-tsa-na in Tibetan) was
recognized by Padmakara as a reincarnation of an Indian pandita. He
was among the first seven Tibetan monks and was sent to India to
study with Shri Singha. Shri Singha in turn entrusted Vairochana

with the task of propagating the Mind Section and Space Section of Dzogchen in Tibet. He is one of the three main masters to bring the Dzogchen teachings to Tibet, the two others being Padmakara and Vimalamitra. Vairochana's chief disciples were Yudra Nyingpo, Sangtön Yeshe Lama, Pang Gen Sangye Gönpo, Jnana Kumara of Nyag, and Lady Yeshe Drönma. An especially renowned disciple was the old Pang Gen Mipham Gönpo, whose disciples attained the rainbow body for seven generations by means of the oral instructions entitled Dorje Zampa, the "Vajra Bridge." Tsele Natsok Rangdröl, Terdag Lingpa Gyurmey Dorje, and Jamgön Kongtrül Lodrö Thaye are regarded as reincarnations of Vairochana.

Vajra (rdo rje) "Diamond," "king of stones." As an adjective it means "indestructible," "invincible," or "firm." The ultimate vajra is emptiness; the conventional vajra is the ritual implement of material substance.

Vajra Kilaya (rdo rje phur ba) One of the main yidams of the Nyingma School, belonging to the Eight Sadhana Teachings.

Vajra master (rdo rje slob dpon, Skt. vajracharya) A tantric master who is adept in the rituals and meaning of Vajrayana. The master from whom one receives tantric teaching and empowerment. Can also refer to the master who presides over a tantric ritual.

Vajra Seat (rdo rje gdan, Skt. vajrasana) The "diamond seat" under the Bodhi Tree in Bodhgaya where Buddha Shakyamuni attained enlightenment.

Vajra Thötreng Tsal (rdo rje thod phreng rtsal) "Powerful Vajra Garland of Skulls." One of Padmasambhava's names.

Vajra Varahi (rdo rje phag mo) "Vajra Sow." A sambhogakaya manifestation of the female buddha Samantabhadri. She is also one of the chief yidam deities of the Sarma Schools, as well as a wisdom dakini.

Vajradhara (rdo rje 'chang) "Vajra-holder." The dharmakaya buddha of the Sarma Schools. Can also refer to one's personal teacher of Vajrayana or to the all-embracing buddha nature.

Vajradhatu (rdo rje dbyings) Indestructible innate space.

Vajradhatu Mandala of Peaceful Deities (zhi ba rdo rje dbyings kyi dkyil 'khor) An important sadhana of Mahayoga. See also Forty-two peaceful deities.

Vajrakaya (rdo rje sku) The unchanging quality of the buddha nature. Sometimes counted among the five kayas of buddhahood. *See also* Five kayas of fruition.

Vajrapani (phyag na rdo rje) "Vajra Bearer." One of the eight great bodhisattvas and the chief compiler of the Vajrayana teachings. Also known as Lord of Secrets.

Vajrasattva (rdo rje sems dpa') A sambhogakaya buddha who embodies all of the five or hundred buddha families. He is also a support for purification practices.

Vajrayana (rdo rje theg pa) The "vajra vehicle." The practices of taking the result as the path. *See also* Secret Mantra.

Vehicle (theg pa, Skt. yana) The practice of a set of teachings, which "carries" one to the level of fruition. In Buddhism there are mainly three vehicles: Hinayana, Mahayana, and Vajrayana.

Vidyadhara (rig pa 'dzin pa) "Knowledge-holder." Holder (Skt. dhara) or bearer of knowledge (Skt. vidya) mantra. A realized master on one of the four stages on the tantric path of Mahayoga, the tantric equivalent of the eleven levels. Another definition is the bearer of the profound method, the knowledge that is the wisdom of deity, mantra, and great bliss.

Vidyadhara Accomplishment Tantra (rig 'dzin grub pa'i rgyud) One of the Eighteen Mahayoga Tantras. *The Golden Garland Chronicles* names this scripture *The Tantra of Six Vidyadharas* (rig 'dzin drug pa'i rgyud).

Vidyadhara level of longevity (tshe'i rig 'dzin, tshe la dbang ba'i rig 'dzin) The second of the four vidyadhara levels. Corresponds to the path of seeing. The practitioner's body turns into the subtle vajralike body, while his mind matures into the wisdom of the path of seeing. It is the attainment of longevity beyond birth and death.

Vidyadhara level of mahamudra (phyag rgya chen po'i rig 'dzin) The third of the four vidyadhara levels. The stage of the path of cultivation. The practitioner emerges from the luminosity of the path of seeing in the form of the wisdom body of the unified state of the path of training.

Vidyadhara level of maturation (rnam par smin pa'i rig 'dzin) The first of the four vidyadhara levels. The beginning of the path of seeing. The practitioner has reached stability in the development stage and his mind has "matured" into the form of the yidam deity, but he is yet to purify the remainder of the physical elements.

Vidyadhara level of spontaneous perfection (lhun gyis grub pa'i rig 'dzin)   The fourth of the four vidyadhara levels. Corresponds to buddhahood, the path beyond training. The final fruition and state of a vajra holder endowed with the spontaneously perfected five kayas: dharmakaya, sambhogakaya, nirmanakaya, vajrakaya, and abhisambodhikaya.

View, meditation, conduct, and fruition (lta ba sgom pa spyod pa 'bras bu)   The philosophical orientation, the act of growing accustomed to that (usually in sitting practice), the implementation of that insight during the activities of daily life, and the final outcome resulting from such training. Each of the nine vehicles has its particular definition of view, meditation, conduct, and fruition.

Vimalamitra (dri med bshes gnyen)   A master in the Dzogchen lineage and the crown ornament of five hundred panditas, who attained the indestructible form of the rainbow body. He received the transmission of Dzogchen from Shri Singha and Jnanasutra. Vimalamitra is regarded as one of the three main forefathers for establishing the Dzogchen teachings in Tibet, especially the Instruction Section, which he chiefly transmitted to five people: King Trisong Deutsen, Prince Muney Tsenpo, Tingdzin Sangpo of Nyang, Kawa Paltsek, and Chokro Lui Gyaltsen. Having translated these extremely profound instructions, he concealed the texts at Samye Chimphu for the sake of future generations. On his departure to the Five-Peaked Mountain in China, Vimalamitra made the promise to return once every century in order to clarify and propagate the teachings of the secret, innermost essence, Sangwa Nyingtig. The oral lineage of his teachings on the Instruction Section was continued by Tingdzin Sangpo of Nyang, who also concealed one set of the scriptures. One hundred and fifty-five years after Vimalamitra departed from Tibet, an emanation of him named Dangma Lhüngyal took out the hidden texts. They are now included in the collection known as *Vima Nyingtig*, the "Heart Essence of Vimalamitra." In his role as lineage holder of Nectar Quality from among the Eight Sadhana Teachings, he is counted among the eight vidyadharas of India, the receiver of the Eightfold Volume of Nectar Quality. According to this lineage, he was born in Elephant Grove, an area in the western part of India. He was learned in both the common and extraordinary topics of knowledge and received teachings on the tantras from Buddhaguhya and many other illustrious masters. Having practiced, he reached the accomplishment of the vidyadhara level of mahamudra and wrote numerous treatises, mainly on the teachings connected to the Magical Net.

Vinaya ('dul ba)   "Discipline." One of the three parts of the Tripitaka. The Buddha's teachings showing ethics, the discipline and moral conduct that is the foundation for all Dharma practice, both for lay and ordained people. *See also* Tripitaka.

Vishuddha (yang dag)   The heruka of the vajra family or the tantric teachings connected to that wrathful deity. One of the Eight Sadhana Teachings of the Nyingma School.

Vishuddha Heruka (yang dag he ru ka)   *See* Vishuddha.

Vishuddha Mind (yang dag thugs)   *See* Vishuddha.

Vishva (sna tshogs)   Variety, manifold purposes. In this book, the Vishva Temple at Samye used for teaching arts and crafts.

War Goddess of Shangshung (zhang zhung gi dgra lha)   A protectress of the Bönpo doctrine. She was subjugated by Padmasambhava and given the name Great Glacier Lady of Invincible Turquoise Mist.

Wheel of Yama (gshin rje'i 'khor lo)   Tantra belonging to the Sadhana Section of Mahayoga, focused on a wrathful form of Manjushri.

White Skull Naga Forefather (klu'i mes po thod dkar)   Another name for the protector Nyenchen Tanglha.

Wind of karma (las kyi rlung)   (1) Another word for conceptual thinking. (2) The inevitable force of the ripening effect of former deeds.

Wisdom dakini (ye shes kyi mkha' 'gro ma, Skt. jnanadakini)   Enlightened female being, the root of activity among the three roots. *See also* Guru, yidam, and dakini.

Wish-fulfilling jewel (yid bzhin nor bu)   A gem that grants the fulfillment of all one could desire; thus the Buddha, one's personal master, and the nature of mind are often referred to as a wish-fulfilling gem.

World-system ('jig rten gyi khams)   A universe comprised of Mount Sumeru, four continents, and eight sub-continents.

Wrathful Blue Lotus Tantra (khro bo pun da ri ka'i rgyud)   One of the Eighteen Mahayoga Tantras, focused on Vishuddha Mind. Found in the *Nyingma Gyübum,* vol. RA.

Yaksha (gnod sbyin)   A class of semidivine beings, generally benevolent, but sometimes wicked. Many are powerful local divinities; others live on Mount Sumeru, guarding the realm of the gods.

Yama (gshin rje)   The Lord of Death. A personification of impermanence, the unfailing law of karma, and one's inevitable mortality.

Yamantaka (gshin rje gshed)   *See* Manjushri Body.

Yangleshö (yang le shod)   *See* Cave of Yangleshö.

Yarlha Shampo (yar lha sham po)   Important Dharma protectors of Tibet, especially for the Chö teachings.

Yeshe Dey of Nanam (sna nam ye shes sde)   Also known as Bandey Yeshe Dey of Shang (zhang gi bhan dhe ye shes sde). Prolific expert translator and disciple of Padmasambhava. He was a monk, both learned and accomplished, and once exhibited his miraculous powers by soaring through the sky, like a bird.

Yeshe Tsogyal (ye shes mtsho rgyal)   The different versions of her biography give varying details about her place of birth, the names of her parents, and so forth. In his *Ocean of Wondrous Sayings to Delight the Learned Ones,* Guru Tashi Tobgyal states that her father's name was Namkha Yeshe of the Kharchen clan and that she was born in Drongmochey of Drag. At first she was one of King Trisong Deutsen's queens, but later was given to Padmasambhava as an empowerment fee to be his spiritual consort. During the empowerment of Assemblage of Sugatas, her initiation flower fell on the mandala of Kilaya. Through this practice she became able to tame evil spirits and revive the dead. She was the chief compiler of all the inconceivable teachings given by the great master Padmasambhava. Having remained in Tibet for two hundred years, she departed for the celestial realm of the Glorious Copper-Colored Mountain without leaving a corpse behind. In *The Precious Garland of Lapis Lazuli* (p. 352), Jamgön Kongtrül says:

> Yeshe Tsogyal was a direct incarnation of Dhatvishvari Vajra Yogini in the form of a woman. She served Pad-

masambhava perfectly in that life, engaged in sadhana practice with incredible perseverance, and attained a level equal to Padmasambhava himself, the "continuity adorned with inexhaustible body, speech, mind, qualities, and activities." Her kindness to the land of Tibet surpasses the imagination, and her compassionate activity, which is no different from Padmasambhava's, continues unceasingly.

Yeshe Yang (ye shes dbyangs)   Early Tibetan translator predicted by Padmasambhava. The chief scribe for writing down the termas of Padmasambhava. He was an accomplished yogi, able to fly like a bird to the celestial realms. Also known as Atsara Yeshe Yang of Ba (sba a tsar ye shes dbyangs) or Atsara Yeshe. *Atsara* is a corrupt form of the Sanskrit *acharya*, "master."

Yidam (yi dam)   A personal deity and the root of accomplishment from among the three roots. The yidam is one's tutelary deity, a personal protector of one's practice, and guide to enlightenment. Traditionally, yidam practice is the main practice that follows the preliminaries. It includes the two stages of development and completion and is a perfect stepping stone or bridge to approaching the more subtle practices of Mahamudra and Dzogchen. Later on, yidam practice is the perfect enhancement for the view of these subtle practices. *See also* Guru, yidam, and dakini.

Yoga (rnal 'byor)   (1) The actual integration of learning into personal experience. (2) *See* Yoga Tantra.

Yoga of shape (dbyibs kyi rnal 'byor)   A synonym for the development stage; the practice of visualizing the form of the deity.

Yoga of vidyadhara life (rnal 'byor tshe'i rig 'dzin)   The tantric practice of attaining immortality by accomplishing the vidyadhara level of longevity.

Yoga Tantra (rnal 'byor rgyud)   The third of the three outer tantras: Kriya, Upa, and Yoga. It emphasizes the view rather than the conduct and regards the deity as being the same level as oneself.

Yoga vidyadhara level of longevity (rnal 'byor tshe'i rig 'dzin)   *See* Vidyadhara level of longevity.

Yogi (rnal 'byor pa, Skt. yogin)   Tantric practitioner. In this book, the word yogi often holds the connotation of someone who has already attained some level of realization of the natural state of mind.

Yogic (rnal 'byor gyi) Of or pertaining to Vajrayana practice, with emphasis on personal training as opposed to scholarly learning.

Yogic discipline (rtul shugs) Additional practices for a tantrika in order to train in implementing the view of Vajrayana in daily activities; for example, feast offering.

Yudra Nyingpo (g.yu sgra snying po) One of the twenty-five disciples of Guru Rinpoche; the reincarnation of Lekdrup of Tsang. Born in the region of Gyalmo Tsawarong, he was brought up by Vairochana and reached perfection in both learning and yogic accomplishment. He is counted among the 108 lotsawas and is one of the main lineage holders of the Mind Section of Dzogchen, from the great translator Vairochana.

Zi stone (gzi) Divine agate.

Index

INDEX

Index

Index

INDEX

INDEX

The Art of War, by Sun Tzu. Translated by Thomas Cleary.

The Awakened One: A Life of the Buddha, by Sherab Chödzin Kohn.

Bodhisattva of Compassion: The Mystical Tradition of Kuan Yin, by John Blofeld.

The Book of Five Rings, by Miyamoto Musashi. Translated by Thomas Cleary.

The Buddhist I Ching, by Chih-hsi-Ou-i. Translated by Thomas Cleary.

Cutting Through Spiritual Materialism, by Chögyam Trungpa.

Dakini Teachings: Padmasambhava's Oral Instructions to Lady Tsogyal, by Padmasambhava. Translated by Erik Pema Kunsang.

The Diamond Sutra and The Sutra of Hui-neng. Translated by A. F. Price & Wong Mou-lam. Forewords by W. Y. Evans-Wentz & Christmas Humphreys.

The Essential Teachings of Zen Master Hakuin, translated by Norman Waddell.

The Experience of Insight: A Simple and Direct Guide to Buddhist Meditation, by Joseph Goldstein.

A Flash of Lightning in the Dark of Night: A Guide to the Bodhisattva's Way of Life, by Tenzin Gyatso, the Fourteenth Dalai Lama.

Great Swan: Meetings with Ramakrishna, by Lex Hixon.

The Heart of Awareness: A Translation of the Ashtavakra Gita. Translated by Thomas Byrom.

I Am Wind, You Are Fire: The Life and Work of Rumi, by Annemarie Schimmel.

Insight Meditation: The Practice of Freedom, by Joseph Goldstein.

Lieh-tzu: A Taoist Guide to Practical Living, by Eva Wong.

Ling Ch'i Ching: A Classic Chinese Oracle, translated by Ralph D. Sawyer & Mei-chün Sawyer.

Living at the Source: Yoga Teachings of Vivekananda, by Swami Vivekananda.

Living with Kundalini: The Autobiography of Gopi Krishna.

The Lotus-Born: The Life Story of Padmasambhava, by Yeshe Tsogyal.
Translated by Erik Pema Kunsang.

Mastering the Art of War, by Zhuge Liang & Liu Ji.
Translated & edited by Thomas Cleary.

The Myth of Freedom and the Way of Meditation by Chögyam Trungpa.

Nine-Headed Dragon River, by Peter Matthiessen.

Rational Zen: The Mind of Dogen Zenji. Translated by Thomas Cleary.

Returning to Silence: Zen Practice in Daily Life, by Dainin Katagiri.
Foreword by Robert Thurman.

Seeking the Heart of Wisdom: The Path of Insight Meditation,
by Joseph Goldstein & Jack Kornfield.
Foreword by H. H. the Dalai Lama.

Shambhala: The Sacred Path of the Warrior, by Chögyam Trungpa.

The Shambhala Dictinary of Buddhism and Zen.

The Spiritual Teaching of Ramana Maharshi, by Ramana Maharshi.
Foreword by C. G. Jung.

Tao Teh Ching, by Lao Tzu. Translated by John C. H. Wu.

Teachings of the Buddha, revised & expanded edition. Edited by
Jack Kornfield.

*The Tibetan Book of the Dead: The Great Liberation through Hearing in the
Bardo.* Translated with commentary by Francesca Fremantle &
Chögyam Trungpa.

Vitality, Energy, Spirit: A Taoist Sourcebook.
Translated & edited by Thomas Cleary.

Wen-tzu: Understanding the Mysteries, by Lao-tzu.
Translated by Thomas Cleary.

Zen Essence: The Science of Freedom.
Translated & edited by Thomas Cleary.

The Zen Teachings of Master Lin-chi. Translated by Burton Watson.